Arrogant Aussie

The Rupert Murdoch Story

ARROGANT AUSSIE

The Rupert Murdoch Story

by Michael Leapman

Lyle Stuart Inc.   Secaucus, New Jersey

To Times past, present and future

Library of Congress Cataloging in Publication Data

Leapman, Michael, 1938–
  Arrogant Aussie.

  Originally published as: Barefaced cheek.
  Bibliography: p. 280.
  Includes index.
  1. Murdoch, Rupert, 1931–   2. Times (London,
England) 3. Newspaper publishing—Australia. 4. News-
paper publishing. I. Title.
Z533.3.M87L4 1985   070.5′092′4 [B]   84-24093
ISBN 0-8184-0370-5

Published by Lyle Stuart Inc.
Published simultaneously in Canada by
Musson Book Company,
A division of General Publishing Co. Limited
Don Mills, Ontario

Queries regarding rights and permissions should be
addressed to: Lyle Stuart, 120 Enterprise Avenue,
Secaucus, N.J. 07094.

Manufactured in the United States of America

Contents

Preface

If there were a club for ex-editors of Rupert Murdoch's publications, it would be the least exclusive in the international news business. Editing a Murdoch publication is a high-risk occupation. Researching this book I interviewed dozens of these ex-editors and would generally include the broad-ranging question: "What do you think of Murdoch?" It is the kind of query that can provoke either meaningless generalizations or penetrating insights. One ex-editor thought about it for an unusual length of time before replying: "Let me just say that I wouldn't like to *be* Rupert Murdoch."

On the face of it that is a curious response. Here is a man controlling significant segments of the news media of three of the most important English-speaking nations, clearly enjoying the political influence that entails; a man with an effectively limitless personal fortune, lavish residences in the center of three glamorous world cities as well as a good supply of places in the country. Although his first newspapers in South Australia came to him through inheritance, he has the satisfaction of knowing that the international empire was his own creation, and much of it was in place while he still had time to enjoy it. Why should he attract any adverse emotion other than envy?

Yet that ex-editor's view is not quirkish. Anyone who reaches a position of public prominence picks up enemies and critics along the way. Few have provoked such passionate denunciation as Rupert Murdoch.

"The Press Lord of Mass Ignorance" is one of the labels attached to him by media critics, who are among his own favorite targets for scorn. His racy tabloid *New York Post* has been described as more of a social problem than a newspaper. He has been accused of flagrantly debasing journalistic standards that many have worked a lifetime to sustain.

Although he affects unconcern at such criticism, he and his family do find it wounding. The contradiction between his manifest success and his adverse reputation is part of the subject of this book.

An author who writes about so controversial a figure, without his cooperation, obviously runs the risk of basing his conclusions primarily on the evidence of disgruntled former employees and others who nurture grievances against the man. I have avoided that by taking care to include, among the 120 people I have interviewed during my research on three continents, those who admire Rupert Murdoch as well as those who do not. That is why, when an earlier version of this book appeared in England, the critics praised its objectivity and candor.

Many of those I interviewed, especially current employees of the Murdoch organization, would talk only in strict confidence. I therefore feel it best to name none of my sources, but I offer my sincere thanks to all, and to the many others who helped.

Prologue

It is no accident that Allen and Co., perhaps the best-known investment bankers in New York, have their offices in the Columbia Pictures building on Fifth Avenue, instead of in the traditional financial center around Wall Street. They moved there when they bought control of the troubled film company in 1973, leading it to prosperity before having to steer it through the much-publicized David Begelman scandal a few years later. Although Allen's have more than 100 institutional clients in numerous fields of business, they have caught the public eye over the years through their connections with high-profile companies in show business and the media.

On the fourth day of 1984, a few days before the first of that year's January snows, Stanley Shuman, the executive vice-president of Allen and Co., stayed at the office well after business hours. He was waiting for three men to join him. All three were important figures in a particular area of American business, but, as far as Shuman was concerned, one was of far greater importance than the others.

Rupert Murdoch was Allen and Co.'s only overseas client and one of their most active. An Australian newspaper publisher, he had met Shuman by chance eight years earlier and the two had become firm friends and colleagues. Shuman admired Murdoch's determination, his decisiveness and above all his ability to identify business opportunities where others saw none. That skill, allied with Shuman's financial prowess, had enabled the Australian, in less than ten years of operating in the United States, to become a force to be reckoned with, even feared.

Rupert Murdoch was not universally popular. Indeed, many prominent citizens found his newspapers tawdry, an insult to the intelligence and aspirations of their readers. But the papers were, for the most part, successful, and by now nobody underestimated Murdoch's prowess as a businessman. As for Shuman, Murdoch reciprocated his regard and assistance by appointing him to the board of both News Corporation, his international company, and its offshoot, News America.

The Australian was in a state of some excitement as he entered the Fifth Avenue office on that January evening. The other two men at the meeting came from the glamor sector of corporate America, where Murdoch had long felt that he too might have a place. They were Steven Ross, chairman of Warner Communications, the film and leisure conglomerate, and Herbert Siegel, chairman of Chris-Craft, a company whose varied interests include television. Both felt most at home in the glittering world of Hollywood and Broadway and enjoyed an exuberant life style that placed them in newspaper gossip columns almost as often as on the financial pages.

The gathering was intended to be a peace conference. But before the four had been together long, it had turned into a declaration of war.

Murdoch and Ross had met twice before in recent months. The Australian, ever alert for opportunities of profitable expansion, had been seeking to augment his American newspaper and magazine holdings by venturing into television. He was specifically interested in satellite television, a new technique that would allow numerous TV channels to be beamed from satellites into individual homes equipped with small and cheap receiver dishes.

Such an operation would need a reliable source of programming. The previous summer Murdoch heard that Ross was planning to merge Warner's part-owned cable TV subscription service with a rival channel, and had asked whether he, Murdoch, could be included in the deal and use the service on his satellite operation. The answer was no.

Shortly afterwards, Murdoch suspended his satellite plans, taking a loss—unusual for him—of some 20 million dollars. At about the same time, he began buying significant quantities of Warner shares on the stock market.

The Warner stock price had tumbled since 1982, when it stood at a high of $63¼. The boom in video games in the late 1970s had persuaded Ross to acquire Atari, the leading manufacturer in the field, which had made tremendous profits for a few years. Suddenly the boom collapsed and the profits turned to a loss of $424,700,000 in the first nine months of 1983. At its low point, the price of the stock was down to $19. Murdoch, whose business career has been characterized by an instinct for buying cheap, had by the end of September acquired about a million shares, or 1.6 percent of Warner's stock.

"We welcome Mr. Murdoch as one of our shareholders," said Geoff Holmes, a Warner spokesman, but two months later that welcome had become decidedly muted, and was transformed into alarm, verging on panic. In early December Murdoch notified the Securities and Exchange Commission that he now owned 6.7 percent of the company, making him the largest single shareholder, with a stake valued at nearly 100 million dollars. On December 7th he spent another three million to bring his holding close to 7 percent, and two days later he went to see Ross, who, like the father of a bride interviewing a suitor of suspect reputation, asked about his intentions.

Murdoch could not answer the question precisely because he was not yet clear in his own mind just what his intentions were. He told Ross the share purchases were an investment. Ross wished the Australian would take his investments elsewhere. He explained that Murdoch's reputation for interfering in the editorial management of his newspapers, and the fact that most of his publications served the bottom end of their markets, might offend the best creative people at Warner's film and TV studios and make them susceptible to job offers from rival companies. Moreover, there were strict rules about the cross-ownership of newspapers and television stations serving the same areas. Murdoch's control of the *New York Post* might clash with Warner's cable franchises in New York, causing trouble with the Federal Communications Commission.

Murdoch gave Ross none of the assurances he sought. The Warner chief had therefore to look to his defenses.

A few days after Christmas, Ross disclosed his plan. He had made a deal with Siegel by which new Warner shares amounting to 19 percent of the company's capitalization would be issued to Chris-Craft. In return, Warner was to receive 42.5 percent of Chris-Craft's television subsidiary. This thwarted Murdoch in two ways. To begin with it diluted his existing holding in Warner and made it for all practical purposes impossible for him to acquire a controlling interest. Even if he did he would fall foul of the FCC over the TV stations Chris-Craft owned, for there is a law preventing non-Americans from controlling an interest greater than 25 percent in a TV station.

Murdoch was furious and a little bewildered by the maneuver. This was his first major corporate battle in the United States and such tactics were new to him. His favorite way of acquiring assets—chiefly newspapers—was to buy them from their existing owners. Usually they were failing papers that he could get cheaply and, more often than not, revive through vigorous marketing.

Until now, such stock-market assaults as Murdoch had made were confined to Australia, where company values were lower. His most notable was a bid in 1979 for the Melbourne Herald newspaper group—once controlled by his father. He didn't get it because the Fairfax group in Sydney allied themselves with the Herald and entered the market against Murdoch, who cuttingly described the rescue as "two incompetent managements throwing themselves into each other's arms at the expense of their shareholders." He could afford to sound superior, for after two days of hectic trading on the Melbourne exchange he had emerged with a profit of three million Australian dollars.

His immediate response to the Warner/Chris-Craft deal had been to buy more Warner shares and file a statement of intent with the Justice Department to acquire between 25 percent and 49.9 percent of the company. If he went for the higher figure it could cost him some 900 million dollars—about two-thirds of his 1983 revenues. Then, on the afternoon of January 4, a few hours before the meeting at Allen and Co., he initiated a legal tussle by filing suit with the FCC to have the Chris-Craft deal blocked, on the grounds that Warner had a half share in the Warner-Amex cable system and Chris-Craft had interests in four traditional TV stations, and it was against the rules for companies to have a stake in both kinds of television.

The tone of Murdoch's complaint did not suggest that compromise was in the air. In an attempt to show that Warner was not a suitable company to control TV stations, he brought up the case of two Warner executives convicted in 1982 of fraud in connection with the purchase of stock in a theater in upstate New York. He said the convictions were "relevant information regarding the character of Warner." A Warner source told the *Wall Street Journal* with apparent relish: "All of what happens in the next ten days will be a big game of spitball as everyone sues each other and tries to throw monkey wrenches into the other's plans."

The atmosphere, then, was inauspicious for Ross and Siegel to sue for peace on that January evening. The four men who gathered in the offices of Allen and Co. were all high-stakes players. For Shuman, the host, the occasion was a little embarrassing, for he was also a long-time acquaintance of Ross. He had been involved in the formation of Warner Communications in 1971 from a merger of the old Warner Brothers film studio with Ross's Kinney National Service Inc., whose most prominent business until then had been parking lots. And one of the unsuccessful suitors for Warner had been Herbert Siegel, a former talent agent enraptured by the movie business, who had in his time made a play for most of the major Hollywood studios.

Murdoch could have been forgiven for feeling pleased with himself as he sat around the negotiating table in Allen and Co.'s office suite. In New York you have not truly proved yourself as a major-league tycoon until you have played a role in a multi-million-dollar takeover struggle, and he could scarcely have chosen a more prominent corporation to cut his teeth on.

He had arrived in New York a little over ten years earlier, the culmination of a journey that had begun in Adelaide, South Australia, where he inherited a daily and Sunday newspaper on the death of his father in 1952. From that base he had penetrated, first, the highly competitive newspaper market in Sydney, Australia's largest city. Then, at the end of the 1960s, he moved to London, where he bought Britain's best-selling—and most scandalous—Sunday paper and a struggling daily. He soon turned the daily into the leader in its market, primarily through the innovation of printing a photograph of a nude woman every morning on page three.

When he and his young wife Anna moved into a Manhattan apartment in 1973, he had no specific business project in mind. Partly the move was a reaction against what he saw as his ostracism by the stuffy British establishment, who resented his papers prying into those sex scandals that rock the upper echelons of British society and government from time to time. But he could see, too, that there must be scope for an energetic manipulator to acquire newspapers on favorable terms in America, just as there had been in Britain and Australia.

Rupert Murdoch felt he understood the way Americans did business, and liked it. Americans were direct, open and accessible. There was none of the thick overlay of social snobbery that he found so distasteful in London.

His first American purchases were three newspapers in San Antonio, Texas, in the burgeoning Sunbelt. Next he launched the *Star,* a racy tabloid sold mainly in supermarkets, which after an uncertain start proved a formidable rival to the successful *National Enquirer.* His big American breakthrough came in 1976, when he bought the *New York Post,* the city's only evening paper, from its long-time owner Dolly Schiff. Soon afterwards he out-maneuvered his friend Clay Felker for ownership of *New York* magazine and the *Village Voice.*

During the next few years his main advances came in Australia and Britain. In Australia he gained control of television stations in Sydney and Melbourne, coming as close to forming a national network as the regulations allowed, and getting himself a half share in the country's main internal airline into the bargain. In London in 1981 came his most startling acquisition in a career laced with the unexpected—the prestigious London *Times,* the organ of the British establishment, and its sister paper the *Sunday Times.* Barely had he digested those than he was back in action in America, buying the *Boston Herald* and, in 1984, the *Chicago Sun-Times,* for which he paid nearly 100 million dollars, the most he had ever spent for a newspaper.

Probably the best thing that ever happened to Murdoch, as far as his American business was concerned, was his chance meeting with Stanley Shuman in 1976. They both had children at the Dalton School, one of New York's finest educational establishments. They would chat at parents' meetings and found that they had much in common. When he was planning to buy the *New York Post,* Murdoch called Shuman and asked for his advice on the finances of the deal. That was the beginning of his association with Allen and Co., and the reason why the four men were meeting in their offices that night.

It was Shuman, indeed, who had first suggested to Murdoch that he should invest in Warner. Now his old acquaintances Ross and Siegel were there to propose that the investment should be liquidated. Siegel pointed out that if Murdoch were to sell all his shares to Chris-Craft at the then prevailing price, he would emerge with a handy profit of more than 25 million dollars. Murdoch declined. He preferred to fight on. And in interviews over the next few days he implied, as was his custom, that he was acting not primarily to serve his own interest but for the sake of the entire financial community, making a principled stand for proper corporate behavior.

"I'm still very angry about it," he told *Business Week* a few days later. "We told them when we bought stock. We are clients of theirs overseas [through the Australian TV stations]. Then we woke up to find that paranoia had overtaken them. There is a question about whether those people can run TV stations. I'm not even sure they could get a casino license.... I don't think [Warner] is well run. Look at the results. I don't know whether it is bad management or lack of management, but it is run by dealmakers rather than managers."

He said he expected to continue his fight to upset the Chris-Craft deal. "Someone can beat you up or run over you, but if you don't give them a few bruises in return, they can do it to the next person who comes along. It is also important for News Corporation to show that it won't be pushed around. It would be very bad for News Corp. for people to think we are a patsy that can be run over and disenfranchised in this way."

In early February his mood was unchanged. He told the *New York Times:* "When someone's trying to run you down, you try to protect yourself, so that, the next time, someone else doesn't try to run you down."

By now both sides had employed teams of lawyers. Suits and counter-suits were filed not only at the FCC but also in Federal Court in Delaware, where Warner is registered.

Murdoch accused Warner management of racketeering and provoked a flurry of controversy by assigning reporters from the *New York Post* to seek damaging information about Ross's private life and business record. Then, when it seemed that the trenches had been dug for a long war of attrition, Murdoch, despite his brave talk, thought it prudent to make a tactical withdrawal. In mid-March he agreed to sell his Warner shares back to the company for $31 each, eight dollars above the price at which they were trading and $6.50 more than the average price he had paid for them.

The word "greenmail" was beginning to be employed on Wall Street to describe the process, where corporate raiders demand a high price for backing off. Murdoch's profit came to $41,500,000 and Warner reimbursed him eight million dollars for his expenses. In return, he promised to buy no Warner shares for ten years. The deal differed from the one he had so contemptuously rejected in January only in terms of its price—16 million dollars more than the earlier offer.

Not bad for a beginner. Only in a strictly technical sense could it be argued that he had been beaten up and run over. Certainly nobody was calling him a patsy.

ONE

Puff the Magic Founder

You don't realize that there's a great deal of iron behind the boyish exterior.

—Maxwell Newton

Sir Keith Murdoch spent the last few years of his life worrying about two matters: money and his son Rupert. His wife Elisabeth, nearly twenty-five years his junior, would certainly outlive him, and he was not sure that he had provided sufficiently for her and their four children. As for Rupert, Sir Keith was never convinced that his son had the tenacity and application to assume his mantle as probably the most influential newspaperman in Australia.

In the event, only the first of these fears was justified. After death duties, the only business venture Rupert and his mother inherited was a paltry evening and Sunday paper in Adelaide, capital of South Australia. Though chairman of the giant Herald and Weekly Times group in Melbourne, Sir Keith owned only a few shares in it. Paradoxically, the greatest favor Sir Keith did for his heir was to die in 1952 at the fairly early age of sixty-six, when Rupert was twenty-one and still at Oxford. The young man soon returned to become the "boy publisher" of the Adelaide *News* and was never anything but boss of his own show. If he felt that he had somehow been maneuvered by his elders out of a larger inheritance, he had a working lifetime ahead to prove his worth and expand the empire. Sir Keith's legacy of time, and a lingering sense in Rupert

17

that he had been cheated of part of his patrimony, proved a more potent spur to achievement than anything tangible Rupert could have been bequeathed.

Sir Keith had been a distinguished correspondent in the First World War and was, in an Australian context, something of an old-world aristocrat. The son of a Presbyterian minister from Scotland, he had forged a successful career in journalism entirely on the strength of his determination and ability. He had served five years as a district reporter for the *Age* in Melbourne, despite being hampered by a serious stammer. In 1908, aged twenty-three, Keith Murdoch took himself to London and spent a frustrating eighteen months trying to break into Fleet Street; his Melbourne references secured him many interviews but his stammer deterred editors from hiring him.

Returning to Australia in 1910, he had five years to wait for his breakthrough. Then he was appointed manager and editor of the United Cable Service, an Australian news agency in London. World War One was a year old and thousands of Australian volunteers were fighting in the Dardanelles. Murdoch was asked by the Australian government to investigate their mail facilities, but when he got to Gallipoli he found that not only the mail was a subject of concern. He was appalled at the conduct of the war and was encouraged in his dismay by Ellis Ashmead-Bartlett of the London *Daily Telegraph,* who persuaded him that things were much worse than anyone had admitted in London or Melbourne, and that the situation was deteriorating. Working under strict military censorship, the British reporter had been unable to hint at any of this in his dispatches. Murdoch agreed to smuggle out a report by Ashmead-Bartlett, although he had, as a condition of being allowed to visit the front, signed a specific undertaking not to try to skirt the censor.

Another British correspondent "squealed" and the despatch was taken from Murdoch at Marseilles, before he reached London. Yet he remembered much of it and wrote it in a letter to the Australian Prime Minister, recommending the dismissal of Sir Ian Hamilton, commander of the Allied forces at Gallipoli. "The conceit and complacency of the red feather men are equalled only by their incapacity," he wrote. The letter reached prominent British politicians and Sir Ian was dismissed. Through that incident

Murdoch became intimate with the powerful in Britain and Australia.

In 1916, when the new Australian Prime Minister Billy Hughes visited Britain, Murdoch arranged private meetings with members of the establishment. Thus, when the fast-maturing journalist returned to Australia in 1921, as editor of Melbourne's afternoon paper the *Herald,* he was already an influential figure. In London he had forged a close friendship with Lord Northcliffe, founder of the *Daily Mail* and the father of British popular journalism. Murdoch took many of Northcliffe's ideas with him to the *Herald.*

He soon established himself as a tough and competent editor of strict conservative views. Within a few years he had become editor-in-chief of the group, now including a morning paper, the *Sun News-Pictorial.* In 1928, at the age of forty-two, when he seemed to be settling into confirmed bachelorhood, he met and married a young debutante, Elisabeth Greene, at nineteen less than half his age. The Greenes were a highly respectable Melbourne family—her father Sir Rupert was a steward at the races. Murdoch doted on his young wife and as a wedding present he bought her a charming farm near Langwarrin, some thirty miles south of Melbourne. They called it Cruden Farm, after the town in Scotland where his father came from.

Helen, their first child, was born in 1929 and Rupert, their only son, two years later. Two more daughters, Anne and Janet, came in 1935 and 1939. In his book *In Search of Keith Murdoch,* Desmond Zwar paints an idyllic picture of family life at Cruden, with the children playing under their father's feet as he genially and single-mindedly dealt with work he had brought home from the office. That is also how Dame Elisabeth remembers it at a distance of over forty years, but it is not the entire story.

Sir Keith was born in the Victorian era and ran his household in the patriarchal tradition. He was specially strict with his heir Rupert. Against the boy's will, he was sent to Geelong Grammar, the most exclusive boarding school in Australia. In the holidays when he returned to Cruden he was not allowed to live in the house but made to camp out in a hut in the garden— "Rupert's sleep-over" — unequipped with heat or running water or electricity, in the belief that this would strengthen his character and self-reliance; though he was allowed indoors for a shower. This strict regime lasted for eight years, until he was sixteen.

Sir Keith often worried about Rupert's capacities, and he would discuss his fears with masters at Geelong. The boy was an introverted student with few friends. Sir Keith, who had become managing director of the Herald and Weekly Times group a year after his marriage and was knighted in 1933, hoped to bequeath to his son a lucrative newspaper empire but was unsure whether he would prove worthy of it.

It might have been hard for Sir Keith to accept that he was himself a large part of Rupert's problem. For the conservative nature of the newspapers he ran made him the butt of satire and scorn from fashionable young radicals, including many of Rupert's school-mates. He was nicknamed "Lord Southcliffe" (after Lord North-cliffe, the publishing tycoon) and his name was inserted into pastiche music-hall songs. The boy's cocksureness, later to develop into ruthlessness, probably originated as a defense mechanism against such barbs.

Ironically, the ruthless streak that so worried Sir Keith was one of the qualities to which he owed his own success. For, as a newspaper executive, Sir Keith had a short way with incipient competition. In 1933 the *Argus,* a successful Melbourne morning paper, decided to launch an evening paper, the *Star,* to rival the *Herald.* Many senior people on the *Herald* were lured to the new paper, including Crayton Burns, a reporter whose son Creighton was many years later to edit the *Age.*

When Burns gave his notice at the *Herald,* Sir Keith called him in and said: "I hear you're leaving us. Are you dissatisfied?"

Burns replied that he was being offered more money and a better job at the other newspaper.

"But what are you going to do when I run it off the streets within twelve months?" Sir Keith asked.

Burns joked that his son would by then be fifteen and could sell copies of the *Herald* on street corners. Sir Keith's boast was not quite justified; the *Star* survived two years and five months before folding. Burns had jumped back to the *Herald* a few months earlier.

An intriguing insight into Sir Keith's desire for power came with World War Two, when he was made Director-General of

Information and introduced rules that gave him the right effectively to control the press. After an outcry he was forced to withdraw them.

His worries about his son persisted even after Rupert was awarded a place at Worcester College, Oxford, to study politics, philosophy and economics. The London correspondents of the *Herald*—first Rohan Rivett and then Douglas Brass—were deputed to keep an eye on the lad, and Sir Keith exchanged voluminous correspondence with him. He regarded Rupert's letters as tests of his ability as a journalist. When one would arrive sketchy and ill thought out, he would be cast into gloom, but a well-turned letter would delight him. His widow, Dame Elisabeth (she was made a Dame of the British Empire in 1963) recalls that, shortly before his death, Sir Keith looked up from a letter in which Rupert was describing a meeting of the Labour Club, where he was active. "He's got it," declared the proud father, rather in the manner of Professor Higgins in *My Fair Lady*.

Rupert enjoyed his time at Oxford, where he struck up a friendship with his history professor, Asa (now Lord) Briggs, that has lasted to this day. In the 1970s he donated a substantial sum to the refurbishment of the library at his old college, Worcester, now headed by Briggs.

The most famous incident of his undergraduate career was his unsuccessful campaign to be elected secretary of the Labour Club. The rules were that candidates and their friends must not indulge in any electioneering or open campaigning, but Rupert disregarded them. He canvassed vigorously and even sent out campaign liter-ature with the slogan ROOTING FOR RUPERT written boldly on the envelopes. His opponents complained to the chairman of the Labour Club, Gerald Kaufman, later a cabinet minister, and he set up a tribunal to investigate the matter, whose members included Shirley Catlin, later Shirley Williams, another minister in the making. They found that Rupert had indeed broken the rules, and he was barred from contesting future elections.

When Sir Keith died as Rupert was about to leave Oxford in 1952, his mother assumed the role of monitor of his achievement. She did not do so consciously: she had never interfered in Sir Keith's business affairs and would not in Rupert's, despite his tender age.

When the executors of the estate decided to sell Sir Keith's share of the *Courier-Mail* in Brisbane, leaving only the *News* and the *Sunday Mail* of Adelaide in family ownership, she did not question their judgment, though Rupert would have preferred it otherwise. But when the owners of the rival Adelaide paper, the *Advertiser,* sought to buy the *News,* she resisted out of a sense of loyalty, suppressing her doubts—inspired by Sir Keith—about Rupert's business capacity.

Rupert knew of those doubts and was determined to show them unfounded. Throughout his career, he has operated as though his mother's approval was paramount among the criteria for making decisions. Even today, they talk by phone two or three times a week, wherever he is.

Before leaving Britain to establish himself on the *News* in Adelaide, Rupert spent a few months as a junior sub-editor on the *Daily Express.* Sir Keith had been friendly with Lord Beaverbrook, the paper's Canadian proprietor, and had asked if his son could be "blooded."

Under the editorship of Arthur Christiansen, the *Express* had become a model for middlebrow popular newspapers—bright and readable but maintaining a stronger grip on sober reality than its down-market rival the *Daily Mirror.* Beaverbook put Rupert in the care of Edward Pickering, managing editor in charge of night production of the paper, who slotted the young Australian in at the bottom end of the subs' table, never entrusting him with any big stories.

Among the other subs, Rupert was best known as an enthusiastic gambler on horse racing in both Britain and Australia, a frequent visitor to the sports desk to check on the latest results. Professionally, he impressed Pickering as a trainee of promise, though some of his colleagues on the subs' table were skeptical. Certainly he was the only *Express* sub-editor who would repair home to the Savoy Hotel after finishing his shift.

Most successful journalists will admit, if pressed, that one figure early in their career exercized an important influence on them, teaching them much of what they know. There is evidence that for Murdoch the tall, lean Pickering, the epitome of a Fleet Street professional, was that person. It would explain why, nearly thirty years later, he plucked Pickering from retirement and placed him in an influential position on *The Times* of London, his latest and then his most troublesome acquisition.

Rupert was only twenty-two when he went to Adelaide and assumed the title of publisher of the *News.* So he had—and took—plenty of time to establish himself. In commercial matters he would generally defer to his elders on the board. The journalistic side of the paper was in the hands of the charismatic and mercurial Rohan Rivett, a liberal, campaigning editor admired by Sir Keith, who had placed him in charge of the *News* a year before his death.

Rupert already knew Rivett fairly well. They had met while he was at Oxford and Rivett was the London correspondent of Sir Keith's Melbourne *Herald.* The young undergraduate would visit the Rivetts at their house in suburban Sunbury-on-Thames. An engaging guest, he would roister energetically with the Rivetts' children. Once he shared a motoring holiday with Rohan and Nan Rivett and a woman friend.

For a few years Rupert was content to watch and learn. The rival paper in Adelaide was the *Advertiser,* controlled by Sir Lloyd Dumas, one of the "white knights" who dominated South Australian society. The *Advertiser* had offered Rupert and his mother 150,000 pounds for the family holding in the *News* just after Sir Keith's death and when this was refused they tried to run their rivals out of business by launching a Sunday paper against the profitable *Sunday Mail,* which the *News* published.

After a couple of years of ferocious and expensive competition a truce was called and the two organizations decided to merge their Sunday interests by publishing the *Sunday Mail* jointly, each owning half the stock and sharing costs and profits. This went against Murdoch's competitive instinct; he agreed to it only with reluctance.

As if to purge himself, not long afterwards he made a hugely optimistic takeover bid for the *Advertiser.* Although he offered 14 million pounds—a substantial sum in the late 1950s—there was no real hope of success. The Herald and Weekly Times group in Melbourne were the largest stockholders in the *Advertiser* and it was never likely that they would agree to sell. The eager Murdoch waited outside the *Advertiser* building while the board were having their crucial meeting. As the directors emerged, he approached Sir Lloyd Dumas, the chairman, and asked him what had happened. Sir Lloyd marched on and into his car, staring through the upstart as if he were not there.

Murdoch had already plunged into what was to become the most consistently profitable aspect of his operations, television. Roy Thomson, the Canadian tycoon, had not yet made his famous remark that owning a television station was a license to print money, but its truth was already apparent to Murdoch. In 1958 he made a successful application for the license for Channel 9 in Adelaide and hired Bill Davies from a local radio station to run it. It was an instant money-maker and Davies became one of the solid, unflappable men who have formed a sound base for his organization, freeing Murdoch to lead its imaginative forays.

By now Murdoch had bought his first paper in another state, the *Sunday Times* in Perth, Western Australia. He tackled the venture with the enthusiasm that has become his hallmark, traveling to Perth almost every week to supervise the paper's production and quickly improving its circulation and profitability. He was also starting to flex his muscles on the *News,* and as he did so he became increasingly irked by Rivett's restraining presence. The two differed over whether the paper should carry advertisements on the back page. Murdoch was in favor, because of the extra revenue it would generate, but Rivett wanted to keep the whole page for sports. Murdoch waited until the Rivetts were on holiday in Spain before he made the change; but he wondered to himself why he should have to indulge in such subterfuge on what was, after all, his own paper.

In 1959 the *News* became involved in a contentious issue that divided opinion in South Australia and was to have a profound effect on the young publisher as well. An aborigine named Rupert Max Stuart, a funfair worker, was tried and convicted of murdering a nine-year-old girl, and sentenced to death. His appeal to the South Australian Supreme Court was turned down.

As the date of the execution approached, doubts grew as to the validity of the conviction. The prosecution's case rested almost entirely on a "confession" Stuart had made to the police, and there were questions about how this had been obtained. New witnesses were found whose accounts suggested that Stuart could not have committed the crime. The execution was postponed several times while the case was heard by the Privy Council, the final court of appeal, but they too found no reason to alter the sentence.

Rivett, a socialist and humanitarian, became convinced that justice had not been done and began campaigning in the *News* for a reprieve and a commission of enquiry into the trial and sentence. Murdoch, at that time also a socialist, backed him to the hilt. At Oxford, Murdoch had been a prominent member of the Labour Club and here in Adelaide he continued his left-wing associations. With Rivett, he would attend social evenings organized by Don Dunstan, an up-and-coming Labour politician who was to become one of South Australia's most notable premiers. Adelaide's embattled radicals would attend, and impassioned political discussions would take place. On one occasion in the early 1950s, at Dunstan's invitation, Murdoch addressed a meeting of the local Fabian society, an intellectual social club.

So although the *News* under Murdoch and Rivett did not give formal editorial support to the Labour Party, it could be relied upon to take a radical line on issues such as colonialism and human rights. The Stuart case was just such an issue. Rivett sent reporters to the remote northern part of the state and into Queensland to find witnesses who had not come forward at the trial, and the story was never absent long from the columns of the *News.* James Cameron, a leading liberal British journalist of the day, now turned his attention to the case in the London *News Chronicle,* describing Rivett as "the Zola of South Australia." He commented: "Hundreds of uneasy Australians all over the nation, stirred and challenged by the Adelaide *News,* are now keenly watching the cause of a pauper black man who could so easily have gone into limbo unnoticed."

The very opposite of praise came from the "white knights," the Adelaide establishment, who viewed Rivett's campaign as irresponsible rabble-rousing. But it had its effect. Sir Thomas Playford, the veteran Premier of South Australia, announced a Royal Commission to look into the case. But even this did not still the criticism. When the names of the three commissioners were announced, it emerged that one would be Sir Mellis Napier, a

seventy-seven-year-old judge who had presided over the High Court
when it rejected Stuart's appeal, and another was Mr. Justice Reed,
the trial judge.

The *News* declared that the naming of the judges and their
terms of reference "arouse the gravest doubts and fears among all
those who know something of the history of the case." Those doubts
appeared to be confirmed when, not long after the commission
began its hearings, Stuart's chief counsel, J. W. Shand, walked out
because he felt they were not being conducted fairly.

The way the *News* reported this incident was later to be the
subject of a long court case. The front page headline quoted Shand
as saying: "THESE COMMISSIONERS CANNOT DO THE JOB." Two
posters on the Adelaide streets shouted: SHAND QUITS: "YOU WON'T
GIVE STUART FAIR GO" and COMMISSION BREAKS UP—SHAND
BLASTS NAPIER. Two weeks later, on September 2nd, 1959, Sir
Thomas Playford told Parliament that the headline and the posters
were "the gravest libel ever made against any judge in this state." In
particular he pointed out that the words in quotation marks in the
headline were not a precise quotation from Shand. Asked why no
libel action was taken, Sir Thomas said it would be considered "at
the appropriate time," when investigations into the Stuart case were
over.

The next day, September 3rd, the *News* ran a front page
editorial which, it emerged later, had been written by Murdoch.
Although it contained an element of apology, it was rambunctious
stuff that showed the proprietor just as committed to his paper's
campaign as his editor was. It was headlined: LET'S GET THE
RECORD STRAIGHT. It read in part:

"The *News* has AT NO TIME alleged any crime by any member
of the government, the Supreme Court, or even the South Australian
police. However, we conceive it as our duty to report all statements
in such an important matter." The editorial went on to admit its
mistake in publishing as a quotation the challenged front-page
headline. "Mr. Shand did not use these words and the headline
should never have been published and we regret that it was." It was
also incorrect to suggest in the poster that Mr. Shand had singled out
Sir Mellis Napier for attack. But after these apologies the editorial
reached a rousing conclusion: "We have never claimed that Stuart is
innocent—merely that he must be shown to be guilty beyond all

doubt before being hanged. The *News* sees it as its duty to fight always not only for justice to be done but for justice to appear to be done. WE MAINTAIN THIS STAND AND WILL CONTINUE, WITH PRIDE, TO FIGHT FOR THIS IDEA."

Stuart's sentence was commuted to life imprisonment. In January 1960 Rivett and News Ltd., Murdoch's company, were charged on nine counts of libel, including three of seditious libel—a charge rarely used, which involves uttering a libel with the purpose of bringing some part of the machinery of the state, including the administration of justice, into contempt. The penalty was a fine or term of imprisonment at the judge's discretion.

At the trial, Rivett stated that Murdoch had not only written the September 3rd editorial but had also suggested the wording for the controversial headline and for one of the two posters. He had approved the other poster, "YOU WON'T GIVE STUART FAIR GO," before it was distributed. He added that Murdoch had asked him to point that out to the court.

At the end of the ten-day trial, the jury dismissed eight of the nine charges—those of seditious libel had already been ruled out by the judge. They disagreed on the ninth charge, concerning the "FAIR GO" poster. Ten weeks passed before the state decided to drop that charge as well. Then the *News* published an editorial affirming confidence in the state's judicial system, its judges and the commission.

Five weeks later Murdoch dismissed Rivett as editor—a notable landmark in the young publisher's career for two reasons. To begin with, Rivett was the very first of what was to become a flood of editors removed from their posts by Murdoch. Second, the dismissal marked the end of the Stuart affair and the involvement of the *News* in it. It was significant as the last time a Murdoch newspaper entered into a human rights campaign with anything like that commitment or fervor. His proprietorial style from then on was to engage in power politics, supporting one politician or party against the other, seldom straying beyond the formal party struggle.

Although the *News* had won glory in liberal circles for its Stuart campaign, its effect on advertisers and probably on most readers was negative. What was the point in bucking the establishment, especially when the establishment controlled most of the advertising and much else in the state? Where was the profit in it?

The style, too, of Rivett's dismissal was one that would become familiar later. Murdoch dictated a curt, three-line letter and sent it round to Rivett's office, where a secretary opened it. She burst into the editor's office in tears. Rivett, shaken, left immediately and was never again to occupy an executive post in newspapers. Soon afterwards he became director of the International Press Institute in Zurich.

By the time Murdoch had gritted his teeth and purged himself of the unpleasant experience, the Stuart affair was a long way from being his central concern. Adelaide was pushed into the back of his mind by his move into the big time, to Sydney, to trade blows with such heroic newspaper proprietors as the Fairfaxes and the Packers. If you sought to pick the most significant year in Murdoch's career, this one, 1960, would stand out. In February he had nibbled at the fringes of the city by buying the Cumberland group of giveaway suburban weeklies for one million pounds. Three months later came the really big break, when he began negotiations to buy the *Daily Mirror,* one of the city's two evening papers.

This broadening of the Murdoch interests almost certainly contributed to Rivett's downfall. There was a period when Rivett thought he might go with his proprietor to Sydney but, after the nerve-racking turmoil of the libel trial, Murdoch did not feel confident enough in him either to put him in charge of the *Mirror* or to leave him in Adelaide deprived of his own restraining influence.

The sale of the *Mirror* to Murdoch was an act of extraordinary misjudgment by the Fairfaxes, owners of the *Sydney Morning Herald* and the *Sun,* the rival evening paper to the *Mirror.* It was not long before Rupert Henderson, Fairfax's all-powerful managing director, started to regret the day he agreed to it, and in ensuing years the Fairfax group was to spend millions of dollars mitigating its effect.

Their motive was to prevent any of what they then saw as their serious rivals from strengthening their position. The *Mirror* had been owned by Ezra Norton, who had inherited a batch of decidedly racy papers from his father, John Norton. For years he had wanted to sell his papers—including low-grade weekly rags in Sydney, Melbourne and Brisbane—and in 1948 had come close to agreement with the Mirror group in London (who the following year bought the Melbourne *Argus* instead, to their subsequent regret).

Though fierce rivals, the Sydney newspaper barons recognized a community of interest. In 1958 Norton told Henderson of his plan to sell out. Henderson and the Fairfax management were obsessed by the fear that one of their two dreaded rivals would move in. Sir Frank Packer, who owned the *Daily Telegraph,* and the *Sunday Telegraph,* would dearly have loved an afternoon paper to gain maximum use from his presses—an economy that Fairfax already enjoyed with the morning *Herald* and the evening *Sun.* Henderson wanted to prevent that and was also determined that the Herald and Weekly Times group in Melbourne, which Sir Keith Murdoch had built into the largest newspaper group in the country, should not be allowed to gain a toehold in Sydney.

The simplest response to Norton's approach would have been for Fairfax to buy the *Mirror* and then close it, leaving the afternoon field clear for the *Sun,* but Henderson and the Fairfaxes, conscious of their reputation as the most respectable of the city's newspaper groups, were unwilling to face the public obloquy that such a blatantly self-interested move would have provoked. Instead, they created a new company, O'Connell Pty Ltd., to run the old Norton papers. Though nominally independent, it was controlled by Fairfax.

By 1960 it was apparent that the ruse was not working. Because of the ambiguity of its ownership, the *Mirror* lacked the stomach for the head-to-head fight with the *Sun* that was its only chance of competing effectively. Its circulation slipped—as did that of the sister *Sunday Mirror.* Murdoch, sensing an opportunity, approached Henderson, who looked on the deal with initial favor because of the respect he had had for Sir Keith. Perhaps because he had known Rupert as a boy, he could not persuade himself that he presented any substantial threat.

Henderson had already displayed his avuncular attitude to Murdoch when the young newcomer to Sydney went to ask him for help in printing *New Idea,* the women's magazine that had come with the Cumberland group. It was printed on primitive letterpress machines and as a result looked shoddy compared with its competitors. Henderson agreed to print the magazine on Fairfax's more advanced rotogravure, and to do it at bargain rates until it reached an economic circulation. Then the price of the printing would be raised to a realistic level. But before that point was reached, Murdoch had put in his own rotogravure plant and printed *New Idea* on that, having established it with Henderson's cut-price help.

Others at Fairfax warned Henderson against selling the *Mirror* to Murdoch. Sir Warwick Fairfax, the chairman, was opposed and Robert Falkingham, the shrewd company treasurer, wrote a memorandum denouncing the plan in strong terms:

"I do not think we should contemplate selling to Murdoch at any price," it began. He went into detail about the dangers as he saw them. Murdoch would cut advertising rates, do backdoor deals with the unions and not stick to agreements. Murdoch had already attacked the Fairfax group in one of his new suburban papers. "We would make a greater capital profit and would better protect our own operations by adhering to our original intention of reconstructing the *Mirror* as a widespread public company, with ourselves holding only enough shares to prevent another paper getting control," Falkingham wrote.

But Henderson was determined to go ahead. Falkingham went on holiday and on his first day away received a message to ring the office. "Come back right away," Henderson told him. "I've agreed to sell the *Mirror* to Murdoch."

Arriving at the office late in the evening, Falkingham found both sides supported by teams of high-powered lawyers. The negotiations were concluded at about 1:30 in the morning. Murdoch put in a jubilant phone call to his old rival Clyde Packer, Sir Frank's eldest son. One version of the occasion has him dancing a jig in Henderson's office after the deal was made.

Although Murdoch was about to slough off the influence of Rivett, he still felt the need, as he always has, for a man of serious substance somewhere near the top of his organization. His father had plucked Rivett from London to take charge, and it may have been a subconscious reflex action that persuaded Rupert to do something similar. Douglas Brass, a dour New Zealander, was London correspondent of the *News*. Murdoch brought him back as group editorial manager based in Sydney. In the relation between the two there were some similarities to that between Murdoch and Rivett but there was one crucial difference: while Rivett had been in place when the young Murdoch arrived back from Oxford, Brass was his own appointment. After Rivett, he was careful never to let anyone in his organization rise to a position that was not ultimately dependent on his patronage. There were ups and downs in relations between Murdoch and Brass, and in the 1970s Brass left for a while, but until he retired in 1981 he was an influential figure.

When Murdoch acquired the *Mirror,* its circulation was in decline and its image uncertain. Founded during World War Two, by 1953 it had established a lead of 11,000 over the *Sun,* in a total market of just over 600,000. But the *Sun* revived after the Fairfax group bought it and it had overtaken the *Mirror* by the time Norton sold out five years later.

Under the O'Connell ownership the *Mirror* wilted further and was 13,000 behind the *Sun* when Murdoch arrived on the scene. Norton's *Mirror* had been a racy tabloid. In the O'Connell period it was toned down to be closer in approach to the more sober *Sun,* but this had only resulted in fudging its identity. Murdoch, influenced by Brass, at first tried to take it further in that more responsible direction, but circulation charts showed that this was not what readers wanted. So Murdoch took it back down market, though it never became as lurid as in Norton's day. Soon it was a viable competitor to the *Sun.* It was a lesson Murdoch was to put to good effect when he took over the London *Sun* nine years later.

Freed from Rivett's overpowering influence, the new Sydney press baron no longer felt inhibited from playing the role to the hilt. The *Mirror* was indisputably his paper and its executives his people, there to please him. An early victim was Robert Hughes, the *Mirror's* cartoonist and art critic. Murdoch did not like his work and suggested he take a hefty pay cut. Hughes left and is now the highly respected art critic of *Time* magazine in New York.

Murdoch would visit the composing room almost daily, at first to watch the metal type being placed in the page forms.

"What size is that headline?" he would ask. "Wouldn't it be better to take it down a size?" And he would scribble an altered wording to fit the smaller letters.

Many found this an engaging habit, evidence that the proprietor was not too grand to roll up his sleeves and muck in with the lads. For the editors, though, it was an irritation, especially on the *Sunday Mirror,* where the weekly rhythm, leading to a climax only once every seven days, is different from that on a daily paper.

A former *Sunday Mirror* executive put it like this: "You'd slave your guts out over the paper for the first four days of the week, see nothing of Rupert, and on the fourth or fifth day Rupert would bowl in, be very nice and breezy and so on, but he'd want to push you a bit, inject an idea or two of his own into it. I'd be irritated about this, frankly. I used to think that he was a bit of a dilettante. He had nothing to do with it for most of the week and then suddenly he'd show up and expect to run it."

He still likes to second-guess his editors even from thousands of miles away. In New York, it can take a week for his Austrlian papers to reach him, but he will telephone editors about editions they have long confined to the darker recesses of their minds and say: "Your front page headline's all wrong."

Another restraint Murdoch left behind in Adelaide was too great a care to avoid the sensational in the name of accuracy. The cut-throat competition between Sydney's two evening papers gave him, he felt, a license to stretch the facts. The *Mirror* had, after all, always done it, and the *Sun* had few scruples that he could detect. At the end of 1961, the *Mirror* sent reporter Brian Hogben, later to climb to a senior position in the organization, to Hollandia, Dutch New Guinea, to report a local war. The *Sun* had also sent its own man, and when Hogben had not been heard of for a while his colleagues were terrified they would be scooped. So they invented the kind of story they thought he might write and kept it on ice for a while. It was a colorful piece about cannibalism and shrunken heads, stuffed with hackneyed jungle clichés. When the editors' nerve could hold no longer, they published the story in the paper under Hogben's byline. There is no evidence that the decision was made by Murdoch personally: it was probably Douglas Brass, as editorial director, who gave the go-ahead, but working, as he did throughout his career, within Murdoch's guidelines. When Hogben received a copy of the paper he sent a furious telegram to his office: "Nearest shrunken heads to Dutch New Guinea are in Sydney."

The two other Sydney newspaper groups, Fairfax and Packer, had lucrative television stations there as well. When in 1962, the government decided to introduce a third Sydney station, Channel 10, it seemed to Murdoch that he was the logical person to own it. He found an impressive band of backers and made a plausible bid, but he was not awarded the license, probably because of the opposition of Sir Robert Menzies, the veteran Prime Minister, symbol of the old Australian establishment that Murdoch instinctively opposed.

Thwarted, he decided to attempt entry into Sydney television by an oblique route. Apart from the three main channels, there were a number of small stations in the suburbs whose transmission range included part of the Sydney metropolitan area. By law these could not be owned by anyone who ran a central Sydney station, so they usually belonged to groups of local businessmen. The Sydney stations saw them as potential opposition and used their muscle to prevent them getting major American programs that were then—and still are—the staple of Australian television fare.

As Murdoch told the story in a 1967 television interview, Channel 4 at Wollongong, a small town south of Sydney, was on the brink of bankruptcy for this reason. The big stations, he claimed, had told the American distributors: "If you sell any single program to Wollongong you won't sell any to us. So you take the 25 pounds for half an hour there and don't get the 2,000 pounds from us." So the owners of Channel 4 made an appeal to him.

"I was tempted by the thought that if it was true that the Wollongong station was too close to Sydney and could in fact one day compete with a Sydney station this might be an opportunity to get in and try out. So I went in. But I realized that to have any hope at all of doing this, of making people change their viewing habits in Sydney—they'd have to even change their antennae around—I'd have to have the most attractive programs.

"So I went over to America and bought every new program from every network that was available for a year and spent very nearly three million dollars to buy Australian rights. I knew we could show them in Adelaide and, through Ansett [owners of Melbourne's Channel 10], in Melbourne. . . .

"Meanwhile the existing people here sat around and said they'd let me go broke, that I was making my really fatal mistake, that I would go broke. However Sir Frank Packer at some stage must have slid away because he rang me up and our paths crossed at San Francisco airport and then later he rang me—I was in Honolulu and he was in New York—and he said: 'Let's do a deal.' So I went back to New York and he agreed to sell me a 25-percent share interest in Channel 9 in Sydney and Channel 9 in Melbourne. This doesn't give

me control or much say in it...but still it's a very important
investment and it got me off the hook. But then I think the original
thought occurred that I might really have overstepped myself in
taking this gamble in Wollongong—looking back at it now I think
they were probably right then."

Murdoch hates standing still. After he had owned the Sydney *Mirror*
for a couple of years he could see it was holding its own in its battle
against the *Sun,* and he looked around for other opportunities.
Along with his two Sydney papers he had bought two weeklies, both
called *Truth,* published in Brisbane and Melbourne. They were as
far down market as you can get without straying across the line into
simple pornography. "Rapes in Nigeria, that kind of thing," was
how one senior executive put it dismissively. The Melbourne *Truth*
survives today, though no longer under Murdoch's ownership,
making much of its profit through advertisements for massage
parlors.

However dismal his Brisbane and Melbourne papers, they did
mean that, taken together with his operations in Sydney, Adelaide
and Perth, he had printing capacity in every state capital. He was
therefore uniquely placed to try something that Australian newspapermen had regarded as an impossible aspiration for years: the
creation of a national newspaper.

Because of the distances involved, such a paper could not
economically be distributed from a single printing plant. But the
technology of the day did allow the printing of a newspaper by photo
composition. Whole pages could be photographed and converted
into lightweight matrices which could be flown from a central point
to printing presses in all the capitals.

It was a seductive idea and the obvious place to mount such an
operation was Canberra, the purpose-built federal capital, sited
between Sydney and Melbourne. The paper would, after all, be
specializing in federal politics and overseas news, and Canberra was
the diplomatic and political hub of the nation. The snag was that, in
a small town of only 40,000 inhabitants, there was not much of a
local population to provide a solid advertising and circulation base.

Moreover, Canberra already had a paper of its own, the
Canberra Times. It was a dim little tabloid selling 16,000 copies a
day, but it did make a stab at covering national politics and it

obviously had to be put out of business if a new paper was to get an economic level of local Canberra advertising. The *Canberra Times* was owned by Arthur Shakespeare, son of the man who had established it in 1926 when the federal government was moving into the new city.

Shakespeare had no children and was worried about what would happen to the paper when he died. He discussed the matter with Henderson in the late 1950s and they reach an understanding that the Fairfax group would be informed of any move to sell. In the meantime Fairfax were thinking of printing a Canberra edition of the *Sydney Morning Herald* which might have developed into the national daily people were talking about. To protect their flanks from an outsider, Fairfax made a secret agreement with Shakespeare by which ownership of the *Canberra Times* would pass to Fairfax if any rival appeared on the scene.

To strengthen his paper, Shakespeare hired a new editor in 1962. He was Dave Bowman, who had left the Adelaide *News* and worked for six months on the *Sunday Mirror* in Sydney. Murdoch rather liked it when people left his organization on their own initiative rather than waiting to be fired. It was evidence of sturdy independence; he would never want to close the door on re-engaging them. He was polite to Bowman at their farewell interview.

"Got a chair of your own, eh? Good. I wish you a lot of luck." Then he added something that may have been a hint of what he had in mind, though it was to be two years before the *Australian* came into being: "Arthur Shakespeare has got it all to himself down there. I wouldn't want to wake up one morning and read in the paper he'd sold it. I'd like to hear about that in advance."

Bowman's brief was to modernize the *Canberra Times,* broaden its outlook and put it in better shape to withstand the competition that Shakespeare and the Fairfax group were convinced would come. One afternoon in 1963, when Bowman had been in Canberra for less than a year, he received a message that Murdoch had arrived and wanted to see him. They shook hands like old friends. Murdoch had really called to see Shakespeare, but he was out, and in any case he seemed delighted to chat to his former employee about old times and his present position.

The affable Bowman took him on a tour of the office and the printing plant and discussed the problems of the paper: it was always, for instance, being produced late because of inadequate capacity in the composing room. Murdoch was absorbed, and when the tour was over he told Bowman: "You might like to come and work with me." Bowman shrugged off the suggestion, and only several months later, when the rumors of Murdoch's plans began to harden, did the true purpose of the reconnaissance visit dawn on him.

The opening of Parliament at the beginning of the year, towards the end of the Australian summer, is an important social occasion. The Governor-General hosts a reception in King's Hall in Canberra. Newspaper owners and other prominent Australians are invited. By the beginning of 1964 it was known that Murdoch had bought some land in Mort Street, only a few hundred yards from the office of the *Canberra Times*. At the King's Hall reception, Murdoch and some of his senior men found themselves in a group that included Shakespeare. It was a large circle of about a dozen people, standing shaking their drinks idly, trying not to feel awkward. To relieve a pause in the conversation, Shakespeare, a short and peppery man in his sixties, suddenly snapped at Murdoch: "What are you going to do with that property in Mort Street?" Murdoch paused for only an instant before roaring, "Run you out of business!" and cackling loudly. Everyone in the circle joined in the laughter, but at least two of them—Murdoch and Shakespeare—knew it was no joke. Not long after that Shakespeare flew to Sydney to invoke the agreement with Fairfax.

Murdoch had already begun planning Australia's first national daily. To run the editorial side, he hired Max Newton, managing editor of the *Financial Review*. This specialist paper, owned by the Fairfax group, had just made a successful transition from weekly to daily under Newton's talented leadership, but he was a volatile, plain-speaking man and he had fallen out with the Fairfax management. When Murdoch hired him for the new venture, he took with him Jules Zanetti, his deputy at the *Review*, and hired a number of other senior journalists. They all met to plan the new paper in Murdoch's suite on "Mahogany Row," the nickname given to the executive offices at his Sydney headquarters. They had endless inconclusive discussions and it soon became plain that Murdoch planned to do it very much his own way.

The first thing they had to decide was a name. Each of the eight or nine men sitting in the room had his own idea. Names like National Inquirer, Canberra Star, National Chronicle were thrown up and considered. Suddenly Murdoch piped up: "I've had a thought. What about calling it the *Australian?*" The consensus was that it was a boring name. The others quickly dismissed it and went back to discussing their own suggestions. But it soon dawned on them that what Murdoch had said was not a passing idea at all. He had decided that was going to be the name of the paper and had chosen that oblique way of telling them.

His new employees quickly learned this as one of his techniques. At a planning session Murdoch pulled a telegram from his pocket. "I've just had a cable from this man in London offering his services. Name's Chandler. Anyone ever heard of him?" Nobody had and Murdoch put the cable back in his pocket. The talk switched to other matters and the others assumed that was the end of the matter. But a few months later Solly Chandler, formerly with the *Daily Express* and at the time with the *Daily Sketch* in London, arrived and started to sit in on the planning meetings. Neither he nor Murdoch would be specific about his role. When the paper started he became copy taster, with the job of looking at incoming news stories and evaluating them. Zanetti, whose tasks were supposed to include finding a story to lead the paper with—not easy in a country with no tradition of national journalism—would discover towards the end of the day that Chandler had been working away on a front page lead different from his, and Chandler's would normally take precedence. He was an example of Murdoch's penchant for putting a "spoiler" into a newspaper's hierarchy, believing that the resulting tension keeps people on their toes. When Zanetti complained to Murdoch about how wasteful it was of resources and energy to pit people against each other like that, the proprietor would smile.

"Survival of the fittest, that's how you run a newspaper," he would declare. "You've been reading too many of your management books." Zanetti did not find a way of handling the technique and soon asked to quit his executive post. At the end of 1964 he was sent to London.

The early days of the *Australian* amounted to the most concentrated period of excitement in Murdoch's life. Starting a new paper is not something anyone gets to do very often, but this was one facing problems nobody in Australia had tackled before: how to edit one paper to capture the whole nation's interest and, more practically, how to ensure that it reached audiences separated by many hundreds of miles.

It had, too, to find a national advertising constituency. City papers attract local classified advertising and page after page of display panels for department stores, supermarkets and entertainments. At first Murdoch hoped local Canberra advertising would provide a solid financial base for the project, but the improvement of the *Canberra Times,* charging only 60 pence a line for classified ads, ruled that out. The *Canberra Times* changed from a broadsheet to a tabloid just before the *Australian* was launched. Readers did not like the change much and its effect, combined with the appeal of Murdoch's new paper, distributed free for its first few days, was to push sales of the *Times* down to around 12,000 at its worst. But then as the *Australian* began to falter, the *Times* regained health and it became apparent that it was not to be displaced as the local daily paper of the capital. Murdoch's paper had reached sales of over 200,000 in its first heady days, but quickly sank to around 50,000.

Adrian Deamer, later to become the *Australian's* most controversial editor, gave a graphic account of the early days in a lecture at Melbourne University in 1971, soon after his rancorous dismissal. The chief practical problem was flying the plastic matrices from Canberra for printing in Melbourne and Sydney. In winter, Canberra airport often gets fogbound around midnight. Murdoch would go and plead with the pilots to make the trip anyway; if they would not, the matrices had to be driven to Cooma, more than an hour's drive away, for the flight to Melbourne, while those for Sydney were taken all the way by road.

"It was exciting and entertaining," Deamer said. "Real frontier newspaper stuff right out of an old B class movie—with Mr. Murdoch, in the early days, standing on the tarmac in his pajamas egging the pilots on, convincing them and [airport] officials that the fog was really only a light mist. But it was not the most reliable way to produce a newspaper, and reliability, however dull it sounds, is the first requirement of a newspaper."

In a television interview in 1967, Murdoch called the launching of the paper "the greatest challenge and the biggest task that has been put before me I think in life yet...the biggest and most exciting thing." On the same program Max Newton described an evening when he was having a drink with Murdoch, who told him: "I've got where I am by some pretty tough, larrikin* methods, but I've got there. And what I want to do is produce a newspaper that my father would have been proud of."

Newton, who quickly fell out with his new proprietor, said: "Throughout the planning period Rupert was excellent. I think he gets more fun out of planning things than actually the business of doing them. He's not very good at managing things....

"Rupert was excited and at the top of his form. He was happy. It was when we got started that he started to get unhappy because he was continually afraid that somebody—myself—was going to, as it were, take over, I think. Another thing of course was that while he had this great ability as managing director to get into the detail of the organization, he carried this to extraordinary lengths. The first four or five months, up until the time I left the organization, Rupert would quite often be seen down on the stone making up the paper....Very unnerving. This is the sort of work that should be done, as you know, by a sub-editor earning about twenty-five pounds a week.

"Mr. Murdoch was known around the office after a while as 'Puff the Magic Founder'...not a vicious or a satirical comment on him but an indication I think that a certain cynicism quickly grew up because the paper didn't live up to its own promise, and the staff who'd been quite excited at the prospect of working on a great newspaper felt that somehow they'd been cheated and the paper wasn't anywhere near so good as they'd been led to believe."

It was an uncertain start and the temperamental Newton, who has some larrikin characteristics himself, was its first victim. The production problems, combined with the differences over editorial content, made it impossible for two strong individualists to work together for long.

On that 1967 television program, which remains the best documentation of the early days of the *Australian,* Murdoch said bitterly: "It frankly proved a lot bigger job than I expected. We ran

---

*Larrikin: boozy, uncultured Australian. Though the more cultivated citizens affect shock at their excesses, they secretly admire them as part of their distinctive heritage.

into opposition from quarters we didn't expect, heartbreaking opposition at some times. It's been a pretty buffeting two years that I've had, getting a paper established. People who've made a life out of criticizing newspapers, calling for something better, have been turning on you and making a full-time occupation of looking for spelling mistakes in the one paper that's been trying to satisfy them."

And Newton took up the narrative: "When I met Rupert it seemed a very exciting thing. Here was a young bloke prepared to spend a lot of money doing something that was probably going to be very good. At least we hoped it was. One didn't realize at the time, meeting Rupert, who on first impression gives you this sort of 'I'm just a simple boy, you know—I'm a very likeable kid' thing, you don't realize that there's a great deal of iron behind the boyish exterior, and he's a very tough proprietor who I think in the course of the period of the *Australian* sacked more journalists than I think I've ever seen sacked in my whole career. He's a tremendous sacker. But of course he's also a tremendous hirer. He's always sacking them and hiring them."

The words were prophetic for Newton, who, some fifteen years after he left the *Australian* following a blazing row, was hired by Murdoch as a financial commentator for his *New York Post.*

Murdoch defended his record in the television interview: "Just because I haven't managed to get the right working relationship with every single editor I've appointed doesn't for a minute suggest that I'm ruthless. In fact if you'd known the precise reasoning at the time...and the sort of settlement these people got. I think one would consider me—a lot of people did consider me—rather ridiculously soft....I'm far too easy-going as a rule."

His secretary vouchsafed: "He suffered intensely with every staff change he had to make....There were no heads rolled before he made enquiries as to how the person would be placed...nothing ruthless—it may have appeared to be that outside because he has to have a face outside, otherwise he'd be taken for a ride."

One of the remarkable aspects of Murdoch's career has been the consistency of his techniques, attitudes and weaknesses. His failure to get the right working relationship with many of his editors has dogged him to this day, most notably leading to the spectacular break with Harold Evans on the London *Times* in 1982. And the fear of being taken for a ride—if we can assume that his secretary was speaking with her master's voice—persists too.

In March 1956, a few years after taking over at the *News,* Murdoch married Patricia Booker. Nearly thirty years later people who knew him and Pat observed that the couple were not well matched. She could not cope with his dynamism and unpredictable schedule, and, soon after they moved to Sydney in 1960, the marriage began to break up. It was an unhappy business, conducted with suspicion and ill-feeling. Their daughter Prudence was especially wounded, and lawyers were hired to negotiate a financial settlement.

Not long afterwards, Murdoch met Anna Torv, the eighteen-year-old daughter of immigrants from Latvia. She was a trainee reporter on the *Mirror* and one of her first jobs was to report the night-club circuit. They are said to have met first at a Sydney night-club called Chequers. Murdoch had gone there with Douglas Brass, who introduced him to Anna. Soon they were seeing much of each other, and when Murdoch went to Canberra to start the *Australian,* Anna was one of the Sydney reporters sent there to help launch it.

Because Murdoch was, for the next few months at least, going to be spending most of his time in Canberra, Anna wanted to work there, and she went to see Jules Zanetti, the assistant editor, to ask for a job. She and Murdoch had kept their relationship so discreet that Zanetti knew nothing of it. He had already been warned against poaching staff from other papers in the group, so he turned down her request. Next day Murdoch called on him:

"I believe that girl Anna Torv was in to see you," he observed. Zanetti said that she was and that she had been after a job.

"Did you give her one?" he asked, and Zanetti said he had not, that he had already been having problems with the Mirror organization and had no plans to make things worse. Murdoch looked at him quizzically but said nothing.

Later Anna went to Zanetti again. Slow on the uptake, Zanetti did not recognize his conversation with Murdoch as an instruction to hire her. So when she asked him: "Hasn't Mr. Murdoch spoken to you?" he replied that yes, her name had been mentioned, but there was still no job.

That night Murdoch came to see him again and said simply: "That girl Anna Torv. Hire her." Zanetti did. She was soon given one of the most coveted assignments for young reporters, a berth on the gossip column.

They married in 1967 in Sydney and Anna has proved an ideal wife for Murdoch—competent and self-contained, an excellent organizer and hostess, bringing order to a home life which, because of his business demands, must necessarily be erratic. She had learned these skills as a child. Her parents were separated and, as the oldest of the children, she had been almost a surrogate mother to her brothers and sisters, living with their father in the western suburbs of Sydney. There are three children from Murdoch's second marriage.

The period of Adrian Deamer's editorship, from 1968 to 1971, is regarded by many as the high point of the *Australian*'s history. Now published from Sydney, where production difficulties were fewer than in Canberra, the paper reached a circulation of 143,000 in the early months of 1970 and was making a tidy profit. But a recession and a price increase combined to push the circulation down, and, under a succession of short-term editors, it has seldom looked as if it were recovering.

Deamer was an editor of decided views, not an easy man to work with, but he did impart to the paper a clear political philosophy that it had hitherto lacked. He was, in one sense, lucky that his term of office coincided with Murdoch's thrust into Britain, so he was less subject to proprietorial interference than were Newton and the early editors.

In the end, though, the fact that Murdoch was visiting Australia ever more rarely was a factor in Deamer's dismissal. Just as he had not felt able to trust Rivett on his own in Adelaide, Murdoch wanted an editor whose views he could rely on. One of the results of the growing multi-national nature of the organization has been the appointment of safe, colorless editors: yes-men may not be too strong a word—mice who can be trusted not to play irresponsibly during the cat's long absences.

Under Deamer, the paper had found a constituency among intellectuals at the universities. Deamer, admittedly a biased witness, put it like this in his 1971 Melbourne lecture: "They were intensely devoted to the paper in a way that I have never come across before. They felt somehow that the paper belonged to them and they cared about it, argued about it, disagreed with it but kept on buying it."

But Murdoch and his most influential lieutenants were not happy with what they saw as a growing leftward drift. Bruce Rothwell, a conservative formerly with the *Daily Mail* in London, had been brought in to edit the *Sunday Australian,* launched in February 1971 and modelled on the London *Sunday Times.* The new paper had not been a success in its first months and Rothwell was keen to increase his influence in the organization. He reported to the proprietor that, under Deamer, the *Australian* was too obsessed with liberal causes, and Murdoch listened.

Deamer said that the gist of Murdoch's complaint was that the paper had become too intellectual and too political. "It was anti-Australian, it preferred black people to white people, it wanted to flood the country with Asians. He complained it took up every 'bleeding heart' cause that was fashionable among the long-haired left. It was not interested in the development and progress of Australia. It criticized the political leaders he supported. It was dull, it was a knocking paper, and it stood for everything he opposed and opposed everything he stood for."

A year later Murdoch gave the same Melbourne lecture, inevitably seen as a reply to Deamer. "There is a tendency," he said, "for many journalists to bring their commitments with them and impose them on their work." He ended with a succinct statement of his publishing philosophy: "The public certainly has no duty to support newspapers. It is the duty of the publishers to provide the type of newspaper the public wants to read."

Looking through the files of the paper for June 1971—the month before Deamer left—it is easy to see what irritated Murdoch. The front page was generally dominated by two issues that had become the subject of left-wing protest—the Vietnam war and the Springbok (South African) rugby football tour of Australia. The Premier of Queensland had declared a state of emergency to help his police maintain order while the Springboks played there. When the Australian Prime Minister, Billy McMahon, offered the use of an air force jet to fly the team from Perth to Adelaide, Deamer ran a front page editorial headed, "Cynical misuse of a Prime Minister's power." Other editorials urged that a proposed South African cricket tour be banned by the government—but the paper also denounced violent demonstrations against the rugby team.

On July 24th, 1971, a short announcement appeared on the front page headed: "New posts on the *Australian*." It said that Bruce Rothwell was now editor-in-chief of the *Australian* and Evan Williams of the *Sunday Australian*. Deamer was not mentioned at all. It was as though he had never existed.

Rothwell's brief was to broaden the appeal of the *Australian* by making it less political—moving it towards the *Daily Express* model rather than the *Observer*. Business coverage was strengthened to attract wealthier readers for the pleasure of advertisers. The university audience gradually drifted away, but was not replaced by an equivalent number of new readers.

TWO

Go North, Young Man

Rupert is a gentleman.

—*Sir William Carr*

When you have newspapers in all the main Australian cities, as well as the country's only national daily, and you are still comfortably under forty, what next? Australia has scarcely more than fourteen million people and there is a limit to how many words they can read. Yet the other big Australian press magnates—the Fairfaxes, the Packers and the rest—had never thought seriously about expanding beyond their own hemisphere. They were content to slug it out among themselves in their existing markets, gaining satisfaction from a comparatively marginal redistribution of the spoils in their favor.

Murdoch, when he worked briefly at the *Daily Express* in London before returning to Adelaide, was impressed with the slickness, the self-confidence and the success of the operation. He thought it significant that it was all in effect the creation of a single dynamic man, Lord Beaverbrook, who had come to Britain from Canada armed with great energy and unrestricted by the fusty conservatism that afflicted most British commerce. Again, the most recent major acquisition in the British press had been by another Canadian, Roy Thomson. He had bought the badly-managed Kemsley Newspapers—including the *Sunday Times*—in 1959 and added *The Times* itself to the stable in 1966.

The trouble was that the family dynasties that owned much of the British press depended too much for their success on the managerial competence of whichever generation happened to be in charge. It was a hazardous business. There was nothing to guarantee that the son of an accomplished entrepreneur would inherit his father's commercial sense.

Some of the groups had drifted and atrophied and were ripe for the injection of bold new ideas from outside. Did it always have to be Canadians? Just because an Australian had never done it was no reason why one should not try.

Murdoch's ambition to make himself felt on Fleet Street had been growing for years. Soon after his move to Sydney he decided to do something about it. Through his London bankers, Morgan Grenfell, he began to buy shares in the International Publishing Corporation (IPC), publishers of the *Daily Mirror.* Though he had worked on the *Express,* the *Mirror* was the paper he really admired. It seemed to him, as to many others, the epitome of what a tabloid should be—racy, irreverent and with a red-blooded quality. His *Mirror* in Sydney was frankly modelled on it.

Like an art collector who has never been able to afford anything more than a reproduction Picasso, Murdoch longed to move up in the market and buy an original. To extend the metaphor, when his chance did come, he had to decide whether to hold out for the Picasso or settle for an original by a lesser artist.

The *News of the World* was unique in nearly every respect. Its six-million copy sale every Sunday gave it the largest circulation of any paper in Britain. It sustained this by a peculiarly British mixture of titillation and ingenuousness. Its stock-in-trade on the "news" pages was stories about sexual crimes or indiscretions among the respectable classes, with as much explicit detail as was allowed by a somewhat arbitrary and often changing yardstick of taste. Mixed with this were frequent "revelations" about prostitution, preferably taking place in seemingly innocent suburban houses.

The world created by the *News of the World* was one where torrid lusts and passions were acted out in unsuspecting day-to-day surroundings. The reader was supposed to wonder whether that mild man opposite in the pub was the one who had lured his teenage niece to the bicycle shed and there made her do unspeakable things.

And was the mousy woman shuffling down that tree-lined street going to turn in at number thirty-five, pull on black fishnet stockings, draw the chintz curtains and start her day's work entertaining a succession of furtive male customers in bowler hats and raincoats?

The paper had been more or less controlled by the Carr family since 1891. Sir Emsley Carr, editor for fifty years until he died in 1941, had created the formula that had remained essentially unchanged since. His son, Sir William Carr, had, by 1968, been chairman for sixteen years. Then fifty-six, he ran the firm as a family concern and saw nothing wrong in using its resources for his personal comfort and amusement. The family enjoyed company boxes at Ascot races and the Covent Garden opera. There were company golf courses in Surrey and Spain where Sir William played. The paper owned thoroughbreds and a stud farm and sponsored a race at Goodwood. Carr would host regular black-tie stag dinners at the company flat at Cliveden Place in London's exclusive Belgravia district—one floor below his own plush quarters. All this affected profitability and the share price, and that was compounded by an unadventurous record of expansion. While other newspaper companies had branched into a variety of profitable sidelines, Carr ran the *News of the World* conservatively. Diversification had been almost exclusively in print-related businesses and television, though there were small interests in chemicals, transportation and engineering, plus the Townsend Hook paper company. But profits, at below 2 million pounds, had dropped by nearly one million pounds over five years. And the paper's circulation had fallen by a quarter from a peak of well over eight million in 1950.

Carr drank too much and his health was a worry. He suffered from a painful and debilitating aneurism, a swelling of the main artery. He owned 32 percent of the shares. The second largest block, 25 percent, was held by his cousin, Professor Derek Jackson, a slightly eccentric scientist and inventor who had married six times and now lived in Paris. He was a difficult man to get on with and was not on especially friendly terms with his cousin William. The Carrs were a quarrelsome family. Sir William had only managed to gain control after the war by dint of a cleverly executed campaign against his relatives. That was why Jackson did not consult him before announcing that he was going to sell his holding, then resisted his cousin's blandishment to change his mind.

It was alarming news for Carr, for unless the Jackson shares fell into friendly hands he could easily lose control of the company. So he instructed Hambros, his bank, to offer Jackson the then market price of twenty-eight shillings a share.* Rothschild's, handling the sale for Jackson, said it was not enough, and sought another potential buyer. The family feud came to the surface here, too, because Jacob Rothschild, who ran the firm, was married to Serena Dunn. Her father, Philip Dunn, had been chairman of the *News of the World* in the 1940s as a representative of the Jackson interest—and he was the man Sir William had ousted to gain control.

Rothschild's found a customer for the shares in Robert Maxwell, the ebullient, high-flying Labour Member of Parliament who had achieved great success with Pergamon Press, a group devoted chiefly to publishing scientific and technical books and journals. As the Pergamon share price climbed in the 1960s, the company expanded into other publishing, printing and overseas ventures. The ownership of a national newspaper seemed a logical next step. Maxwell bid 37s. 6d for *News of the World* shares that then stood at 29s. 3d. A few days later they were up to 49s. 6d.

Carr and his portly editor Stafford Somerfield, close friends and drinking companions, reared back at the thought of sharing control with the abrasive, assertive Maxwell. They were not keen to share with anyone, but certainly not with this naturalized Czech who would surely try to turn the paper into a vehicle for his party. Somerfield delivered a harsh attack on Maxwell in an editorial published on October 20, 1968, just four days after his interest became known.

"Why do I think," he asked, "it would not be a good thing for Mr. Maxwell, formerly Jan Ludwig Hoch, to gain control of this newspaper which, I know, has your respect, loyalty and affection—a newspaper which I know is as British as roast beef and Yorkshire pudding?"

---

*Before the reform of the British currency in 1971, there were twenty shillings (s) to the pound and twelve pence (d) to the shilling. Now there are 100 pence (p) to the pound.

Somerfield claimed that the paper's editorial stance was independent—though it was an independence standing very much to the right of center. He pointed out that leaders of all parties had written for it.

"I, as editor, as those before me—there have only been six of us since 1891, we don't change very often—have been able to direct this policy because of the complete backing of the chairman of the board, now Sir William Carr, who has followed a great family tradition. Would this attitude and policy be continued by a complete stranger, as far as Fleet Street and this newspaper are concerned, a man with no newspaper experience and a Socialist MP?

"Mr. Maxwell has gone on record as saying that if he gained control he would not change the policy of the paper. But what guarantee is there of this? Mr. Maxwell has also said that he would cease to be a Socialist MP if he gained control.... But is it possible for him to support the Socialists one day and become completely impartial the next? I do not think so. I believe that Mr. Maxwell is interested in power and money. There is nothing wrong with that but it is not everything."

Then he went back to his point about Maxwell's nationality: "This is a British newspaper, run by British people. Let's keep it that way."

The harsh tone of the editorial alienated many who had formerly sympathized with Somerfield and Carr. David Steel, the young Liberal MP, summed up the prevailing attitude in an article in the *Guardian:* "What a revolting piece of chauvinism. Mr. Maxwell is not everybody's cup of tea and he knows it, but he is as disgustingly British as anybody I know. He even has a Rolls-Royce with a telephone in it." In his book *Banner Headlines,* Somerfield defended himself by saying that, to him, the situation was akin to 1939. "I was at war and, when at war, I saw no point in throwing friendly leaflets."

Rupert Murdoch had been alerted to the forthcoming fight over the *News of the World* by his friend Lord Catto, of Morgan Grenfell. It was not easy to decide whether to get into the bidding, for he knew that if he did so he would have to give up his ambitions with respect to IPC. He thought that if he continued to buy IPC shares steadily he could be in a position to bid for the company within ten years. (In fact it was sold to Reed International in 1970.) Should he hang on, or go for the here and now? Waiting was not really part of his nature. On hearing from Catto, Murdoch instructed the London bureau of his Australian newspapers to send to Sydney all news and press comment on the rumored Maxwell bid. When the bid became public he was in Melbourne preparing to go to the races. He flew immediately to London, pausing in Sydney to pick up his luggage and relevant documents. He arrived in such secrecy that it took his London office a day to discover he was there.

Murdoch, Catto and Harry Sporborg of Hambros had devised a clever plan to outflank the confident Maxwell. Instead of entering the contest as a third party, Murdoch would in effect shore up Carr. In return, Murdoch would become joint managing director, with Carr staying on as chairman and consultant. The plan was put to Carr at a breakfast meeting on Tuesday, October 22nd, at his flat in Cliveden Place. Sporborg convinced him that it was the only way to keep some control of the paper for his family. Next day Murdoch's News Ltd. began buying shares, and it was only then that his interest became known publicly.

Even Somerfield, a director of the company, had not not been told. The first he knew was when, early the following morning, a friend on the *Daily Express* telephoned him and said: "Your savior is here. It's young Rupert Murdoch from Australia."

By October 24th, 1968, Carr and Murdoch between them owned fractionally more than half the shares, but Maxwell was not finished. He complained to the Takeover Panel, a self-policing body of the London Stock Market, which did not approve of companies buying their own shares to frustrate a takeover offer. Dealings in *News of the World* shares were suspended and remained so until Christmas. During that two months the battle between Murdoch and Maxwell became increasingly acrimonious, with each side accusing the other of dirty tricks. Murdoch's Australian papers launched an investigation into the operation of encyclopedia salesmen working for a Maxwell company there.

Maxwell suspected people working for Murdoch of spreading a rumor that he was bankrupt. Maxwell and his ally, the respected financier Sir Isaac Woolfson, tried to persuade Carr that Murdoch's intentions were dishonorable. "You will be out before your feet touch the ground," Maxwell told him. "Bob, Rupert is a gentleman," Carr replied.

When dealings were suspended, Murdoch had only 3½ percent of the shares—a stake of less than one million pounds in a thirty-million-pound company. On October 26th he revealed his clever plan in full. New shares would be created in the *News of the World* by merging some of his Australian properties into it. All the new shares would go to Murdoch, giving him 40 percent of the issued shares. His understanding with Carr contained three safeguards: that he and Carr would be joint managing-directors, that a member of the Carr family would remain chairman of the company for the foreseeable future and that he would not seek to increase his shareholding to give himself absolute control.

Many financial commentators agreed with Maxwell that the deal with Murdoch violated rule thirty-three of the Takeover Code. This stipulated that companies could only take allies to defeat takeover bids if it was not prejudicial to the interests of shareholders. Murdoch's offer of a link with a random bunch of his Australian papers seemed intrinsically less beneficial to shareholders than Maxwell's cash offer. Professor Jackson arrived from the Continent to see the Takeover Panel and to side with Maxwell: but the Panel had precious little power to intervene even if its rules had been breached. Anthony Crosland, President of the Board of Trade in the Labour Government, commented: "As there are very few sanctions at the Panel's disposal, it will have to rely mainly on the respect shown for its views." Maxwell remains convinced that the Panel could and should have acted but did not do so because the City establishment was against him, largely on account of his politics.

The Carrs were an old-fashioned upper-class family. Almost the first thing they had done in response to Maxwell's bid was to foregather—nineteen of them—in the company flat and have their picture taken, to underline their solidarity. Although Murdoch was in no sense their kind of person, he was still to be preferred to the flash Maxwell, the known and feared quantity. The grating Australian accent was unfortunate but that presumably would soften in time. The spirited Lady Carr took it upon herself to try to smooth some of Murdoch's rougher edges, to make him acceptable socially. It started well enough when she invited Dame Elisabeth Murdoch to lunch at the Cliveden Place flat. That went splendidly: there was a woman who obviously knew how to behave. But the enterprise foundered when she made the bold move of asking Rupert to lunch at the Coq d'Or, a classy Mayfair restaurant. It was the first time she could remember taking a strange man out to lunch and it was not a success. She found him lacking in small talk and a sense of humor. That need not have mattered—it holds good, after all, for many prominent society people—but the moment she knew there was to be no taming the Austrlian beast came early on, during pre-lunch cocktails, when he summoned the waiter to ask for a cigar and began puffing before the first course. She recognized then, before his business behavior confirmed it, that Murdoch was not the good news the Carrs had hoped for.

Scenting victory, Murdoch now made the first of the crucial variations to his agreement with Carr. He was to become sole managing-director, not joint, and Carr would be chairman. In a letter to Carr, Murdoch said he still hoped members of the Carr family would continue to serve as chairman—an aspiration that, within a year, was dashed.

By now the contest between Maxwell and Murdoch was being given press coverage similar in spirit, if not in scale, to a soccer cup final. The match was fixed for Thursday, January 2nd, 1969, in the Connaught Rooms in London, where shareholders would vote on the Murdoch merger. The Takeover Panel had ruled that shares acquired since Maxwell's bid should not count for voting purposes. This meant that the balance of power as between the Jackson shares (twenty-five percent) and the Carr shares (thirty-two percent) lay with the small shareholders who had not sold out.

There was never much doubt that Murdoch would emerge the winner, and although Maxwell could see this as well as anyone, he put on a show of resistance. He even thought of joining forces with Lord Thomson, the Canadian owner of *The Times* and the *Sunday Times,* to buy out News Ltd. in Australia. Then Maxwell provoked three members of the *News of the World* pension fund, which owned 600,000 shares, to seek an injunction preventing the fund's trustees from voting in Murdoch's favor. The injunction was refused on the eve of the shareholders' meeting.

At the meeting, Murdoch made a three-minute speech claiming that great benefits would flow from a liaison between the Australian and British newspaper groups. He paid tribute to Sir William Carr, repeating his intention to keep him on as chairman. Then Maxwell gave a typical rough-and-tumble performance, attacking the record of the company and the tactics of their bankers. His own offer, he maintained, would provide great benefits for shareholders.

After some angry exchanges, Carr persuaded him to sit down. The vote by a show of hands was overwhelmingly in Murdoch's favor, and after a tally according to numbers of shares held, Murdoch was ahead by more than a million votes. "The law of the jungle has prevailed," said Maxwell, but perhaps the most apt remark came from Professor Jackson: "I regard the *News of the World* board as raving mad."

Safely in charge, Murdoch did not take long to flex his muscles. On January 21st, less than three weeks after the shareholders' meeting, he sent Carr a handwritten letter. Beginning with some solicitous remarks about the chairman's health, he went on to announce that he was planning to buy some of the Jackson shares, which Rothschild's were putting on the market. He explained that if he did not take his chance now he would miss out, but stressed that his plan did not change in any way the understanding the two had reached. Since a key feature of the understanding had been that Murdoch would not seek a majority of the shares, it was hard to credit that disclaimer.

This was the first of a series of swift moves by which Murdoch secured sole control of the company. Carr remained ill and inactive for weeks after the change, and Murdoch could have used that as an excuse to ease him out. Instead, he chose to make precisely the opposite argument, saying that the prospect of Carr's recovery made it imperative for him to act. The company had always been run on patriarchal rather than on formal commercial lines, and Murdoch feared a more active Carr would provide a focal point for disaffection by the resentful "old guard" —chief among them editor Stafford Somerfield, already showing signs of resistance.

On March 2nd Murdoch wrote to Carr that his improved health and increased contacts with senior executives of the company left him, Murdoch, no alternative but to point out that there could be only one executive boss. While respecting Carr's position as chairman of the board, he did not intend a situation to develop where there could be confusion about the chain of command.

It took only three more months for Murdoch to get around to the logical climax of the pressure he was putting on Carr: he asked him to resign as chairman and a director and proposed to take over as chairman himself. Less than seven months earlier he had written that he would hope Carr or members of his family would remain as chairman: but now he wanted to tighten his personal control. This time he did use the argument that Carr's health had prevented him from carrying out his duties. After an acrimonious correspondence between lawyers, the terms of Carr's departure were agreed, and at the annual meeting on June 19th, 1969, giving no hint in his dignified statement that he had been forced out, Carr resigned as chairman. Murdoch's control was now complete. Carr became seriously ill again not long afterwards and was more or less an invalid for the last seven years of his life. When Carr died in 1977, Murdoch offered to pay for a memorial service for him, but a proud Lady Carr refused.

With Murdoch indisputably at the helm, any remaining family atmosphere at the *News Of The World* quickly evaporated. He was not coy about declaring his contempt for the talents and energy of many of the journalists he had inherited. Somerfield remembers breaking to him the upsetting news that Jack Miller, the paper's television and radio correspondent, had dropped dead the previous night. "Well, it wasn't from overwork," Murdoch snapped.

(Murdoch has never felt it necessary to be hypocritical in talking about the dead. In the mid-1960s he was visiting Perth, Western Australia, shortly after Zell Rabin, the young editor of his Sydney *Daily Mirror,* had died of cancer. A group of journalists in a bar were expressing their sympathy. "Not to worry, the new editor's much better," declared the buoyant Murdoch.)

Because Somerfield insisted on keeping control as editor, the influence Murdoch was able to exert on the style and content of the paper was, at first, minimal. In any case, it was not his intention to alter its essential character, and his first big row with British press critics and opinion-molders came over a story of a traditional *News of the World* nature.

Five years earlier the paper had paid £26,000 for serial rights to the memoirs of Christine Keeler, a call-girl whose liaison with War Minister John Profumo had discredited the Macmillan government in 1963. Now Keeler had written the story for a second time, with extra juicy details revealed, and the papers were bidding for it again.

It would not be such big money as last time, but, six years after the event, interest in this distinctively British scandal was still high.

Somerfield read the new version, liked it and showed it to Murdoch. On July 22nd Murdoch wrote to him enthusiastically, urging him to buy it, though the "dirty" bits in the early parts should be held out. He did wonder, at that early stage, whether it might stir emotions so strongly that the paper and the company might be damaged.

The letter went on to suggest that the story was probably worth about £10,000 but that he would be prepared to go up to £15,000. The final purchase price was £21,000 and an extra 150,000 copies were printed in anticipation of demand. Murdoch's letter to Somerfield shows that he was aware of the storm likely to erupt when the series began to run. Emotions were indeed stirred strongly, particularly in those high Conservative circles that sought to forget the embarrassment of 1963 and to whom Profumo, who had now devoted his life to good works, had become a respected figure, well on the way to rehabilitation. For anyone to reopen these old sores— and especially an outsider who could not expect to appreciate the nuances of British life—was unsporting and reprehensible.

Yet even given all that, the outcry seemed out of proportion with the offense. The Press Council—inspired by Denis Hamilton of *The Times* and the *Sunday Times*—condemned the series, and Cardinal Heenan, Britain's senior Catholic, withdrew from a commitment to write an article for the paper. Somerfield, accustomed to such controversy, was a bit too blasé about it for Murdoch, sensitive about the impression he was creating in his new country and worried that he might be gaining a reputation that would inspire resistance to his making further acquisitions in Britain. Discussing Heenan's response in an interview with the *Daily Mail* Somerfield ventured that he would have thought the Cardinal would welcome the idea of talking to fifteen million sinners. Next day Murdoch dashed off an angry, hand-written note. He said he was appalled by Somerfield's remarks and had apologized to Cardinal Heenan. In the future Somerfield should either say nothing or clear his statements with Murdoch first. There was, he insisted, a lot more at stake than one newspaper.

The last observation was a reference to his negotiations to buy the *Sun,* about to be wound up by IPC. But Murdoch's own performance as spokesman, as defender of his right to publish salacious scandal, was not crowned with success. In television interviews he came across as sanctimonious and muddled.

"We can forgive Mr. Profumo," he told interviewer David Dimbleby. "We can do what we can to see that he's rehabilitated because he has tried very hard. By all means forgive the individual; but you can't forget." Dimbleby quoted back at him his reported remark that "people can sneer as much as they like, but I'll take the 150,000 extra copies we're going to sell" and asked whether he was not lining his pocket with sleazy material.

"I don't agree it's sleazy for a minute," Murdoch snapped back. "Nor do I agree that it's unfair to the man. I have the greatest sympathy with him, but it doesn't alter the fact that everybody knows what happened. Certainly it's going to sell newspapers."

Murdoch's most notorious interview was with David Frost on London Weekend Television. His advisers were divided about whether he should accept the invitation from a man skilled at advocacy interviewing, at acting as barrister at the trial of his victims and persuading the studio audience to be the jury and pass sentence. He claims he was misled as to the nature of the program.

He was assured by David Frost that no other guest would be in the studio, and that was true, but what Frost concealed, according to the Murdoch camp, was that a filmed interview with Cardinal Heenan would be inserted into the proceedings. Frost maintains that Murdoch was told about that and agreed to it. The trouble, according to Frost, was that Murdoch was too shrill in his own defense. Had he admitted graciously that he might be blameworthy in some respects, the issue could have been shelved and the discussion broadened. His stubborn insistence that he was right meant that the interview was stuck on the one subject—and Murdoch's defense was inadequate.

It was the first Independent Television program to go out live in color, and after a joke or two about that ("to viewers watching in color, we hope you will both like it very much indeed"), Frost asked the studio audience whether they approved of the publication of the Keeler memoirs. Only nine out of 230 did. That result encouraged Frost to maintain a high moral tone throughout.

Murdoch first sought to defend publication of the series by saying that the early part of the book, containing much explicit sex, had been largely excised from the serialization. The articles would concentrate on Miss Keeler's role as a scapegoat and "the parliamentary side of it, the behavior of the Labour Party in it: very interesting indeed." Frost was able to point out how unfortunate it was that the only episode to have appeared thus far was taken entirely from the first part of the book and that the front page teasers for ensuing weeks had concentrated on titillation rather than on any redeeming social message.

Then Murdoch was caught out in claiming that the new work represented the first time the affair had been put into proper context. Frost referred him to a book by Wayland Young, from which the Keeler work had quoted extensively. Murdoch had to confess he had not read it, and fell back on the alternative argument that it was possible to tell the same story several times. Frost was quick to point out the inconsistency. Then, in response to Murdoch's revised claim that some facts may be new to some readers, Frost asked: "But what new facts? Like this: 'Stephen brought Bill round and we spent a very amusing evening, Bill running after us and trying to pinch our bottoms'?"

That was only the first segment of the program. It would scarcely seem possible for things to go downhill for Murdoch from that low point, but they did.

Frost next showed the interview with Cardinal Heenan he had filmed earlier in the day. The contrast with the live section of the program was startling. Here was Frost cozy and respectful, giving Heenan the chance to expound at length his moral principles and his reason for withdrawing from his agreement to write for the *News of the World*. Heenan's main concern was for Profumo, a sinner who had worked hard to rehabilitate himself. He pointed out that many of the people Profumo was working with in London's improverished East End probably read the *News of the World*. "I think they were profoundly wrong in raking up the past of this excellent man Profumo and putting it in the homes of the people whom he is now trying to help."

When the time came for Murdoch to comment on this, he confessed to being "incredibly shocked." He said angrily: "This easy glib talk that the *News of the World* is a dirty paper is downright libel and it is not true and I resist it completely." People only said it, he maintained, because the paper was so successful.

John Addey, Murdoch's public relations man, was in the audience applauding these sallies, and now Frost turned on him. "Your PR man's doing a wonderful job over there. He's made more noise than the other 230 people put together.... Still, that's what he's paid for."

By now Frost had dropped any pretense of being an impartial moderator and was assuming the unambiguous role of prosecutor. When Murdoch sought to defend the Keeler series as a "cautionary tale," Frost retorted: "A cautionary tale about the best way to make 21,000 pounds?" Murdoch came back: "You make that every week. Don't show horror about that. Come on, let's be grown up about it." And Frost declaimed, to the applause of the audience: "What money I make I don't make by means of exposing a man like John Profumo in that way."

Frost now had the bit between his teeth. He described a visit he had made to Toynbee Hall, Profumo's charitable settlement in the East End, where ex-prisoners, drug addicts and the needy were given a helping hand. "If... you were to damage that man and that work, could you forgive yourself? Because you're a decent man....There is a man doing a fantastic job of work and you are threatening that work by this story and you still haven't given us one good reason for taking that risk."

Murdoch tried valiantly to keep his end up. He said the fuss had been "whipped up by members of the sort of establishment that don't want to be seen with Mr. Profumo anywhere." He added that as long as Profumo was alive people would associate his name with the scandal, and Frost snapped back: "If everybody knows, you don't need to tell the story again, do you?" Then, reading from the page one promotion for the series in the *News of the World* ("a night with the Russian huggie bear"), Frost stormed: "It's pathetic to say that that's a social document of our time." And he ended the interview on a scarcely impartial note: "Your PR man's going mad again. Your PR man is the only person who's applauded. You must give him a rise."

Reading the transcript of the interview after a gap of thirteen years, Frost's tendentious needling comes across as sharply as Murdoch's equivocation, confusion and sophistry. But it is easy to see how damaging it was to Murdoch at the time, and why for years he regretted agreeing to appear. That he did agree speaks for his confidence in his ability to defend what he felt, probably sincerely, to be utterly defensible.

He believed he had been framed. In an Australian television interview two years later, he said: "I was damned upset because I had been told by him and everyone else that it was going to be a nice pally talk. It didn't turn out quite the way I had expected. I'd been lulled into a state of unpreparedness."

Anna, who was with him, is said to have turned on Frost in the hospitality room after the program and hissed: "We've had enough of your hospitality." And as he strode out of the building, according to people who were with him, Murdoch vowed: "I will buy this company—and Frost will be out." Not long afterwards he fulfilled that promise, and those who know him are convinced that the incident, which wounded him deeply, was a factor in his decision.

There were other attacks, and he responded to them with spirit. When the *Observer* criticized his paper as being dirty, he hit back by describing as salacious an *Observer* article on how women get sexual fulfillment from riding horses. He went to see David Astor, then editor of the *Observer*, for peace talks, but relations stayed cool. Again, a few years later, he was to make a strong bid for Astor's paper, but it is possible to make too much of the element of vengeance in his attempted acquisitions. He is, after all, a man who has often felt himself slighted, and who makes a habit of bidding for whatever paper is going.

Murdoch believes today that it was a tactical error to publish the Keeler memoirs, so far as his personal standing in Britain was concerned. He has no doubt it was the the right decision for the paper: it was a mainstream *News of the World* story, it increased circulation and he saw nothing ethically wrong with it himself. But he knew that if he was to become an accepted and respected newspaper proprietor he would have to come to terms with the British establishment that, rightly or wrongly, believed him to have behaved caddishly in raking over Profumo's anguish.

In public he affected a swaggering disregard for such matters. What did acceptance into the inner circles of power matter to him? he would ask rhetorically. But to his friends it was clear that it did matter. It was in many respects the Rupert Stuart case all over again: he was being ostracized for a quite legitimate piece of journalistic enterprise by one of his papers, and he hated it. As he told Somerfield, "There is a lot more at stake than one newspaper."

After his clear humiliation at the hands of Frost the furor died down, but for some time afterwards there was a stiffness when he entered polite society, and Anna, according to friends, was wounded by a few social rebuffs.

The clash with Somerfield over his Heenan remark was not their first. Relations between the two had always been uneasy and neither made much effort to improve them. An early row, which set the tone for subsequent ones, came in May 1969, when Somerfield broke a holiday in Spain on being told by a colleague that, in his absence, Murdoch was making radical changes to the paper.

The two men's versions of the dispute conflicted. Somerfield says Murdoch had wanted to take the leader page out of the paper altogether and only agreed to replace it when Somerfield arrived in the office during the print run, but in a letter to Sir William Carr on May 22nd, two days after the event, Murdoch wrote that the editor's version was seriously inaccurate in detail.

Murdoch's letter was in response to a pompous memorandum that Somerfield had sent to all directors about editorial responsibility: "The Editor is the servant of the board, and contractually answerable to the board and the managing director. But this does not mean that the chief executive, acting independently of the board, can take his chair, seek to discharge his functions or introduce fundamental changes in the paper, without consultation."

Unused to receiving notes of this kind from his editors, Murdoch suspected that Somerfield was seeking a showdown that would end in a handsome payoff. But the two men patched up their relations and tolerated each other uneasily for the rest of that year. The affair of the Keeler memoirs thrust them together temporarily, despite the Heenan incident, and for the last months of 1969 Murdoch was engrossed in his purchase of the *Sun* from IPC. With that under his belt, he returned to Australia for two months around Christmas. Before leaving, he gave a lunch at the Ritz for senior colleagues and asked Somerfield to sit next to him. During the meal he thanked Somerfield for what he had done. The now wary editor wondered if anything sinister lay behind that friendly remark.

He had to wait until Murdoch's return to find out. Arriving in his office on a morning in February 1970, Somerfield was told that Murdoch wanted to see him at noon. In a short interview, he asked for his resignation. Somerfield fled to a pub round the corner, told his friends, and in a couple of hours it was headline news in the evening papers. The remaining seven years of his contract were paid off—a lump sum of around £100,000. Somerfield, then 59, was never to work in Fleet Street again, though he later bought a magazine about pedigree dogs which he edited from Ashford, Kent. His consolation was in knowing that he was the first of the line of Murdoch ex-editors in Britain.

One characteristic of the *News of the World* that damaged its profitability was that its presses were used only once a week. Nearly all its rivals had daily sisters to share overheads. Soon after taking control of the paper, Murdoch had spoken of launching a daily, to use the presses more economically. He believed in saying things like that, often and with conviction, simply to strike terror into the opposition, but few doubted he would some day carry out the threat. As it was, the chance to start a new daily came faster than he had anticipated.

The *Daily Mirror* had, in 1961, bought Odhams Press, publishers of the *Daily Herald* and the *People*—the main Sunday rival to the *News of the World*. The motive for the purchase was not to acquire the two newspapers but the string of profitable magazines that went with them. The *Herald* had the largest circulation of any daily paper in the 1930s, but had declined steadily since—weighed down, many thought, by a formal commitment to support the policies of the trade union movement. In 1964 Hugh Cudlipp, Chairman of Mirror Newspapers, had masterminded a revamping of the still sagging *Herald* as the *Sun,* a paper aimed at affluent young people, as the publicity said, "born of the age we live in." The commitment to the unions was dropped and optimism ran high, but the paper was not a success. Starting with the *Herald*'s old circulation of about 1,500,000, it never rose consistently above that, and by the middle of 1969 it was down to 850,000. IPC had lost £12,702,000 on the *Herald* and the *Sun* since 1961.

One of the architects of the *Sun*'s marketing concept had been Bert Hardy, deputy advertising director for the *Sun* and the *People*. Market research had indicated that the better-educated and more sophisticated working class were growing out of the traditional, wham-bang tabloids and wanted something a bit more intelligent. The size of the paper symbolized that—midway between a tabloid and a broadsheet. There was an emphasis on youth and leisure, especially in a twelve-page weekend supplement. They even had a name for their target audience: the growth generation. But either the market research was wrong or the concept was inadequately fulfilled, for the twelve weekend pages dwindled to almost nothing and the paper languished. Bert Hardy left IPC at the end of 1968, after twenty years, to join Rupert Murdoch. He was the first British executive Murdoch hired. The second, also from IPC, was Alex McKay, an Australian who had worked for Murdoch's father.

In the summer of 1969 the board of IPC decided to sell the *Sun* or, if they failed, to close it. The first person to declare an interest was Robert Maxwell, thwarted over the *News of the World* and still keen to break into Fleet Street. Maxwell's idea was to keep the paper's commitment to Labour and run it on a lower budget than was customary, not aiming for a mass circulation that would make it a rival to IPC's *Daily Mirror*. On this understanding, and because some jobs at least would be saved, IPC were prepared to give him the title for nothing, but the unions, to nobody's surprise, were less than enthusiastic, not just because of the precedent lower manning levels would set, but because they did not think Maxwell was a proprietor they could rely on.

Murdoch kept himself informed about all this and in August he felt the time was right to stake his claim. First he flew to Rome to see a holidaying Richard Briginshaw, head of NATSOPA, one of the most difficult of the print unions. Assured of his support, he wrote to IPC asking to start negotiations to take over the *Sun*. Hugh Cudlipp wrote back saying that as long as the discussions with Maxwell had not formally come to an end he could not start talking with anyone else—leaving the implication that as soon as Maxwell pulled out he would start doing business with Murdoch. Most of the IPC directors did not see much of a threat in a Murdoch purchase: like the press barons of Sydney nine years earlier, they were convinced he would be letting himself in for a heavy loss.

A few—notably Frank Rogers, the managing director—had their doubts, but Cudlipp could not see that he had any alternative. To close the paper when a buyer was ready to take it might on the face of it assure the commercial future of the *Mirror,* but it would be unacceptable to the unions, who could take revenge on the *Mirror* and its sister papers.

Maxwell pulled out and Cudlipp started talks with Murdoch. At first Murdoch was pressing to be given the title for nothing, as Maxwell had been offered it. But Rogers went to see him at the *News of the World* office in Bouverie Street and told him, first, that he did not personally favor any deal at all and, second, that he would certainly not agree to giving it away. The final modest price was under a million pounds. The rump of the editorial staff joined Murdoch, although most senior executives stayed with the Mirror group.

(As for Maxwell, it took him 15 years to maneuver himself back into a position where he might be able to avenge his double defeat at Murdoch's hands. After making passes at virtually every national newspaper in Britain, he eventually acquired the *Daily Mirror* group in July 1984, and thus owned the only paper that could challenge the dominance *The Sun* had by then achieved at the popular end of the market. With the *Mirror* came the *Sunday Mirror* and *Sunday People,* competing with the *News of the World.* A lively battle was anticipated between the two tough tycoons with very different personal and business styles, but equal reputations for ruthlessness.)

Murdoch knew precisely what kind of paper he wanted the *Sun* to be. He was convinced that the *Mirror,* by far the best-selling tabloid, was not as good as it had been when it was the object of his most fervent desire. Now, he felt, it was the soft underbelly of the popular market. It was suffering to an extent from the affliction that had led to the demise of Cudlipp's *Sun.* It was getting above its readers, trying to push them up-market against their will. To do this it had introduced special sections—the Inside Page, Mirrorscope—that sought to deal with serious issues in a way its readers could comprehend; but they were out of tune with the rest of the paper. You turned a page and it shouted at you: "This is the serious bit."

Murdoch thought readers must resent this and would enjoy the chance of buying a tabloid that did not keep reminding them how little they knew—a tabloid modeled on the *Mirror* of the 1940s and 1950s, before it had become seized by ideas above its station. Moreover, he thought Cudlipp's reputation as the guru of tabloid journalism greatly exaggerated. In Murdoch's view, Cudlipp's abilities had peaked when he edited the *Sunday Pictorial* in the 1940s.

Murdoch is never shy about seeking advice—even if sometimes an inquiry about what *you* think is simply a pretext to test his
own opinion. When he asked around Fleet Street whom he should
appoint editor of his new paper, two names kept cropping up, both
ex-*Mirror* men. Larry Lamb, a Yorkshireman of forty, had been a
protégé of *Mirror* editor Lee Howard, who saw him as a future
editor. But Cudlipp did not at that time share Howard's view: he
thought Lamb a little too self-confident, too ambitious for comfort.
Sensing that this could bar his way to the top *Mirror* job, Lamb had
accepted an offer to join the *Daily Mail* as Northern editor in
Manchester. Bernard Shrimsley, another who had felt shunted aside
in the jostle of senior *Mirror* executives, had spent the previous year
revamping the *Liverpool Daily Post*. Murdoch invited Lamb for
dinner at Rules in Covent Garden, where they sat for nearly four
hours swapping ideas for the new tabloid. Then they moved on to
the *News of the World* office. It was one o'clock before Lamb left.
Murdoch told him he still had a few more people to see and would
be in touch.

Three hours later Murdoch phoned Lamb at home and told him
the job was his. They met again later at Murdoch's flat in Sussex
Gardens, Paddington. By coincidence, Lamb told Murdoch he
would like to hire Shrimsley as his deputy.

The first issue of the new *Sun* appeared on November 17th,
1969, and Murdoch invited senior people from Fleet Street and
elsewhere, advertisers and politicians, to a celebratory party, to
watch Anna push the button to start the presses. The ceremony was
timed for nine p.m. but because of production delays it was after
eleven when the button was pressed and the run began. It was an
exciting evening, with a flushed Murdoch in his shirtsleeves and his
friends congratulating him raucously. But they were only his
friends.

Hardly any of the invited VIPs turned up. Murdoch guessed
that this was partly to do with the Keeler business a few months
earlier but, more practically, because Cudlipp had chosen to throw a
rival party at the *Mirror* at the same time. If you were an advertiser
or a person who needed Fleet Street's goodwill, and you were being
made to choose sides, it was no contest. Far more important to
butter up Cudlipp, the established star of the Street, than this gauche
newcomer, this unknown quantity.

Around midnight some copies of the *Sun*'s first edition were delivered to the Cudlipp party, smudgily printed and full of typos. Cudlipp cast a professional eye over what Fleet Street regards as the salient parts of a tabloid: the front page, the back, page three and the center spread. He hurled it down on the table and shouted to Howard across the room: "Lee, we've got nothing to worry about." Within a year the *Sun*'s circulation had doubled and soon after that it passed two million, chiefly at the expense of the *Mirror.*

The feature by which the *Sun* became best known was the daily picture of a bare-breasted woman, usually on page three, but that did not begin until nearly a year after the launch. It was not Murdoch's idea, nor indeed a conscious stratagem at all. Lamb simply decided to do it one day and the reaction was so positive he thought he should carry on with it. The *Mirror* felt obliged to do the same for a while.

People on the *Mirror,* and others of the Fleet Street establishment, were unhappy about the *Sun*'s success. They felt wounded, not so much because their circulation was suffering but because they had been obliged to come down market to stop the *Sun* from driving them off the street altogether. Mirrorscope and the Inside Page were quickly killed off and the *Mirror* was competing stridently on the *Sun*'s terms. It had dozens of capable tabloid journalists on the staff and it competed effectively.

It was not until 1976 that the *Sun* caught up with the *Mirror* in circulation. Many felt and said that the *Sun,* by its success, had set back responsible popular journalism by years. In a radio interview an embittered Cudlipp said: "Someone will always be found to scrape the bottom of the barrel," but later he was able to take a more philosophical view. He told Simon Regan, a biographer of Murdoch: "Murdoch is in the tradition of Beaverbrook and Thomson—rustling 'colonials' who could in fact teach their grandmothers how to suck eggs. There was room at the top for a new force in Fleet Street: Rupert's it."

It was not just the editorial content that made the *Sun* a commercial success. Murdoch is a frugal publisher, resenting unnecessary expenditure as though it were all his own money. For years Fleet Street had grown used to extravagant practices, particularly the employment of many more people than were needed to produce the papers. Some journalists on the popular tabloids were paid comfortable salaries and generous expenses for writing perhaps only one article a week. Murdoch introduced more rigorous scrutiny. And he did not see fit to waste money providing luxurious working conditions: the staff of the new daily paper were crammed into the *News of the World*'s existing Bouverie Street premises. He does not stint, though, when it comes to promotion. Many attribute the *Sun*'s success in large measure to expensive but effective television advertising.

Murdoch's next expansion in Britain was into television. In 1966 a consortium of big-name television stars and businessmen, with David Frost prominent among them, got together to bid for the license to operate London's commercial television from Friday night to Sunday. They won the contract on the strength of their names and of a program prospectus that assumed an unsatisfied taste among British viewers for weekend fare of a more cerebral nature than they had hitherto been offered, emphasizing plays, documentaries, news and interview programs.

It was a laudably ambitious notion, but it was illusory. The creative people put into management jobs proved weak in organizational and commercial skills. London Weekend Television was overstaffed, under-organized and losing a packet of money. The traditional view of program planners had been correct: what people wanted to watch on Saturday night was light entertainment. As audiences dropped so did advertising, and by 1970 the company was on the brink of collapse, seeking a savior.

Whether or not the threat he made after his disastrous Frost interview was a factor, Murdoch became interested in the travails of London Weekend and in 1970 bought a block of shares. His foothold established, he was approached by the directors and asked whether he would inject some capital and his company's management skills. They proposed a new issue of shares which Murdoch would buy, giving him about forty percent of the share capital: a replica of the *News of the World* deal.

Murdoch has never been too lucid about his precise motive for accepting this offer. If he saw it as yet another British media company throwing itself into his arms, he must have been unfamiliar with the rule of the Independent Broadcasting Authority that makes it impossible for any single shareholder to gain effective control of a commercial TV station. But by now Murdoch had come to enjoy the actual challenge of reviving failing institutions. And in LWT he saw some parallels with Cudlipp's *Sun,* an information outlet that had gone astray through making over-optimistic assumptions about the intellectual level of its audience.

Not that he ever sought to bring London Weekend as far down market as his British newspapers. Indeed, one other attraction of the deal was that it irked him to be identified in Britain only with those two papers. He was not ashamed of them: far from it. But he saw himself as someone who could operate across the cultural board. The *Australian* was his token of respectability, but to him it was more than a token. It was just accidental that most of his papers operated at the popular level: he was not exclusively a purveyor of opium to the masses, at least not in his own eyes.

Because of the rules limiting the extent to which newspaper owners could control television companies, Murdoch could play no formal executive role in London Weekend. But for some months at the end of 1970 he effectively ran it and seconded his best British manager, Bert Hardy, to restructure the commercial side, especially advertising sales. In his familiar style, Murdoch dismissed those executives he felt to be responsible for the mess the company had gotten into. That was easy, but what he now needed was someone who could take over and guide London Weekend into calmer and more prosperous waters.

When the consortium had been formed in 1966, John Freeman had been asked to join it. A protégé of the socialist writer Kingsley Martin, Freeman had succeeded him as editor of the weekly journal the *New Statesman* in 1961. Then he had become renowned as a remorseless television interviewer. Soon after Harold Wilson became Prime Minister, he appointed Freeman High Commissioner to India in 1965. Since he was still in that job in 1966—and would in 1969 become ambassador in Washington—Freeman turned down the initial approach from LWT. But he did say, in what now seems a fit of prescience, that if they would ask again when he was free, he might be ready to consider it.

Less than a month after Freeman's return from Washington in early 1971, Frost asked him whether he would be interested in coming to LWT as chief executive. Freeman said he might well be, but wanted to be assured that the move had the approval of

Murdoch, whom he knew had the real power. He did not want to go in as the nominee of one faction in an internal squabble. Murdoch—whom Freeman had met only once before, at dinner with the Carrs in 1968—telephoned from Australia and Freeman accepted.

The two quickly became friends, despite their obvious differences of temperament. While Murdoch is impetuous, Freeman had a calm, diplomatic mien even before he became a diplomat.

Murdoch, very much in charge, held Freeman's hand for the few months it took him to learn the ropes, then left him to his own devices. Freeman proved a shrewd choice as chairman. The company's health improved dramatically and it kept its franchise; it is now one of the strongest ITV license holders. Murdoch quit the board when he began to get involved in the United States and nominated Bert Hardy to represent his interest. In 1979, when he needed cash to acquire a television station in Sydney, he sold nearly all his shares in LWT, at a comfortable profit.

And David Frost? He switched his allegiance to the BBC not long after, and sold his shares in 1976. Now he is back with the commercial channel—a shareholder and announcer with the morning company, TV-AM.

THREE

The Uses of Power

Rupert Murdoch will probably never be played by Jason Robards.

—Ron Powers, CBS press critic

If you sit long enough under an apple tree in autumn, a ripe apple will fall either into your lap or on your head. Like Sir Isaac Newton, Rupert Murdoch could probably benefit from either eventuality, but in the case of the Sydney *Daily Telegraph* and *Sunday Telegraph* in 1972, the fruit fell painlessly within reach.

For some time the Packer organization had been worried about the Telegraph newspapers. The problem was that their chief competitor, Fairfax, was getting maximum utilization of its presses by printing the *Sydney Morning Herald* in the morning, the *Sun* in the afternoon and the *Sun-Herald* on Sundays. Sir Frank Packer was growing old and control of the group was moving to his younger son Kerry, who did not share his father's sentimental attachment to the papers that had made him a power in the city. Kerry could see that the only way to make money out of the *Telegraph* was to start a new evening paper to share its overheads. But even had he wanted to enter the cut-throat contest between the *Mirror* and the *Sun*, it was simply not feasible to distribute an evening paper from the *Telegraph* plant, sited in Sydney's congested commercial center. The Packer television and magazine interests made a comfortable profit on their own. The sensible, if agonizing, course was to get rid of the newspapers altogether.

The future of the *Telegraph* papers had for months been the subject of excited speculation among Sydney newspapermen. Angus McLachlan, then the managing director of Fairfax, found himself sitting at a dinner next to Rupert Murdoch, who told him: "Frank's not going to last all that long and you're going to have the Melbourne *Herald* in there." He was playing on the Fairfax horror of competition from his father's old group—an obsession that had led them to sell the *Mirror* papers to him in 1960.

A few weeks later McLachlan, Murdoch and Sir Frank Packer were in London at the same time and met on that neutral territory to discuss what was to become of the *Telegraph*. One scheme was for Murdoch and Fairfax to buy it jointly, and McLachlan undertook to raise it with the Fairfax family on his return. But in the end Sir Frank could not stomach the thought of making a deal with his fiercest rival. Murdoch was the less painful option.

Sir Frank arranged an evening with Murdoch at a championship boxing match, preceded by dinner. When the time came, the old tycoon did not feel up to it, so Kerry went with Murdoch instead. Telling the story later, Kerry gives the impression that the subject of the *Telegraph* came up simply by chance in a general discussion of the newspaper scene, but it is clear that there was a strong element of forethought.

Kerry's first proposition was to sell a half share in the *Telegraph* newspapers to Murdoch and have them printed at News Ltd.'s headquarters, where they would share overheads with the *Mirror* and the *Australian*—a deal similar to the one Murdoch had made years earlier over the Adelaide Sunday paper.

But Murdoch was loath to share. If he was to print the *Telegraph* titles, he wanted to own them. By the time the dinner and boxing were over he had agreed to buy the goodwill of the papers— nothing more—for fifteen million dollars. The staff remained employed by the Packer group, though Murdoch did hire many of them. By not buying the whole staff he avoided responsibility for severance payments—a ruse he must have wished he could call on when buying *The Times* and *Sunday Times* in London nine years later.

Murdoch was now the biggest newspaper proprietor in Sydney. Fairfax had a morning, evening and Sunday paper, while Murdoch had an extra two Sundays as well as the *Australian*. The *Sunday*

Australian, never as successful as Murdoch had hoped, was a casualty of the *Telegraph* acquisition, being merged with the *Sunday Telegraph* a few months later. The *Sunday Mirror* was eventually to go the same way.

The editorial floor of the Murdoch building at the corner of Holt and Kippax Streets, near Sydney's Central Station, is mightily impressive. His four Sydney papers share an open-plan office so large that signs are hung above each section to assist navigation. They are like the labels above shelves in supermarkets but instead of COOKED MEATS and FROZEN VEGETABLES they say AUSTRALIAN NEWS DESK or MIRROR SPORT. It is suprisingly quiet. The background sound is the seductive click of scores of video display terminals. And it is run with rigid economy. People who work there call it "Shoestring International."

Murdoch's growing empire gave him increasing political influence. The remnants of his youthful radicalism, which he was fast growing out of, ensured that his papers supported the Labour Party under Gough Whitlam during the election campaign of 1972. Indeed, Billy McMahon, the Liberal Prime Minister, believed the sale of the *Telegraph* newspapers, his most influential supporters in the press when owned by Packer, was a critical factor in his defeat later that year.

Murdoch admired Whitlam, identifying in him many of his own qualities. He was forthright, he had presence and style. He was the very opposite of the cliquish old politicians, the Menzies gang—and, going back to his Adelaide days, the white knights he scorned so. Whitlam was not an establishment man. Moreover, Murdoch could tell that the country was restless after twenty-three years of stifling conservative rule.

He and Whitlam became close friends in the years leading up to 1972. Murdoch even suggested some planks of Labour's election platform, including the plan to commission an Australian national anthem to replace England's "God Save the Queen" —a typically symbolic enthusiasm they shared.

In a country where Labour had been so long out of office, there was a clear need for them to be promoted as a credible governing party, and Murdoch readily allowed his papers to be used to that end. The theme he developed was that under the Liberal-Country coalition Australia had slumped into comfortable, idle middle age. A reviving dose of radicalism was needed to halt a slide into early senility.

Murdoch's support for Whitlam continued through the next election, in 1974, but very soon after that he turned against him as fervently as he had supported him hitherto. The following year Murdoch was a key figure in the maneuvering that culminated in the unprecedented dismissal of the Prime Minister by the Governor-General, Sir John Kerr, who represents the British Queen as Australia's head of state.

In an election speech in December 1975, Whitlam claimed that an important reason for Murdoch's switch of loyalty was the government's refusal to grant him a bauxite development license in Western Australia, in partnership with Reynolds Aluminum, an American company worried about the long-term future of their existing bauxite supplies from Jamaica. Whitlam vetoed it because his government was opposed to a major extension of foreign investment in Australia's key industries, as well as on environmental grounds.

But there were other reasons for Murdoch's disillusion. He felt that since attaining office Whitlam had deliberately turned away from him. Murdoch likes to be made much of by the powerful. He likes to consult and be consulted, to have easy access. Whitlam had scruples about getting too close to a newspaper proprietor, aware of the danger of being compromised; so he distanced himself.

Murdoch's own explanation is simply that Whitlam in office appeared to be making a mess of things. The Australian dollar was devalued by 12 percent after the 1974 post-election budget. There were scandals over some unorthodox negotiations for government loans through the offices of a Pakistani financier named Tirath Khemlani, and over a relationship between Jim Cairns, the deputy Prime Minister, and a Chinese-born aide, Junie Morosi.

The climax to this period of growing confusion came when the opposition, led by Malcolm Fraser, used its Senate majority to block the supply of funds for the day-to-day running of the government. In the resulting stalemate Sir John Kerr, egged on notably by the Murdoch papers, dismissed Whitlam, appointed Fraser as temporary Prime Minister and called a December election that Fraser won in a landslide.

The role of the Murdoch papers in this affair is on record, but whether Murdoch played a part personally in influencing Kerr to take his constitutionally controversial action is a subject of debate. Much has been made of a weekend party Murdoch gave for his senior journalists at his ranch at Cavan, near Canberra, in November, 1974.

Late on the Saturday afternoon Sir John arrived for a drink. The host and guests sat round the swimming pool and discussed affairs of state. One guest recalls that Sir John wondered aloud how Whitlam could run the country when the Senate was controlled by the opposition, and what would happen if the Senate refused to pass the budget. In fact the 1974 budget had just been approved by both houses and people later pondered Kerr's ability to foresee so clearly the difficulties that did materialize the following year.

The *Australian* led the Murdoch papers in urging Kerr to act. Not for them the agonized doubts that affected other journals about whether he had the constitutional power to dismiss a prime minister who could not engineer the provision of essential government funds. Some of Murdoch's senior people were uneasy about the proposition, but he would not be budged.

Because journalists on the *Australian* would later protest about what they saw as the newspaper's biased coverage of the ensuing election, it is important to stress that while the paper was editorially uncompromising in its opposition to Whitham, some of its commentators, notably Paul Kelly in Canberra, were writing material from the other standpoint and, at least early in November, were still getting it in the paper. On November 5th, for instance, an editorial blamed Whitlam for rejecting a compromise settlement offered by Fraser, who would have agreed to allow the budget to pass in exchange for a commitment by Whitlam to hold an election after six months. If Whitlam were allowed to win this conflict, the editorial said, he would have wrought an enormous extension of the Prime Minister's powers. Yet in the same paper Kelly was discussing ways in which *Fraser* could emerge without utter humiliation, and writing confidently that Kerr would definitely not intervene on either side to swing the balance.

Two days later Kelly stuck to this view, while the leader-writers were becoming more blatant in their appeals to Kerr to act. It was "not a situation he can view with equanimity," they wrote.

Whitlam's "determination to tough it out regardless of the con-
sequences...[is] fraught with danger for the national body politic."

On the morning of November 11th, the *Australian* was explicit
in its advocacy of "positive intervention" by Kerr, despite the risk
that he would be seen to be taking sides. It is hard to conceive that
Murdoch did not have advance knowledge of Whitlam's dismissal,
for that was the day it happened. Mark Day, then editor of the *Daily
Mirror,* recalls that as the only time Murdoch ever gave him a
specific instruction about what to write in his editorial.

"Write a leader for tomorrow more in sorrow than in anger," he
was told. "Whitlam's got to go. You know, talk about the brave
experiment failing." Although the *Mirror* has a much higher
circulation than the *Australian,* the editorial opinions of Australian
tabloids have never counted for as much as those of their British and
American counterparts.

The partisan passions aroused by the dismissal made the 1975
election campaign among the most heated in Australian history. An
enraged Whitlam characterized Fraser as "Kerr's cur." In an
emotional speech to his supporters outside Parliament House he
urged them to "maintain your rage," adding: "Well may they say
'God Save the Queen,' for nothing will save the Governor-General."

In a chapter on the 1975 campaign in her book *The Politics of
the Press,* Patricia Edgar of La Trobe University concluded that
there was "quite clear bias" in the *Australian*'s coverage. After a
close analysis of the content of four major papers, she found that the
paper "published no comment article which was not either neutral
or supporting of its editorial line...No articles appeared in which
opinion disagreed with editorial policy." However, more bylined
news stories were favorable to the Labour Party than the Liberal-
Country coalition, indicating that many reporters were out of step
with the paper's policy.

Coverage can be slanted in a number of ways. Reporting the
election for *The Times* of London, I noted that the choice of pictures
in Murdoch's papers seemed to favor Malcolm Fraser, who invariably looked firm and gritty, while Whitlam looked miserable and
unimpressive. In the book *Fixing the News,* edited by Keith and
Elizabeth Windschuttle, there is a revealing comparison between the
front pages of the first and second editions of Murdoch's *Daily
Mirror* on November 26th, 1975. The headline on the first edition is

GOUGH'S PROMISE: CHEAP RENTS. By the second edition this has been changed to GOUGH PANICS: CHEAP RENTS. And in the same paper on December 3rd, a front-page splash on the loans scandal had a colossal headline GOUGH GUILTY! And in letters a quarter the size underneath, A LIE! SAYS WHITLAM.

In the event, Labour was defeated comprehensively and it is doubtful whether the pro-Fraser campaigns of the Murdoch papers had a really decisive influence. But Whitlam was so angered that he delivered a savage attack on Murdoch at a lunch at the Brisbane Press Club on December 4th, nine days before the election.

"Anybody who works for his papers knows how odious Mr. Murdoch's control is," he said. "Some of his employees have gone around Australia with me and they are finding it very difficult to get their stories published. When stories have not suited him, others have been published.... Some of the people on the *Australian* have courage and it requires courage because the editors of the *Australian* have the shortest duration of anybody.... This expatriate tycoon lives in various places on either side of the North Atlantic."

Whitlam went on to predict that the *Australian* might not survive many more weeks. "Circulation is dropping and the readership is, of course, losing faith. The newspaper is inacurrate and has lost whatever standards and integrity it ever had." He added an appeal for Australian television reporters to "cut up" newspaper owners as David Frost had cut up Murdoch in the interview on British television in 1969.

Next day Murdoch responded in kind. "Mr. Whitlam's comments are highly irresponsible and entirely false. They are scurrilous and defamatory." An editorial in the *Australian* declared, in a misquotation: "Whom the gods destroy, they first make mad. Mr. Whitlam is going out not with a stance of dignity but with a whimper."

Influenced no doubt in part by Whitlam's outburst, journalists at the *Australian* went on strike on December 8th, complaining about unacceptable bias in the news pages. The strike lasted only twenty-four hours, yet it was destined to become one of the most celebrated causes in Australian journalism, the subject of numerous reports, hearings, analyses and inquiries.

It had been building up before November, so it cannot be put down entirely to the passions aroused by Whitlam's dismissal, though they were surely a factor. In evidence before a hearing over one of Murdoch's television license applications in 1980, Robert Duffield, a leader-writer who had been with the paper since its foundation, said it had become clear from the start of 1975 that Bruce Rothwell and Les Hollings, the editor, had been instructed by Murdoch to campaign against Whitlam. He cited cases where he had been told to write anti-Whitlam leaders he thought unreasonable, and picked out some news stories from the *Australian* and other Murdoch papers that were, in his view, unfairly biased.

In August 1975 Duffield asked to be relieved of leader-writing duties and in October he and Barry Porter, a sub-editor on the *Australian* and president of the New South Wales branch of the Australian Journalists' Association, drafted a memorandum to the proprietor that became the basis for what was known as the "Murdoch Mutiny." Written in a self-important, maudlin style guaranteed to enrage Murdoch, it began:

"Our loyalties to yourself, to the *Australian* and to the profession of journalism have made it essential that we approach you urgently. For the three loyalties, which could and should be fused to make a great paper, have become intolerably incompatible.

"We do not dispute your prerogative to decide the editorial policy of the paper; that point is not at issue.

"But we would not be loyal to you if we failed to say that, among the influential Australians with whom we come into daily contact—including and especially the intelligent middle-income earners it is the paper's policy to attract—the *Australian* has become a laughing stock.

"Reporters who were once greeted with respect when they mentioned the *Australian* have had to face derisive harangues before they can get down to the job at hand. It is not so much the policy itself but the blind, biased, tunnel-visioned, ad hoc, logically-confused and relentless way in which so many people are now conceiving it to be carried out, both in the editorial and news columns.

"We can be loyal to the *Australian,* no matter how much its style, thrust and readership change, as long as it retains the traditions, principles and integrity of a responsible newspaper. We cannot be loyal to a propaganda sheet."

The memo went on to specify what it was complaining about: slanted headlines, imbalance in news presentation, political censorship, the distortion of what journalists wrote, the stifling of dissent and impartial opinion. "Many of us are near breaking point," it declared, and asked Murdoch to name an early date for a round-table meeting.

The letter was signed by seventy-five journalists on the *Australian* and delivered to Murdoch on November 2nd. When he had not replied after two weeks, Duffield and Porter wrote saying they were about to publish the letter and to announce his refusal to answer it. By now the election had been called and the campaigning was under way. Murdoch did reply this time, saying: "If you insist on providing ammunition for our competitors and enemies who are intent on destroying all our livelihoods, then go ahead."

After a further exchange of letters the staff met and agreed to take up specific examples of bias with the management. That evening Duffield and Porter were interviewed on television about the issue.

Murdoch clearly saw that as another act of disloyalty and refused to discuss the matter further. The editor, Les Hollings, reacted in a curious way: on the morning after the TV interview, he ordered Duffield to move out of his private office to a desk in the features section.

On December 6th, a Saturday, printers of the *Sunday Mirror* and *Sunday Telegraph* went on strike in protest against anti-Labour editorials in both papers, but returned to work when Murdoch agreed that a letter expressing their views should be published in the *Daily Mirror.*

That weekend, demonstrators burned copies of the *Australian* outside the Holt Street offices. All this unsettled the journalists who, at a meeting attended by over a hundred of them, agreed on a two-day strike at all three of Murdoch's daily papers. Their statement spoke of "very deliberate and blatant bias in the presentation of news," and added: "We have therefore felt it necessary to dissociate ourselves entirely from the desecration of the traditional and historical ethics of journalism."

The papers were brought out by non-union labor that night. The next day an industrial tribunal recommended a return to work in exchange for a promise by Murdoch to meet Duffield and Porter the next morning. It was a heated meeting. Murdoch pushed towards the two journalists a copy of that morning's *Australian* and asked: "Any objections to today's paper?" Porter replied that he had, that the strike had not been covered properly, because it was said to be about objections to *editorial* policy rather than slanted news coverage.

Duffield then pushed a copy of the *Sydney Morning Herald* towards Murdoch and said: "See, the *Herald* got it right."

Murdoch was disgusted. "You dare to show this paper to me?" He rasped. "These people are our enemies, trying to destroy us."

Then he turned on Duffield personally: "'You do this to me after all I've done for you, how I've protected you?"

Duffield, as he admitted in public at a later inquiry, had a history of a drinking problem.

But the meeting did not continue in that rancorous vein. Duffield and Porter were able to tell Murdoch that part of the trouble, as they saw it, was that his key executives were over-enthusiastic in interpreting the company line, sometimes indulging in excesses that Murdoch would not have approved of had he been told in advance. Murdoch said he expected his staff to abide by the code of ethics of the Australian Journalists' Association, which rules out deliberate distortion. And he added that any future complaints of that nature should be taken directly to him.

Several of the paper's senior political writers resigned within months of the election—one of them, Bruce Stannard, during the campaign itself—but Murdoch persisted in trying to minimize the importance of the dispute. In an interview with *The Bulletin,* a Sydney weekly magazine, in December 1979, he attributed the strike to two agitators who did not work for his papers inciting the night shift of the *Australian* to call the strike. "There were about forty people and they whizzed a vote through on them and we lost that night's paper out of it. Nothing else. They were back within twenty-four hours, as soon as they could get a full vote. It was a put-up job."

That is an understatement, both in terms of numbers (he halved the actual number of people taking the strike vote, and the leaders were not outsiders) and in the sense of the importance of the action. Yet his opponents have equally overestimated its significance, because of later controversies in which Murdoch was involved and because of the emotions aroused by the circumstances of the 1975 election.

Two months after the election, Murdoch turned his hand to an unfamiliar skill, reporting; and the effect was sensational. In

February 1976, John Monks and Barrie Watts, in the Melbourne office of the *Australian,* were told to stand by for a call from Murdoch in New York. For three nights they waited until, on February 24th, the call came through. Murdoch spent nearly an hour dictating to Watts.

That morning Brian Boswell, the news editor, had gone into the daily conference with several possible ideas for the front-page main story, or "splash." "Don't worry," Bruce Rothwell told him. "We don't need a splash. We've got one." Boswell knew better than to ask what it was. He would wait to read it in the paper.

It was a tremendous story, bearing in mind the previous year's fuss over foreign loans to the Labour government. It appeared in the issue of February 25th and carried the by-line BY A SPECIAL CORRESPONDENT. It began:

"Secret payments of many hundred thousands of dollars have been promised to the Australian Labour Party to pay for last year's election campaign by the extreme left-wing government of Iraq.

"The leader of the Federal opposition, Mr. Whitlam, and the party's Federal secretary, Mr. David Combe, told the Federal president of the party, Mr. Hawke, and the Federal vice-president, Mr. Egerton, of the promises."

It went on to tell how Iraqi dictator Saddan Hussein al Takrati had "readily agreed" to respond to the appeal and had sent two important emissaries to Australia to see Mr. Whitlam. They were Takrati's nephew and the head of the secret police. The story continued with a detailed description of how the two men's failure to get Australian visas from the British embassy in Baghdad had forced them to travel to Tokyo and obtain them from the Australian embassy there. Staying under false names at the Travelodge in North Sydney, they met Whitlam and Combe before the 1975 election in a block of flats at McMahon's Point in Sydney. Both Iraqis wore machine pistols.

Whitlam, the story continued, had told them he was certain to be re-elected. When he was not, the Iraqis felt sore and had not paid the money, though there was talk of a plan for Whitlam to meet them in London soon.

The detailed reporting must have been Murdoch's own work, although the staff of the *Australian* deduced from stylistic evidence that Rothwell had rewritten at least part of the story. Murdoch has not revealed his source, although many supposed it to be Henry Fischer, the owner of the McMahon's Point flat where Whitlam and Combe met the Iraqis.

In strident editorials, the *Australian* called for Whitlam to resign, but he did not do so, remaining party leader until the following year. All the same, Murdoch had for the time being reached the limit of his political power in Australia, on good terms with the new government of Malcom Fraser and able to claim plausibly that he was to a significant extent responsible for putting it into office. Fraser did not share Whitlam's scruples about the danger of getting too close to the controllers of the media; so Murdoch could, had he felt so inclined, have relaxed a little and enjoyed the fruits of his politicking.

But relaxation is not in his nature. For him, the contest is as sweet as the spoils. Having completed this campaign, his instinct now was to begin another. And in America, where he had been waiting with uncharacteristic patience for his breakthrough for three years now, things were beginning to happen at last.

FOUR

Rupert in Wonderland

Clay Felker is the best editor in America.

—Rupert Murdoch

There was no simple, single reason behind Rupert's and Anna's decision to go to America in 1973. Part of it was that they still felt out of things, socially, in London. For sure, they were asked to more functions than they could possibly attend, but there remained the coolness left over from the business of the Keeler memoirs.

The English establishment is slow to forget and forgive. Polite smiles were laced with a hint of frost. Murdoch came as close as he could to admitting all this in an interview with Alexander Cockburn in the New York *Village Voice* in 1976, although his powerful defense mechanism enabled him to turn the facts round to make it seem as if it were he who was rejecting society.

"I just wasn't prepared to join the system. . . . Maybe I just have an inferiority complex about being an Australian. My wife accuses me of this sometimes. But you've got some money and you tend to send your kids to the school you can most afford; you join the old-school-tie system and you're going to be dragged into the so-called social establishment somehow. I never was. Just as we were being invited round to places we'd catch Lord Lambton in bed or something, and then we'd be barred from everything. . . . It's very difficult not at some point to be sucked into the establishment. The last thing I wanted was to be a bloody press lord. I think when people start taking knighthoods and peerages it really is telling the world you've sold out. I've never been offered one. Well, I've been offered a knighthood a few times but no,I wouldn't take one."

He mentioned, too, the frustration of dealing with the Fleet Street unions. And Anna was still unsettled by the kidnap and murder in 1969 of Muriel McKay, wife of Rupert's senior executive in London. She was unable to erase from her mind that, according to the court evidence of the kidnappers, she had been the intended victim.

These were negative reasons. They would not in themselves have been strong enough unless reinforced by Murdoch's strong drive. Though certain he had not finished his expansion in either Britain or Australia, he saw no immediate opportunities there. America was the only large English-speaking market left to conquer and he was sure he could do it. From what he knew of Americans, he spoke their language in more than merely the literal sense. These were people with his approach to business, single-minded for producing profits, believing hard work to be more important than social prominence.

But in other respects he does not conform to the image of the high-flying American businessman. He is neither extravagant nor expansive. Certainly he has more—and more costly—homes than most, because splitting his time between three continents means he has to have a convenient base in each. But he spends little, for instance, on clothing. "He has thirty-three editions of the same suit," said a colleague. "Dark grey with a thin light red or white stripe and an undemonstrative tie."

He finds expensive restaurants convenient for discussing business but does not scorn more plebeian places. A few years after his arrival in New York he asked George Gordon, then an executive on his weekly tabloid the *Star,* to lunch at Sloppy Louie's, a raffish old fish restaurant on South Street in New York, near the office of the *New York Post.* Though justly famous for its food, it cultivated an air of crowded discomfort and did not then serve alcoholic drinks.

"Want a drink?" Murdoch asked Gordon. When he said yes, Murdoch pushed five dollars into a waiter's hand and said: "Go get us a six-pack of beer from the supermarket."

At the end of the meal a few cans were left over. "You've not finished your beer," Murdoch told Gordon. "Don't waste it." So

Gordon went back to his midtown office in Murdoch's limousine, his overcoat bulging with beer cans.

Although Murdoch has a chauffeur-driven car he sometimes prefers not to use it. Edward Koch, the mayor of New York, is impressed that when he and Murdoch go out to dinner at a restaurant Murdoch usually arrives by taxi and, if the restaurant is fairly near his Fifth Avenue apartment, walks back rather than accept a lift in the mayor's limousine. While nobody would accuse Murdoch of being an ascetic, he certainly has no taste for the high life for its own sake.

Surprisingly few foreign publishers have ever tried to muscle in on the American newspaper market. Roy Thomson, who bought a string of provincial papers in the United States, was a Canadian, and that scarcely counts as foreign. But Murdoch has never been deterred from doing something just because nobody has done it before. Taking a gang of his Australian and British executives with him, he went to America to shop around.

Quite quickly he acquired three newspapers in San Antonio, Texas, in the expanding Sunbelt of the southwestern United States. There is no special significance in his choice of city: it was in truth not a choice at all, but just where a likely-looking property happened to be on the market. At $19,700,000 he thought he was paying too much for them—certainly more than he would have paid in Australia or Britain based on the ratio of price to earnings. It was a start, though, a suitable way of getting the feel of running a newspaper in the United States.

He could scarcely have lighted upon a better place, because Texas has some qualities of the Australian outback. The city was the site of the defense of the Alamo in 1836, when Davy Crockett and his Texas patriots had died heroically in a brave stand against the Mexicans, and it had kept some of its rough-riding properties. Not far from the Mexican border, it had long been a prosperous ranching center, and he knew about those from back home. Enough was familiar here for him to come to grips with.

The papers he bought were the San Antonio *Express,* a morning paper, and the *News,* its afternoon stablemate, and their combined Sunday editions. He gave most of his attention to the *News,* the weaker of the city's two evening papers, competing with the *Light,* owned by the Hearst chain. (By an irony, the Hearst papers had, in the early part of the century, gained the reputation for lurid sensationalism that was shortly to follow Murdoch here.)

Murdoch applied to the *News* the formula that had worked so well in Australia and London—banner headlines, crime, sex and trivia, with a minimum of weighty news. Some of his talented tabloid men were brought from Australia to effect the transformation. In the first year he spent a million dollars on promotion, chiefly on television advertising but also on contests for readers, devoting to them generous amounts of front-page space.

Murdoch has never been inhibited about using his front page to boast of the success of his newspapers. He would print charts showing how he was gaining readers at the expense of the opposition, provoking the *Light* to respond with a full-page announcement in their paper suggesting that the figures were not altogether accurate, that they "jump around like a kangaroo." Murdoch could have been forgiven a quick smile. This was just the sort of insult-trading he was used to from Australia. There were some who had told him he would find America very different from anything he had known; but when it came down to it, the opposition anywhere always acted in the same, predictable way.

Even at this early stage, before he had gained any position nationally, Murdoch was beginning to fall foul of the media critics who saw in the jazzed-up *News* sensationalism of a different order from what they had been used to. One headline that caught their imagination, to be quoted against him time and again over the years, was KILLER BEES HEAD NORTH. The story was of a special kind of bee with a fatal sting, sighted in south and central America. The arousal of alarm in readers on the thinnest of pretexts is a trusted tabloid technique.

Murdoch was to claim, in his 1976 interview with Cockburn, that what he had done with the *News* was simply to strengthen its coverage of hard local news. "We wondered about it and wondered about it and thought, what are people doing for news, where are they getting it?—certainly not from the Hearst papers. We studied the TV programs. The leading channel by a mile was a station that put on two hours of local news every afternoon and was just following the cops around with mobile cameras . . . blood and guts. And we turned the *News* pretty sharply, with lots of crime reporting and the courts. It's a pretty violent city, San Antonio."

The result of all that was to push up the paper's circulation from 61,000 when he bought it to 75,000 by the middle of 1975. That was as much progress as he could make, though. Despite the continued use of prize contests and promotions, the *News* stayed on that figure and the *Light* kept to about 120,000, still the substantial market leader. Worse, his circulation increase had not resulted in any notable improvement in advertising.

Although he claimed to have figures proving that the new readers were from the upper end of the market, the advertisers, judging simply by his product, decided that its audience was not the one they were trying to reach. Murdoch learns fast. By 1976 he was moving the *News* subtly up market, trying to cream the upper end of the *Light's* circulation, and it began to repay his investment. As for the *Express,* it was a morning paper, much less racy, which turned a reasonable profit at a circulation of 80,000. He was content to leave it alone.

Nobody doubted that all this was essentially a training work-out, that he was limbering up for more crucial acquisitions to come. San Antonio was small potatoes. He yearned for national exposure and, since there are no national dailies in the United States (except the specialized *Wall Street Journal* and *USA Today*), he would have to gain it through magazines. He took Bert Hardy with him to size up some publications whose owners wanted to sell, or that might be obtainable even against their owners' wishes. They looked at *Redbook, McCall's,* the *Ladies' Home Journal,* and even the *Village Voice,* though his stable as yet contained no paper catering to anything comparable to its specialized radical and intellectual market. Among newspapers with national clout, he looked at the *Washington Star,* number two in the nation's capital.

He had always preferred acquiring existing publications, no matter how poor a shape they were in, to a so-called "green-fields start," starting something from scratch. It saved money and, important to a man as keen to get on with things as he, it saved time. But he was taken aback by the prices American titles were fetching. In Britain and Australia a rough rule of thumb was to pay ten times a paper's annual earnings. In America they were asking—and getting—up to forty times. It was too much. He would have to go for the green-fields start after all.

The concept of the *National Star* went through several changes. Murdoch's first idea was to create a tabloid news magazine, a down-market *Time* or *Newsweek*. He thought he detected in those two successful publications the same vulnerability he had exploited in the London *Daily Mirror*—they were flying above the heads of their readers. All that polished prose about the arts, society, science, diplomacy and even literature meant very little to middle Americans who had not been to college, he guessed. There must be a market for a paper that would keep them informed, certainly, but would do it in a more accessible way, using the presentational skills of his racy tabloids.

So convinced was he of the logic of this argument that Murdoch, usually careful to be on his best behavior in company, made a rare social gaffe in his enthusiasm to put it forward. At the time of the *Star's* launch, he was taken by a friend to a dinner party at the Park Avenue apartment of Thibault de St. Phalle, an economist whom he was to meet a few years later in more publicly controversial circumstances. Among the guests was Andrew Heiskell, the chairman of Time, Inc.

Over cocktails, de St. Phalle remembers, Murdoch began to round on Heiskell, telling him he did not know how to run his magazine. Heiskell, who can get sensitive about criticism, reacted angrily, and the scene became so heated that de St. Phalle wondered whether his party would break up before the diners had time to be seated. Heiskell was threatening to leave, until reminded that he was de St. Phalle's guest and persuaded to stay. "I found him singularly abrasive," the host recalled of Murdoch later.

In the end Murdoch and his advisers decided not to take on the soft underbellies of the news weeklies but to go instead after a market they thought they understood better. One of the most successful publications in the country is the *National Enquirer,* a weekly tabloid packed with scandalous gossip about film stars and celebrities, recipes, diets and household hints, stories about the occult and emotional domestic dramas, advice for the lovelorn, all packaged so as to appeal to housewives and sold where they were easiest to reach—at the checkout of their local supermarket. It was selling five million copies a week and had no really effective opposition.

Many of the *Enquirer*'s staff were British, veterans of Fleet Street, where that kind of journalism, or something near it, thrived. Murdoch's idea was to go into direct competition with the *Enquirer*, but the *National Star*, first sold only in the northeastern United States, proved a difficult launch. It was harder than he had imagined to get supermarkets to allot space to the paper. Editors came and went in rapid succession, nearly all British and Australian, as were the editorial staff, hired for their skill in stretching a story further than would seem possible without lapsing into plain untruth.

After a year the *National Star* became the snappier *Star*. Murdoch was still casting around for the right formula, but stubbornly rejected the advice of some of his associates to cut his losses and wind it up. It took another three years for it to get established as a profitable enterprise with a confident grip on its market, attracting advertisements for miracle cures, mail-order astrology schools and those other services that rely on the custom of the credulous. Printed in color, it runs headlines such as LOSE UP TO 35 LBS IN 4 WEEKS, HOW TO TURN YOUR HESITANT HUSBANDS INTO WONDERFUL LOVERS, and TIPS TO KEEP YOUR PET EMOTIONALLY CONTENT WITH PATIENCE AND LOVE. By 1984 it was selling four million copies in an average week, only a million fewer than the *Enquirer.*

However successful the *Star* was to become, it was still not the American breakthrough Murdoch was looking for. This kind of periodical, devoted to entertainment, is scarcely part of the news business at all. Certainly it was a distance from his original concept of a poor man's *Time* and *Newsweek*. But though he could not yet call himself a significant force in American journalism, he was confident that the time would come if he could only contain his impatience. By now he had moved his family to New York and was methodically making his entry into smart society. He rented an apartment on East 79th Street, a fashionable enough address in itself but not quite the *most* fashionable.

Where you live is of prime importance if you plan to hold elegant dinner parties or ask friends and potential enemies round for a confidential drink. So he bought himself a duplex right on Fifth Avenue, overloking Central Park, a few blocks north of the famous Plaza Hotel.

He worked at getting himself invited to the right parties, mixing with the right people, especially those who might know of newspapers for sale or be thinking of selling their own. As a substantial overseas newspaper owner, he felt it legitimate to telephone American proprietors out of the blue and ask if he could see their plant. This was how he first came to meet Mrs. Dorothy Schiff, who had owned the *New York Post,* the city's lacklustre evening paper, for nearly forty years and who was known to be looking for ways to give up the reins while assuring the paper's future. He met the redoubtable Katharine Graham, owner of the *Washington Post,* still glowing from its success over the Watergate affair, where its insistent investigative reporting had forced the resignation of President Nixon.

It was at a weekend at Mrs. Graham's home in Virginia that the Murdochs first met Clay Felker, the editor, publisher and indeed the creator of *New York* magazine, one of the publishing success stories of the 1960s and 70s. It had begun as the free magazine section of the Sunday edition of the *New York Herald Tribune,* but when the paper closed down Felker, the editor of the section, and Milton Glaser, its designer, found financial backing and decided to continue it as a separate publication. It developed into a survival guide to New York for the young and affluent. It was scarcely possible to imagine living in the city without it—how would you know what to see, what to buy, how to decorate your apartment? It pioneered what became known as the New Journalism, a style of writing fact in the manner of fiction, practiced by such as Tom Wolfe, Norman Mailer and Gail Sheehy. *New York* set a pattern for city magazines throughout the country, and Felker, tall, sleek, impulsive, impatient and full of creative energy, became a social and journalistic celebrity.

During the Virginia weekend, Mrs. Graham asked Felker to take the Murdochs under his wing, to introduce them to the rich and influential, to ease their way into society. He was glad to help. They would dine together at the restaurants patronized by those with pretensions to celebrity. They would visit each other at home. They went to a championship boxing match at Madison Square Garden.

Murdoch would ask Felker's advice about journalists he was thinking of hiring for his papers. He was always asking questions. Once he telephoned Felker and asked: "What do people do here in the summer?"

Felker said they went to East Hampton, on Long Island. So he acquired a house not far from Felker's and they would exchange visits. Felker had begun what was to prove a long-lasting relationship with Gail Sheehy, one of his writers, and she got on particularly well with Anna. By the end of 1976 the four of them were even talking about taking a skiing holiday together in Switzerland.

The trip was never made, for now Murdoch, after beginning to despair of ever finding a suitable American property to buy, was suddenly confronted with a rush of likely prospects. In less than four months he was to add a New York evening paper and three weekly journals to his American holdings, and to be within a whisker of owning one of the most historic newspapers in Britain.

Dorothy Schiff had for three decades been the most colorful newspaper owner in New York, but by 1976 the *New York Post* had become the drabbest of the three papers surviving from the plague of closures in the 1960s. Although it had the afternoon field to itself, it had never succeeded in establishing a clear identity. It fell between the authority and style of the *New York Times* and the tabloid brashness of the *Daily News*. It was packed with page after page of features and columns, many of them repetitive, taking space from the news. The solid core of the readership were middle class, liberal Jews, and the columns and editorials reflected their attitudes, worthy but dull: a pale bowl of chicken soup.

The *Post* had survived where so many of its more illustrious contemporaries had failed partly because of a cunning move by Mrs. Schiff during the long and debilitating city-wide newspaper strike of 1962/3. She then made a separate deal with the unions, so that the *Post* was able to return to the streets while the other papers stayed closed. A wealthy socialite, she had been given the paper by her second husband George Backer in 1939 and had kept it after their marriage ended. She ran it as a personal fiefdom, keeping it rigidly to its traditional liberalism (it was an outspoken critic of Senator Joseph McCarthy and his Committee on UnAmerican Activities) and maintaining an ever tighter personal grip on its finances, until in the end it was hard to get her agreement for even the most modest editorial expenditure.

Over the years, numerous suitors had come to inquire whether she wanted to sell her paper; she had thought about it, then always politely refused. She was ever conscious of its political tradition and anxious that any new proprietor should undertake convincingly to sustain it. She could never extract such a promise from chains such as Hearst, Newhouse and the Los Angeles Times group, which had made serious inquiries.

Murdoch, when he first came to New York, had looked over the *Post*'s plant but had not maintained contact with Schiff. They were reintroduced a year or so later by Clay Felker. This time the friendship proved more lasting and they began entertaining one another at dinners.

In September 1976 Mrs. Schiff invited Murdoch to lunch in her suite on the sixth floor of the *Post*'s dowdy old building facing the East River, overshadowed by the inelegant bulk of the elevated FDR Drive, interfering with the river view. They did not begin to talk about the *Post* until quite late in the meal—after the coffee, Murdoch was to maintain later.

"I sensed she was very tired," he told Alexander Cockburn. "She said she was very tired. She knew what was necessary to turn the paper and get it done right but she felt she just didn't have the energy left. She really made the opening, though she didn't really mean to, I think."

It was not simple tiredness, although at seventy-three Mrs. Schiff had every right to think of quitting. What weighed on her more pressingly as 1976 progressed was that on January 1st a complex new inheritance law was due to go into effect. She was advised that it might make it difficult for her to pass the newspaper on to her heirs, that it would be better to have the cash in hand.

Murdoch asked her to think of him if she was planning to sell.

"Oh, you'd be interested, would you?" said Mrs. Schiff, according to his account. "Everyone told me you were but you've never said it. Now you've said it."

She liked him. Perhaps he, an outsider anxious to make an impression, could be trusted to nurture the paper with care and respect.

The wheels were in motion. But he did not have to wait idly in his Third Avenue office, scarcely able to contain his impatience to move downtown to South Street. For already another offer had appeared out of the blue, this time from London. It came in a telephone call from Lord Goodman, a respected and influential lawyer and public figure, whom Murdoch had counted among his acquaintances, if not exactly a friend, ever since they met in 1969.

Lord Goodman had an office in the *News of the World* building when Murdoch bought it, and the two men inevitably met. Occasionally Murdoch would ask the corpulent lawyer to act for him in cases where it seemed important to be represented by somebody of such national standing.

Among his public responsibilities, Lord Goodman was chairman of the board of trustees of the *Observer,* one of Britain's oldest newspapers, traditional Sunday reading for intellectuals of the left and center. The paper was owned by a branch of the aristocratic Astor family, prominent on both sides of the Atlantic. (A different Astor had owned the London *Times* until Lord Thomson bought it in 1966.)

David Astor edited the *Observer* until the end of 1975—the last of the owner-editors. Then he stepped down and the job, after a uniquely democratic process of consultation with the journalists, went to Donald Trelford, a man of thirty-eight who had edited a newspaper in Malawi, Central Africa, before joining the *Observer* and becoming assistant to Astor in 1969.

For some time it had been obvious to Astor and his senior colleagues that, with labor and newsprint costs soaring, it would not be possible much longer to finance the paper through his family fortune. Newspapers, especially those operating at the top end of the market, are notoriously vulnerable to fluctuating economic conditions. They need reserves to see them through bad periods and injections of capital for their development. Astor had just about run out of resources. The paper was being operated out of the income from a family trust, the capital of which had been vested in his children and was unavailable to him.

The *Observer* languished for want of financial nourishment. Circulation was down to 667,897 from 730,832 the previous year, lower now than the *Sunday Telegraph* and almost exactly half the figure for the *Sunday Times,* the two rival Sunday papers. Astor, like

Dorothy Schiff, recognized that the days were gone when papers could be run on personal or family fortunes: they needed the resources of a large corporation.

Lord Goodman, informally, began trawling for possible buyers. The most obvious candidate was Lord Rothermere's Associated Newspapers, long searching for a Sunday paper to keep the *Daily Mail*'s presses busy on the seventh day of the week. But Rothermere's papers were Conservative politically and the *Daily Mail* was engaged in intense competition with the *Daily Express*. It was fairly certain, if they acquired it, Associated would bring the *Observer* down-market to compete directly with the thriving *Sunday Express*.

Goodman, who knew the business through his chairmanship of the Newspaper Publishers' Association, was unimpressed with Associated's management. The other main groups had Sunday papers that more or less competed with the *Observer*. That left Murdoch, whose newspapers' politics fluctuated according to circumstances and who owned no quality Sunday newspaper in Britain.

Goodman, who could see clearly what was coming, had discussed with Murdoch earlier the possibility of buying the *Observer*, though it was a tentative sounding and no firm offer or promise was made. Murdoch's mind was more on his American adventures and he dismissed the idea. The *Observer*, a clear second best in its contest with the *Sunday Times,* did not seem an attractive prospect.

After that first talk with Goodman, Murdoch discussed it with some of his senior people in London. Larry Lamb was against taking it any further but Bert Hardy was enthusiastic, making the point that a revitalized *Observer* could become a serious rival to the *Sunday Times,* which he felt had passed its peak. As for Murdoch, he had long been trying to clear up in his mind what he would do if *The Times* and its desirable stablemate the *Sunday Times* came on the market. Those really appealed to him: and he realized that if he acquired the *Observer* he would put himself out of the running for the *Sunday Times.*

A firm decision to look for a buyer for the *Observer* was reached by Goodman, Astor and Roger Harrison, the managing director, at a meeting at Goodman's Portland Place flat in August.

Harrison said Murdoch was the most likely buyer and, he thought, the most desirable. Unaware of Goodman's previous discussion with Murdoch on the subject, Harrison was surprised that the lawyer seemed so certain that the Australian would not be interested, and urged an inquiry. Goodman agreed, went to his study and phoned Murdoch right away. "That's a surprise," he said, returning to the drawing-room some minutes later. "He *is* interested." Hardy's enthusiasm had persuaded him it might be worth a long look.

In his heart of hearts, Goodman was none too happy about the prospect. He had conflicting attitudes toward Murdoch. He enjoyed his company. In their dealings in the NPA he admired the Australian's openness, his lack of cunning. He would say what he thought and stick to it, in contrast to many other newspaper owners who, Goodman would tell friends, he found unreliable and opportunistic, with a low regard for business ethics.

Yet it could not be denied that Murdoch's record in publishing was scarcely one to sustain the belief that he would respect the *Observer's* sober traditions. British readers knew him only through the *Sun* and the *News of the World* and they stood a cultural chasm from the high-minded liberal values of the country's oldest Sunday paper. Murdoch's only paper with much pretension to seriousness was the *Australian,* and that was neither particularly distinguished nor successful.

There was the public relations aspect to consider. The government, through the Monopolies Commission, might want to rule on the sale and it would be hard to persuade members of parliament of Murdoch's suitability. From that viewpoint it would be better to find someone who had a track record with serious newspapers or, failing that, no record in newspapers at all.

There was, too, a more tangible objection. Early in the negotiations Murdoch signalled clearly his intention of appointing new editors if he were to acquire the paper. The two names mentioned were Bruce Rothwell, a former Washington correspondent of the *Daily Mail* who had edited the *Australian,* and Anthony Shrimsley (brother of Bernard), an assistant editor on the *Sun.* Rothwell would be editor-in-chief and Shrimsley editor, with Trelford occupying an undefined middle role as editorial director. Both Murdoch's men professed political views substantially to the right of the *Observer,* but it was not that which worried Goodman chiefly. It was the fact that Trelford had been chosen editor less than a year earlier by a widely-publicized exercise in participatory democracy. For Murdoch to jettison him as his first act on buying the paper would, Goodman could see, seriously alienate the staff. As chairman of the trustees, it was his prime responsibility to see that the tradition of the paper was upheld. Murdoch's stated intention was a threat to that.

Goodman put all this to Murdoch, but he was unmoved. To the argument that Rothwell was not an intellectual, he snapped sharply and incontestably: "Nor's Trelford."

He believed that there were serious flaws in the *Observer* as then edited and that only a change at the top could correct them. Goodman and Astor, sensing a threat to the success of the deal, asked Trelford to fly to New York to see Murdoch. All the negotiations for disposal of the paper had so far been conducted in secret, and Trelford told none of his colleagues why he was going to America. He said he had to give a lecture and was trying to buy Dr. Henry Kissinger's memoirs. When he arrived at Murdoch's office on October 6th, Trelford found his potential new owner none too pleased to see him, feeling that editors should not get involved in these business deals. In their two meetings, Murdoch told Trelford what he had told Goodman, that he did not have a high opinion of the *Observer*'s editorial quality and would want to put his own man in.

On the flight back to London, Trelford was distressed. He wondered what he could do to head off the threat Murdoch posed. It was not just his personal position that concerned him, although as a new occupant of the prized editor's chair he certainly did not intend to surrender it tamely. He was only just starting to enjoy it. It was the wider implication of Murdoch's attitude that worried him more, and he was surprised that Goodman and Astor had not seen through it. For how could Murdoch say with a straight face that he respected the paper's tradition and then bring people from a totally different tradition to run it? It did not seem to him that it had been thought through.

Returning to London, Trelford summoned two of his closest confidants on the *Observer* to a meeting at his Wimbledon home on Sunday evening. He reported on the negotiations and on his meetings with Murdoch and found both men opposed to any deal. He was sure that represented the views of most of the staff.

Trelford told Astor that he and his close associates on the paper were unhappy, and this in turn left Astor depressed. Two weeks after the New York visit, news of the Murdoch negotiations reached, first, the *Daily Mail,* then the other Fleet Street papers. Murdoch was convinced that Trelford had engineered the leak so as to whip up public opinion against his purchase. Trelford denied this. He believed the story had surfaced because Shrimsley had been in New York and had to be summoned back to London to discuss his becoming editor. Contact had been made through the New York office of the *Sun,* and the news had inevitably reached the ears of other British journalists, who maintain close contact in the bars around Third Avenue and 44th Street.

Now things moved quickly. On the morning the first stories appeared, Trelford summoned a staff meeting in the news room and told the whole story. Almost without exception, the reaction to a Murdoch deal was hostile. It was true that Trelford had not tried to put any favorable gloss on it. He told the journalists of an exchange he had with Murdoch over the *Observer*'s meticulous and conscientious coverage of Africa and Asia.

"The Third World doesn't sell newspapers," Murdoch had declared. "Giving the *Observer* to Rupert Murdoch is like giving your beautiful daughter to a gorilla," said one journalist, according to a report in that week's *Sunday Times.* And Clive James, the Australian poet and television critic, pointed out: "Rupert Murdoch was one of the main reasons that people like me have come twelve thousand miles to work in Britain."

Later Lord Goodman gave the staff his version. He stressed the assurance Murdoch had given that the nature of the paper would not be changed. As he was doing so, Trelford was pointedly, though he claims involuntarily, shaking his head. It was clear to everyone what he thought of Murdoch's assurances. It was clear he would try to prevent the deal if he could.

When news of these developments reached Murdoch in New York, he was furious. He felt abused. He had not, after all, sought the *Observer*; its trustees had come looking for him. He was not even sure that he wanted it much. As it had been put to him, he would be doing them a favor by coming in with sufficient reserves of cash to put the paper on its feet. He issued a petulant statement:

> Several weeks ago News International was approached by representatives of the *Observer* to take over the newspaper's business and continue its existence. Friendly and confidential talks were held and advanced to the point where News International expressed willingness to proceed on condition of mutual good will by all parties concerned. At no time did News International seek the *Observer* or any other newspaper. The pre-eminent motive was to preserve the *Observer* itself and the maximum diversity of the British press in general. In view of the breach of confidence that has taken place, together with the deliberate and orchestrated attempt to build this into a controversy, News International is no longer interested.

That seemed final enough, but, almost as soon as the statement had been issued, those who knew Murdoch were expressing doubts as to whether it really meant what it said. Goodman was quickly in touch to ask if he might, in the last resort, be prepared to reconsider. Murdoch did not say yes, but neither did he say no. Only two days after the statement, the *Sunday Times* reported that Murdoch was "thought to be still in the running." But formally that was that, so the search had to begin again.

Whenever newspapers come up for disposal in London there is a cast of consistent suitors whose names enter the reckoning. Sir James Goldsmith, the grocery millionaire, is one. Lord Rothermere of Associated Newspapers is another. There is the controversial publisher Robert Maxwell and the equally unpopular "Tiny" Rowland, head of the conglomerate Lonrho, once described by Mr. Edward Heath, former British Prime Minister, as "the unacceptable face of capitalism."

All these names cropped up this time, as well as more exotic ones. Sally Aw Sian, owner of a thriving newspaper in Hong Kong, was taken so seriously for a while that representatives of the *Observer* flew to see her. Woodrow Wyatt, the flamboyant ex-Labour MP and owner of a group of provincial newspapers, was also in the hunt, or on the fringes of it, as was Olga Deterding, an heiress who appeared often in the gossip columns, and Victor Matthews of the conglomerate Trafalgar House, soon to buy the *Daily Express*. In the end, although the actual price asked for the titles was a nominal one pound, none could contemplate staking a million pounds, the minimum investment thought then to be required to give the declining paper a chance of returning to prosperity—although that turned out to be a substantial underestimate.

Within a fortnight, Murdoch was again the front runner. For the record, he was still protesting that he had withdrawn, but was now willing to add: "If they kick the door down that is another matter." Goodman and Astor were kicking the door with increasing desperation. There seemed no other hope for the paper's survival. Even the staff were coming round, for in the final analysis Murdoch was better than no employer at all. Goodman, though still ill at ease, thought he could persuade Murdoch to keep Trelford as editor, even if nothing was going to dissuade him from bringing at least one of his own men to play a senior role.

Goodman was worried that if they delayed things much longer Murdoch would lose interest again. By Friday, November 12th, the board were on the brink of a decision to invite him formally to be the new owner. They planned to meet the following week to wrap up the details, with the aim of having papers ready for signature by midweek.

Trelford was convinced, as he left the office that weekend after seeing the paper on to the presses, that by the time the next issue appeared it would be under Murdoch's ownership. What he did not know was that Kenneth Harris, a senior journalist on his staff, was dining that evening at Rules in Covent Garden with someone who was about to spark a rapid change of plan.

Douglas Cater, an American intellectual, helped run the Aspen Institute. This think-tank in the Rocky Mountains is funded by Atlantic Richfield (Arco), a large oil company based in Los Angeles. It is characteristic of wealthy corporations to support such endeavors in the arts and sciences. As well as cutting their tax bill, it is thought to soften their sometimes rapacious image.

Cater was passing through London on his way back from a conference in Europe and was at loose ends for dinner on Saturday. He phoned his friend Phil Kaiser at the American embassy, but he was not free. Next he tried Harold Evans, editor of the *Sunday Times,* who was unavailable. (It is intriguing to speculate how Evans would have changed his own professional future had he been free that night; for if Cater had not dined with Harris, Murdoch would have acquired the *Observer* and would have been unable to bid for the *Sunday Times* four years later.)

Harris, then, was Cater's third choice and he was available. When he told Cater what was about to happen to the *Observer*, the American was horrified. He was of the generation that had known the paper's great days in the 1950s. As a liberal, even an American liberal, it had been part of his cultural education. "Who decides these things?" he asked Harris, and Harris said Goodman. "Let's go and see him," said Cater.

They arrived at the Portland Place flat just as Goodman was beginning a late supper with a friend. He was not too pleased to see them, but showed interest when Cater suggested a viable new potential buyer for the *Observer*. Cater had already phoned Jo Slater, a former journalist who was head of the Aspen Institute, and he had undertaken to raise the matter with Robert Anderson, Atlantic Richfield's president. Goodman, who had scarcely heard of Atlantic Richfield or Anderson, found the suggestion far-fetched, but Cater was so persuasive that he agreed to talk on the phone that very evening to Anderson, weekending in New Mexico. Anderson was taken with the idea. The estimated investment needed was paltry by the standards of an international oil company. He asked Goodman to send someone to Los Angeles to talk, and inquired how long he had to decide. "Till Wednesday," Goodman said.

Goodman phoned Roger Harrison at three a.m. and asked him to fly west on Monday. Later that Sunday he phoned Astor, who decided to go too. The pair met Anderson for breakfast in Los Angeles on Tuesday and the deal was in motion. That week, unbeknown to Murdoch, the alternative negotiations went ahead. The hard-headed Harrison had grave doubts about handing the paper to a company with no experience either of the communications business or of the peculiar world of British newspaper publishing, with its archaic industrial practices.

As a businessman, Harrison did not believe in the efficacy of last-minute miracles. Astor, though, was a romantic. What is more, the passionate opposition to Murdoch from the editorial staff had rattled him. Here seemed a heaven-sent chance to do the decent thing after all. He liked the brisk, confident style of the Americans and, more tangibly, he was taken with their pledge that they wanted to leave the paper as it was, with Trelford in the driving seat. It was, after all, his paper to sell.

The prize, if Murdoch ever saw it as that, was slipping from his grasp, and for several days he was unaware of it, until Goodman broke the news in a phone call to New York. Although he had never been as totally committed as in most of his attempted purchases, he could not avoid a feeling of rebuff.

"When I heard, I went right through the gamut of emotions," he told the *Sunday Times* that week. "My first reaction was one of tremendous relief; second of personal grievance and annoyance, partly at myself for being sucked into the thing; and, lastly, I've got to admit that it's all for the best."

It seems an honest enough assessment. Certainly, according to his friends, his sense of personal grievance was apparent. He had long had a suspicion of the British establishment, even before the Keeler affair. He thought they were out to get him; they saw him as a brash kid from the outback, cheeky and bright but not finally of the substance needed to run one of Britain's most important cultural institutions. The outcome seemed to confirm that. An oil company with no experience of publishing had been preferred to someone of his proven expertise. For a man who detests losing anything, this was a painful defeat.

There was a postscript. When Anderson and his executives from Los Angeles came to London to sign the paper for the *Observer,* Goodman gave a celebratory dinner at his rooms at University College, Oxford, where he was Master. The eighteen guests included Anderson and Cater, Astor, Trelford, Harrison and a few people from the college. Harold Wilson, the Prime Minister, was guest of honor, having his first meeting with the new owner of one of the few papers that sometimes gave its support to his Labour Party. Goodman thought it would be nice to have Murdoch along, too. He had behaved quite decently throughout, had been willing to risk his company's funds for what might have been a thankless purpose, and had, at the last minute, been ditched without ceremony. Goodman does not like impoliteness and thought he and his colleagues had been brusque with Murdoch. An invitation to the dinner would be a thoughtful gesture.

Murdoch accepted, although he was not sure what role he was supposed to play. It was a genial and civilized affair and he enjoyed, as he always does, the company of Goodman and the academics among the guests. Everybody was on his best behavior. The Americans were determined to impress on Wilson and the *Observer* people the seriousness, not to say the nobility, of their intentions towards the paper.

The others treated the Americans with the reverence due to rich and powerful people who have virtually materialized from nowhere to effect a last-minute rescue. The atmosphere remained fairly formal and low key—a jet-lagged Anderson was even dropping off to sleep—until near the end, when Goodman invited Wilson to say a few words about the British press.

Wilson can be pompous on these occasions and rose solemnly to start his oration. "I have always," he began, "had a considerable regard for the British press."

Murdoch, in a clearly audible stage whisper, retorted: "Well, you had me fooled." Laughter swept the table, Anderson woke with a start, and Wilson's speech was never to attain the dignity he had intended.

The pain of the rebuff in London was mitigated by its coming almost simultaneously with Murdoch's long-awaited triumph in New York. On the Friday after the miracle at Rules, it was announced that he was to buy the *New York Post*. It had taken only ten weeks for his tentative lunchtime conversation with Dorothy Schiff to be translated into a firm agreement that the paper would be his for around thirty million dollars. He thought it was a little high but, as he explained in the Cockburn interview, it is impossible to value a paper that is not making money. In that year it was on its way to a loss of half a million dollars. He had to guess how much he would make if he made it a success, then allow "for the fact that you're bloody keen to get it and a certain amount of sense goes out of the window and you do the deal."

It was kept secret until late on Friday—too late for the *New York Post* to get the story into that night's paper. Paul Sann, a polished newspaperman of the old school, had been executive editor for twenty-seven years. He had joined the *Post* in 1931. On Friday afternoon Mrs. Schiff called him to her office and gave him the news, adding that Murdoch was keen for him to stay on.

Sann, who had been thinking of retiring the following year, said he was not sure whether he wanted to. Mrs. Schiff replied that Murdoch had expressed a desire for him to stay and that the deal might be jeopardized if he left. Sann was too canny to believe that. It may have been what Murdoch had told her, to assure her that he did not intend any radical change in the paper's character, but it did not square with what he told Cockburn only a few days later. Then he was scathing about American newspapermen in general and those on the *Post* in particular.

"They can't even bloody write... on and on and on and on. Importing English sub-editors is dangerous, but I wish to God the Americans would learn the techniques of English subbing.* The stories in the *Post* are not very well written and they go on too long. There's no subbing. There's no one writing headlines down there. I don't know who the news editor is and who are organizing the stories. It seems to me they're not covering the basics of New York."

On the evening of the announcement Murdoch went to Elaine's, the city's most fashionable restaurant for the media set, to celebrate with Clay Felker and Larry Lamb, who had come from London to be in at the conclusion of the purchase. Felker had invited some powerful and glossy guests. Felix Rohatyn was there, the banker who had organized the city's escape from bankruptcy by means of the Municipal Assistance Corporation. So was Shirley MacLaine, the actress, with her boyfriend Pete Hamill, a trenchant and emotional columnist. They were all giving Murdoch excited advice about what to do with his prize. "I may have paid too much for it," he confided in Felker,"but it was the chance of my lifetime."

Two weeks later Murdoch telephoned and asked Sann to lunch at Christ Cella, a somber but excellent steak house where the well-padded atmosphere resembles that of a gentlemen's club. "Do you know it?" Murdoch asked. "Hell," thought Sann, "I knew it before you were born."

The lunch lasted several hours and Sann found he liked Murdoch, admiring his obvious newspaper expertise. But he was

*Copyediting.

curiously reluctant to discuss the kind of paper he was going to turn the *Post* into. He was much more interested in the staffing, how he could make the journalists more productive without falling foul of the Guild, their trade union. He knew a shakeup would be needed if he was to make the *Post* a tightly-run paper and foresaw that this, rather than the actual journalism, would dominate his initial months as owner.

Murdoch asked Sann what time he arrived at the office of a morning—between four and five a.m. He said he would be getting in at the same time. For the first few days he was as good as his word, but he knew he would not be able to keep that up for long and quickly brought one of his own people over to keep an eye on things. This is a favorite Murdoch technique, to appoint someone to work alongside an existing senior executive with no clear distinction between their areas of authority. Either they work out an accommodation or the weaker party gives up and moves aside.

The man he chose was Peter Michelmore, a deceptively self-effacing Australian with a ferociously independent spirit. He had been the New York correspondent of the *Sydney Morning Herald* until 1975, when Murdoch asked him to be bureau chief in New York for his Australian publications. Next he was one of the many people moved to the *Star* to try to effect a breakthrough there.

When Murdoch bought the *Post* he asked Michelmore to go in and make an initial appraisal of the staff. Michelmore would arrive at the office shortly after Sann at dawn. He would sit and watch and help out and be genial, seldom venturing to suggest any alteration in the way Sann had been doing things over the years. Sann, though, knew he was Murdoch's ambassador and was careful not to cross him. For that reason there were only a few clear-cut differences of opinion between them. The first such provided Sann and the old *Post* people with a signal of the way things were going, confirming their worst fears. It concerned the execution in Utah of Gary Gilmore, the first murderer to be put to death in the United States for nine years. Opponents of capital punishment held a candlelight vigil outside the prison. The reporter's story stressed that it had been a low-key affair but Michelmore insisted on a headline that had the protesters "storming" the prison. Sann objected and the headline survived for only one edition, but for him it was an ominous sign.

After a few weeks Murdoch's pre-dawn appearances in the news room grew less frequent, not because he was in any way growing tired of his new plaything but because he now had yet another acquisition to cope with. *New York* magazine and the *Village Voice* are two weeklies serving different sections of New York society. Although they do not compare in importance with the *New York Post,* his purchase of them was more controversial because it was done without the consent of their owner—and he was Murdoch's old friend and a pillar of New York's café society, Clay Felker.

Felker had inadvertently given Murdoch the idea of buying his publications on the night of that celebratory dinner at Elaine's, after the purchase of the *Post.* In the taxi home he confessed to Murdoch that he was having trouble with his board of directors. In fact, he had been quarrelling with his backers since shortly after he became the magazine's owner. Like many journalists, Felker was naive in money matters and had little patience with those who thought them more important than editorial quality. In 1969 the company he had created went public at the suggestion of Alan Patricof, one of his most important backers, who became president. Felker and Patricof feuded constantly. In 1974 Felker wanted to buy the *Village Voice,* a weekly serving a mainly student and intellectual readership, less affluent than the readers of *New York* but numerous enough for the paper to attract plump advertising and make a profit.

Patricof was unwilling to borrow money for the purchase, so in the end it was effected by an exchange of stock. Carter Burden, a socialite and aspiring politician, had owned the *Voice* in partnership with his friend Bartle Bull. Between them they were given 34 percent of the stock in the new merged company, diluting Felker's own stake.

In 1976, at Felker's urging, the company launched *New West,* a California version of *New York.* Its initial losses exceeded estimates. Felker claims this was because it was so successful that simply printing enough copies to fill the demand cost more than had been anticipated. Patricof, Burden and Bull began to maneuver against Felker and Glaser.

That was the position as Felker told it in the taxi home. It was natural that he should turn for advice to Murdoch, a friend and experienced businessman. He was not astute enough to recognize that what he was doing was like asking an alocholic to sniff your drink. Murdoch said he would think about it and they agreed to meet in a few days.

Nine days later they had lunch together. Murdoch expounded his philosophy that it was no use being a minority shareholder in anything—you had to own 51 percent even if it meant borrowing money. "Then you don't have to take any crap from anybody." He also observed, in what Felker should have seen as a prophetic warning: "You and I could never work together."

Felker had been trying to sound out Burden about selling his stock, but Burden refused to discuss it. Now Murdoch, on the day after his lunch with Felker, instructed his investment bankers to make inquiries of Patricof and the other shareholders. Within a week he was satisfied that he would be able to buy a majority shareholding, but first his conscience dictated that he should try making a deal with Felker. He phoned him in California.

Felker hurried back to meet Murdoch and Stan Shuman, an investment banker. The proposed deal was that Murdoch should buy the company and sell Felker a third share in *New West* alone for a million dollars. Felker said he could not afford that and asked Murdoch and Shuman whether they could help him get a loan. The answer was no.

"I knew then," Felker recalled later, "that they were trying to screw me."

At the end of the meeting Murdoch said to him: "I realize that wasn't a very good deal," and added: "I'll let you know what I'm going to do."

"Felker replied: "I'm going to fight you with anything I can."

Felker detested the idea of working for someone else. What is more, he felt that anyone who could violate a friendship, as he believed Murdoch had done, would not be a satisfactory business partner. He began to make use of his international contacts to seek finance to ward off the bid: Sir James Goldsmith said he might be able to help.

Having disposed of Felker to his satisfaction, Murdoch set about acquiring his majority shareholding. Burden was the key man, the last holdout, playing hard to get. When the negotiations reached their climax in the last days of 1976, Burden was skiing in Sun Valley, Idaho. The Goldsmith talks had come to nothing, but

Felker, back from spending Christmas in the Bahamas with his friend David Frost, had persuaded Katharine Graham to make a counter-bid to Murdoch's on behalf of her *Washington Post* company. She offered $7.50 a share—fifty cents more than Murdoch—but Burden would not for some time come to the phone to discuss it. When he did, he demanded a role for himself in the company. Felker said he could have no such thing and that Murdoch would not give him one either. Over the years Felker had taken no trouble to conceal his contempt for Burden; now he was paying the price. Felker thought he had the legal right to first refusal of the Burden shares, but the fine print of that agreement made it void if the company was operating at a loss—which it was, due to the start-up costs of *New West*.

As his revenge on Felker, Burden agreed to sell to Murdoch at the lower price of seven dollars a share. Murdoch flew to Idaho to finalize the deal. The company formally changed hands on Monday, January 3rd, at a meeting at the Park Avenue law office of Theodore Kheel, the labor lawyer and power broker who represented *New York* magazine. It began in the evening and lasted through the night.

Murdoch lurked in the entrance hall, making occasional forays into the lavatory for conspiratorial talks with his advisers. He was like a small boy pressing his nose against the window of a cake shop, but knowing he had in his pocket enough cash to buy up the stock. Patricof announced that Murdoch had proxies for more than half the shares. Murdoch and Shuman were elected to the board and Kheel was dismissed as the company lawyer.

A group of the magazine's writers were waiting in an anteroom and five of them were invited to the boardroom to talk to the new directors. Passions were high and tempers flared. Gail Sheehy, one of the writers present, described the event in detail in *Rolling Stone* magazine a few months later. She reported that only Murdoch stayed calm. "This is very unfortunate," he said. "Can't we get together, Clay?"

When Felker pointed out that they had once agreed they could never work together, Murdoch answered: "I meant we could never work together as publishers. We could work together if I were publisher and you were editor."

He was now anxious for Felker to stay on. He flattered him as "an editorial genius" and "the best editor in America." He wanted a private discussion between the two of them. Felker said he would take the advice of his staff.

For Murdoch, having the *New York* journalists gathering and holding protest meetings, vowing never to work for him, ridiculing him for being foreign and for publishing (as they saw it) low-grade tabloid newspapers, was essentially a reprise of what had happened with the *Observer* a few weeks earlier. There were two important differences, though. This time he had already secured the deal. Short of a successful legal challenge, which he thought unlikely, there was nothing these pompous intellectuals could do. And this time he genuinely did want the editor to stay, though on his terms. He was not planning, as he was with Trelford, to emasculate Felker by slotting his own man above him in the hierarchy.

By now the takeover bid was the biggest news story in New York. Columns of print were devoted to it in the newspapers and most of the comment was hostile to Murdoch, the interloper doing down the hometown boy. Television cameras were waiting outside every meeting place.

The magazine's writers were expressing in public their determination to resist Murdoch, and attracting general sympathy. But on Wednesday, at a preliminary court hearing on the question of Felker's option, the judge ordered Felker and Murdoch to meet. They did the next day, together with Shuman and Roger Wood, a British newspaperman briefly the youngest ever editor of the *Daily Express* in London, then editor of Murdoch's *Star.* Felker and Glaser reiterated that they could not work for Murdoch, who declared: "I can't back down. After losing the *Observer* I'd be a journalistic untouchable around the world. I can't lose."

He did not. The lawyers confirmed that Felker's first option clause, on which his case rested, was unenforceable because of the company's losses. On Friday the staff, refusing to work, held a somber gathering at a restaurant opposite the *New York* offices, when Felker made his tearful farewell. Murdoch and his senior executives had to bring the magazine out themselves. Some forty staff members and writers eventually resigned. *New York* was never to regain the polish and inspiration Felker gave it, but it survives and makes a tidy profit.

Many have suffered at Murdoch's hands but few have had their career destroyed so comprehensively as Felker, or can so justifiably feel a sense of friendship cruelly betrayed. True, he took nearly a million dollars with him from the settlement, but he was never again to achieve the dazzling success he had with *New York,* the unique and ideal vehicle for his self-expression.

A few months after the debacle he embarked on a new venture with the British newspaper magnate Vere Harmsworth, later Lord Rothermere, heir to the wealthy Associated Newspapers group.

Harmsworth was one of those who had volunteered assistance to Felker in warding off Murdoch, but by the time he arrived on the scene it was too late to halt the sale of Burden's shares. Now he bought control of *Esquire,* a declining glossy monthly magazine for men, and put the team of Felker and Glaser in charge. It did not work and after two years it was sold. Then in 1980 Felker was hired by the *Daily News* to shape their new evening paper *Tonight,* aimed at driving Murdoch's *Post* from the streets of New York. But he could not adapt his magazine techniques successfully to daily newspapers and the evening edition closed after less than a year, with multi-million dollar losses. Another Murdoch victory.

Felker is still a popular and wealthy man, living with Sheehy in a splendid cooperative apartment in the fashionable Sutton Place area of Manhattan; but in the cruel world of the New York media, his two recent failures count for more than his one astounding success. And he has been forced to re-evaluate his naive illusions about friendship.

Meanwhile, downtown, the staff of the *Village Voice* had given their formal support to the *New York* protesters, though with less enthusiasm. Felker was still pretty much an *arriviste* at the *Voice,* not overwhelmingly popular. His appearances on the editorial floor and his interference in policy went down poorly among journalists who, through all their changes of ownership, prized their traditions of rugged independence. So although they had reservations about Murdoch, and had heard alarming stories of the way he operated, they felt that in many ways he could scarcely be worse than their former owner. Anyway, had he not made a pledge that he would not try to move the editors of any of the three magazines, assuming they wanted to stay, for at least two years, or for the duration of their contracts? Surely that was a sign of noble intentions?

Well, no, as it turned out. On the *Voice* the first thing Murdoch did was to try to replace the editor, Marianne Partridge. She had been editor only since August and was not, actually, too popular among her staff. Yet the other journalists, grasping quickly that if he was allowed to get away with this there would be no long-term hope for them, mounted an effective counter-move.

The story has become part of the folklore of New York journalism. Partridge first heard from Murdoch one Sunday a couple of weeks after the takeover was completed. In a brief call, he told her he would be wanting to talk to her. The following day his secretary tracked her down to the compositor's plant at Mount Kisco, New York, where she was supervising the last stages of production of that week's issue. An appointment was made for her to see the new proprietor on Tuesday evening.

Only a few days after his formal acquisition of the *New York Post* he had already installed himself in Dorothy Schiff's green and gold sixth-floor office, a sickly interpretation of the style of the French Empire. (An unflamboyant man, he was later to have it done in a more sober caramel shade.)

Partridge remembers the interview as being highly civilized. Murdoch did not actually say she had to go, but told her he would be hiring an editor-in-chief to supervise things—the Trelford/Sann technique. They chatted about where she had come from and her previous experience in journalism. He kept responding "Oh, oh," as though surprised by what she was saying, or not really listening. He gazed across the East River at the lights just beginning to flicker on in the dusk.

"Manhattan's a beautiful town," he sighed.

"That's Brooklyn," she snapped.

"How can you do this?" Partridge asked, as the news sank in. "Didn't you say you'd keep editors on?" Murdoch replied that she could stay, or he would honor her contract by paying her off.

"That's not honoring my contract," she said calmly. "This is all very surprising. I'm going to have to talk to my lawyer. Perhaps you weren't aware of what was reported as your promise?"

Murdoch made soothing noises and said he was sure it would be sorted out. He thanked her for being so civilized and asked how she was getting home. She said she would take a taxi.

"Call her a cab, call her a cab, call her a cab," Murdoch repeated in a mechanical, preoccupied fashion to his secretary. To stem the flow, Partridge employed an old vaudeville line. "OK, I'm a cab," she shouted. Murdoch, not known for his sense of humor, gave the impression he was unfamiliar with the joke and laughed uproariously. With no cab obtainable he ordered his driver to take her home in his limousine. As she left, he did not really think she was going to give him much trouble.

On the Sunday when he made his first call to Partridge, Murdoch had also approached the man James Brady, the new editor of *New York*, had advised him to hire to replace her. Michael Kramer was a smart, fresh-faced young writer, a coming talent. He had worked for *New York* and was now editing *More*, a monthly magazine devoted to journalism with neither a wide nor a profitable circulation; but it did reach important people in the media and to edit it was therefore a high-profile job. Kramer was in his office on West 57th Street, putting the final touches to that month's issue, which had as its main feature a long article about Rupert Murdoch. At the same time, he recalls, he was watching the Super Bowl on the office television.

The initial phone call came from Brady, speaking from Murdoch's apartment. Could Kramer come to see them? Arriving not long afterwards, he was met in the lobby by Brady and they spoke for ten minutes. Brady said he was to be offered the editorship of the *Voice*.

"What about Marianne?" Kramer asked.

"She's leaving," Brady replied. "She'll be paid her contract."

Kramer assumed it had been agreed with her. He was not to know that Murdoch had not even spoken to her yet.

He was ushered into Murdoch's presence in the living room, where the offer was formally made. They had a brief discussion about the direction the paper would take. Kramer said he wanted a free hand editorially and would try to make it more political, as it had once been. "As long as it's making money I don't care," Murdoch said.

Kramer asked again about Partridge. "She's leaving," Murdoch said. "Didn't Jim talk to you about that?"

Kramer said he would go away and think about it.

On the Tuesday afternoon, shortly before Marianne Partridge went down to South Street, Murdoch summoned Kramer to see him, saying he needed a decision that day. They talked about changes in style that Kramer wanted to make and Murdoch wondered whether they would put him in conflict with Jack Newfield, the talented but abrasive investigative reporter who was one of the *Voice*'s stars.

Kramer said they probably would. He had never got along with Newfield or, for that matter, with Alex Cockburn, a mercurial Englishman who then wrote a brilliant column of press criticism in the paper. (He is the son of the radical journalist Claud Cockburn, who died in 1981.)

Murdoch discussed with equanimity the prospect of his new editor clashing with two of the paper's established writers. That was, after all, the way several of his publications were run. It never did any harm to give people a prod if they seemed too comfortable, too entrenched.

It was not to work out like that, though. Kramer, while prepared to tackle Newfield if need be, was too clever to declare open war from the beginning. The first thing he did, as he got back to the *More* office after dusk, was to phone Newfield at the *Voice*. He told him he was to be the new editor and that he wanted Newfield to stay as his chief political correspondent.

"I don't see how you can do this," Newfield retorted. "What about Marianne?"

Kramer explained what he had been told about Partridge. Newfield said it was not true. He claims to have ended the conversation by saying: "I will kill you with my bare hands"—a remark widely reported in contemporary accounts.

Kramer does not remember that specific threat, but certainly the tone of the exchange was such as to make him worry about whether Partridge was really leaving of her own volition. He tried to phone her but there was no answer. She was down at the *Post*, seeing Murdoch.

As soon as Newfield put the phone down after talking to Kramer, he contacted Alex Cockburn. Though the two were not on the most cordial terms, this was an emergency. Internal differences had to be buried. In any case, Cockburn had access to Murdoch, having done that long interview with him a few weeks earlier.

Cockburn rang Murdoch, told him of their concern, and arranged that he and Newfield should go and see him at his apartment. The pair met in the lobby of the Plaza Hotel and walked the short distance up Fifth Avenue. Murdoch came to open the door and announced: "I'm going to take the wind out of your sails. We're back to square one. Marianne has been reinstated. Come in and have a drink." They did. They reminisced about Alex's father. Murdoch told them how he had been known as "Red Rupert" at Oxford because of his left-wing views.

"It was," Newfield recollects, "a relatively charming hour."

Things had moved quickly after Partridge left Murdoch's office. She went home in a state of shock to her apartment on 59th Street and Second Avenue. She did not want to phone anyone at the *Voice* because it would seem as though she was asking them to put their own jobs on the line for her.

Murdoch telephoned. He wanted to know how she was feeling and suggested a further talk. While she was on the phone to him the doorbell chimed. It was Kramer. He had been trying to contact her for an hour or so and had finally decided to make an unannounced visit. Murdoch said he would ring back.

Kramer's and Partridge's memories of his visit differ. He says that as soon as he heard that she had not agreed to quit he decided to pull out, and this was what he came to tell her. She claims he spent some time trying to persuade her to stand down. Both agree it was a difficult and embarrassing meeting. Kramer paced the room nervously and Partridge offered him something to eat. He declined, so she made herself some soup, and he helped.

Kramer was still there when Murdoch phoned again, this time to tell Partridge that it had all been a terrible misunderstanding, that he had not properly understood the situation at the *Voice,* that she could keep her job after all. "But don't talk to anyone until I've told Michael," he added.

"He's still here," she said, and passed the phone over to him. Kramer, feeling sore and abused—a familiar state of mind for a new Murdoch victim—says it was he who formally ended the short-lived courtship by telling Murdoch that he had accepted the offer only on the understanding that Partridge was leaving willingly, and that now he had found she was not he was not interested.

"I'll get back to you," said Murdoch. That was the last he ever heard from him, although much later Kramer became a political commentator for *New York* magazine.

By his graceful, or at least speedy, withdrawal, Murdoch was starting to absorb the lesson of recent weeks, that outside Australia editors need to be treated with a bit more tenderness and respect than those he was used to. By understimating Trelford he had lost the *Observer*. Now he had risked an unnecessary row at one of his most recent acquisitions by trying to make a change motivated not by any perceived need for improvement in the paper's quality but simply by the desire to make a dramatic announcement of his arrival, a show of strength. He could not tell whether Partridge was a good editor because he did not understand the *Voice* or the concerns of its readers. He understood from its balance sheets that it could turn a modest, steady profit, but its journalism was not of a kind that interested him and he could see now that it was wrong of him to have blundered into alien territory, firing without taking careful aim.

After that nasty shock and his enforced climb-down, Murdoch decided to let the *Voice* go its own way. He changed his relation to it from that of an interfering parent to a kindly uncle, smiling tolerantly if sometimes thinly at its misdeeds. On the day after the Partridge drama, he went down to the *Voice*'s office in Greenwich Village, uttering consoling words to the staff. After that, he watched from a distance, only occasionally picking up the phone to complain vociferously about stories, nearly always stories about himself or his papers.

Murdoch was angry when Cockburn wrote an article scoffing at Paul Rigby, the Australian cartoonist and an old friend, then working at the *Post*. Next day he apologized to Partridge for his outburst through Bill Ryan, his publisher at the *Voice*. Later he heard that Nat Hentoff, one of the paper's sharpest writers, was preparing a critical article about the *Post,* so he phoned and said he did not see why he should be vilified in his own newspapers. Partridge said surely this was proof that he did not interfere editorially in his publications, as his critics charged. He has since used this argument quite often in interviews, citing the *Voice* as an example—almost the only example among his holdings. The Hentoff article did not in fact appear, although Partridge says it had nothing to do with Murdoch's complaint.

Some eighteen months later, with six months of her contract to run, another attempt was made to dislodge Partridge, this time by Ryan. He had already hired David Schneiderman, from the *New York Times,* to take over, but again the staff rallied round Partridge, who would not go, although she would have been paid to the end of her contract. Eighty-two staffers signed a petition, there were threats of mass resignations, and about fifty journalists rounded on Ryan in the office.

"What do you know about the paper?" Joe Conason, a young reporter, shouted at the sleek-suited Ryan. "I've never seen anyone who looks like you buying the paper."

Schneiderman sat in an office uptown for six months, skimming through back issues and mapping his strategy, until Partridge's contract was up. He has been editor of the paper since 1979 and Murdoch is obviously happy with him, although the two do not agree politically. Murdoch knows it would be wrong for the *Voice* to be edited by someone of his own conservative views and he appears to enjoy his infrequent meetings with Schneiderman, when they argue about the city's politics. Occasionally the editor has been on the receiving end of criticism for individual stories, mainly about Murdoch. In 1981 he printed a thinly-veiled suggestion that the *Post* was getting a tax reduction on its South Street office building because of its support for Mayor Koch. After the piece appeared, one of Murdoch's senior henchmen phoned Schneiderman to tell him how badly Murdoch viewed it, but there was no hint of reprisals.

Schneiderman reflected that on the *New York Times* it would have been inconceivable to run such an article about the business affairs of Arthur Sulzberger, the owner. Occasionally, too, Murdoch airs his views about an item that offends his Presbyterian sense of decorum. He described as "nauseating" an article on gay life styles in the West Village. But he understands that the paper caters to a rarefied market and, as long as it makes a profit, he largely lets it be.

Since Schneiderman became its editor, the *Village Voice* has entered a period of stability. Its circulation holds steady at around 160,000.

"Schneiderman, like all editors, has become the ally of the staff against the owner," says Newfield. "The flies always capture the flypaper."

Schneiderman does not quite see it like that: he regards himself as a buffer between Murdoch and his sometimes anarchic subordinates. Murdoch clearly trusts him as much as he trusts anyone working for a paper that relates to nothing he knows about.

While the *Voice* makes money he is prepared to let it do its own special thing. At the very least, it provides a handy argument against those who accuse his press empire of being culturally and politically monolithic. But his real effort in New York has always been expended on the *Post*. Here, many changes were needed to cast the paper in his image, and he lost no time in initiating them.

FIVE

"Sock, Sock, Sock, Day After Day"

No one ever went broke underestimating the taste of the American public.

—H. L. Mencken

Soon after he bought the *New York Post,* Murdoch summoned the editorial staff to a meeting in the news room. As they milled shoulder to shoulder, or sat on the edge of desks for their first glimpse of their new proprietor, he told them: "I want you to forget all you have ever heard about me." After a few months, those who took him at his word wished they had remembered.

A quality of Murdoch's that impresses those who deal with him is his ability to compartmentalize his affairs. When he switches his attention from one of his enterprises to another he can appear completely absorbed in the new subject. Yet he keeps the latest field position of the old one in the front of his mind, ready to switch back. It is an intercontinental facility. After taking off his jacket and writing the front-page headline for the Sydney *Mirror,* he can go back to his office, get on the phone and decide how to deal with an impending industrial dispute at the *Sun* in London, with no discernible shift of gear.

That is how, in the midst of the round-the-clock drama over his acquisition of *New York* magazine, he could still keep track of his more important recent purchase, the *Post*.

One morning in early January, arriving at the *Post* before dawn as usual, Paul Sann had a call from Murdoch, who had been up all night in a lawyer's office wrapping up the details of the *New York* deal. He wanted Sann to come in for a talk. Murdoch had borrowed a cramped room and ordered hamburgers and coffee. He told Sann that his new purchase meant he would have less time to spend at the *Post*, so he was appointing an executive editor to look after things. The man he chose was Ed Bolwell, an Australian who had worked as a teenager for a paper owned by Murdoch's father. But he was not one of the Australian tabloid artists. His record in American journalism had been on its more sober side: he had worked at the *New York Times* and was now a senior editor at *Time* magazine. He was an interesting choice, an indication that so far Murdoch had no intention of pulling the *Post* down market but sought to serve the existing middle-brow readership better.

Murdoch told Sann he wanted him to stay on and was offering him a two-year contract. He had a pad of yellow paper on the desk and pulled it towards him as if to start drafting the document. He offered Sann a cold hamburger. Sann declined both the food and the contract. He was getting close to retirement and was uncertain of what direction the paper would take. He did not want to be tied.

Bolwell, a short, slim man wearing built-up shoes, arrived a week later. Almost right away Sann didn't like him. Bolwell had an unsettling manner, shouting at his staff in a way the gentlemanly Sann would never countenance.

In an interview with *Time*, Bolwell described his philosophy of management: "Running a newspaper is a little like conducting a symphony orchestra. Some people have to be badgered and some coddled to get the best out of them. And you have to stretch. Not to stretch is not to live. I am very competitive."

As Sann remembers it, there was scarcely any coddling and a great deal of badgering during Bolwell's first weeks at the *Post*. The new editor was convinced that the best market for expanding circulation was the commuters who spend an hour or so on the trains of an evening, going home to Westchester or Long Island. Bolwell was one of them himself and insisted on detailed coverage of commuter train delays. One morning he read a reporter's story of a delay that included no explanation for it. "Have you got the president of the line out of bed yet?" he shouted at the reporter. "Have you done that yet?"

Sann hated this style of exerting authority and on occasion would tell Bolwell as much. Always, in front of Sann, Bolwell was deferential, admitting the error and apologizing. The final break between the two came over a matter of professional judgment. Freddie Prinze, who starred in the popular television series called *Chico and the Man,* killed himself in California playing Russian roulette. The story broke too late for the morning papers and Sann saw it as a natural front-page lead. He began to work on it and to get reporters to prepare background articles. When Bolwell came in he was unhappy. He didn't want the story to occupy the whole front page, as Sann had planned. He may have thought that, because it was about a Puerto Rican, it was directed too far down market. It would not be of absorbing interest to the suburban commuters whose attention he wanted to attract.

Looking through the pile of stories, Bolwell found one about a big power blackout at Utica, in upstate New York. What about letting that share the front page lead with Freddie Prinze? Sann was appalled. It would destroy the impact of the dramatic layout he had drawn. Moreover, Utica was nearly 250 miles away, outside the *Post*'s circulation area. Why would New York City readers care?

Bolwell was insistent, so Sann found room on his front page for the power cut. Still furious, the veteran editor went to see Bolwell after the second edition had been locked up. "Look," he told him, "I'm going home now. I won't be back." According to Sann, Bolwell was worried, knowing that Murdoch respected the older man. He hoped Sann would have second thoughts by the morning.

Next day Sann went in to clear up his things. Murdoch called him in and they spoke for two hours, interrupted only by a call from Murdoch's daughter Prudence in London, excited at having secured her first job. He said he would call her back and resumed what appeared to Sann an attempt to persuade· him to stay on. He apologized for Bolwell, again offered Sann a contract and, when that was rejected, asked him to write a regular column. Sann could not be budged. "I had four respectable decades as a newspaper man," he said later. "I didn't want to go out as a guy putting out this kind of newspaper." To save face he agreed to serve as a "consultant," but was consulted only once.

Sann's version of events, of Murdoch's reluctance to see him go, does not square with the recollection of others. On the day of the resignation, Peter Michelmore passed Murdoch in a corridor in the *Post* building. "Paul Sann has just done us a favor," said Murdoch. "He's resigned." It was January 31st, exactly a month after the takeover.

Robert Spitzler, Sann's deputy, left a few months later, followed one by one by most of the old executives. Of the most senior journalists who had run the paper under Mrs. Schiff, only James Wechsler was to remain for the long term. A veteran liberal who had led the paper's fight against the McCarthy committee, he was coming to the end of his career and of his energy to fight. His name appeared on the masthead as editorial page editor for two years before the increasingly conservative tone of the leading articles became a clear embarrassment to him. The title went to Bruce Rothwell, who had effectively been in charge of the page for a long time. Within four years, and until Rothwell's death in 1984, the list of senior editors printed daily contained not a single American name.

Murdoch could rationalize this. "The poor old broken-down *New York Post*," as he described it once, had been brought to that condition by a gang of tired newspapermen drained of inspiration. The only hope for success was to import a new slate of people. While he would have liked to find Americans to do the job, in the end he worked best with the Australian and British journalists he knew.

Bolwell did not last long, although Murdoch could have lived with his short temper and his unpopularity with his staff. In general, he thought editors who did not get on well with their underlings were more effective than those who did. But Bolwell was not producing the paper Murdoch wanted. He had not been trained in the tabloid tradition. It was still afflicted by a lack of professionalism. In July Murdoch asked Bolwell to resign and appointed Roger Wood as editor.

Just after Wood took over, New York became obsessed with a news story of a violent and sensational nature that was to become identified in the minds of readers and critics as characteristic of the changing style of the *New York Post*. Since July 1976 the city had been shaken by a series of motiveless murders of young men and women in middle-class areas of Brooklyn and Queens. They were all shot with a .44-caliber revolver late at night as they sat in the back of parked cars. In eight attacks, six people were killed and seven wounded.

As the attacks continued and the gunman remained at large, the tone of the coverage in both the *Post* and the *News* became increasingly hysterical, reaching a pitch that had not been experienced in the city since "yellow" journalism went out of fashion several decades earlier.

Nobody, they shrieked, was safe from the fiend. The *News* vied with the *Post*, sensation for sensation, but received less criticism because it was perceived that the *Post* was dictating the tone of the coverage and the morning paper, rattled, was simply trying to keep up, as the *Mirror* in London was seen to have reached into the gutter to ward off the *Sun*. It was the *News* that first dubbed the killer "Son of Sam" —the name he used in a letter he wrote to the paper as well as in a note found beside the body of one of his victims.

The last attack came on July 31st, 1977. Wood was away and Murdoch was editing the paper day-to-day, helped by Steve Dunleavy, a young Australian for whom he had a high regard. Dunleavy, brisk and well built, has a liking for the lurid and little patience with considerations of good taste and restraint that might hinder him from writing a story to the very limit of its worth and, some maintain, beyond. "Dunleavy decides what he wants the story to be and then sends reporters out to get it," is how one *Post* reporter puts it.

As Murdoch and Dunleavy rolled up their sleeves to produce fresh sensations daily, Murdoch would say: "There's only one game in town and that's Son of Sam." The *News* had an initial advantage over them in the person of Jimmy Breslin, their much-read Irish-American columnist, a specialist in heart-tugging prose. Son of Sam wrote to him and Breslin quoted from his letters. In one column Breslin forecast that the killer would strike again on July 29th, the anniversary of the first murder. This was one of the aspects of the reporting that angered the *New Yorker,* that mouthpiece of respectable liberal opinion. In a comment published in early August, the magazine maintained that by printing such speculation and making the killer into a celebrity, the two tabloids were encouraging him.

"The Son of Sam has killed six people and wounded seven and he has sold a lot of newspapers," the *New Yorker* wrote. Such solemn knuckle-rapping did not in the least deter Dunleavy from writing an open letter to the killer, in the hope that he, like Breslin, might receive an answer. On August 10th, as the latest of its breathless exposés, the *Post* reported that the Son of Sam wore a wig. NEW WITNESS SAW SAM CHANGE WIG, shouted the headline.

Early the following day, that and similar speculation proved false when David Berkowitz, a twenty-four-year-old postal worker, was arrested and charged with the killings. He had not worn a wig, nor had he invariably adopted a two-handed combat pose before firing, as had also been reported.

All these discrepancies were forgotten in the excitable coverage the papers gave to the arrest. The *News* and the *Post* devoted twelve pages each to the story that day, with twenty separate news items in the *News,* nineteen in the *Post.* The arrest did not interrupt the flow of the story. Breslin and Dunleavy received new letters from Berkowitz in prison.

The *Post* published some old letters he had written to a girlfriend under the front-page headline: HOW I BECAME A MASS KILLER, by David Berkowitz. Murdoch later apologized for that, characterizing the headline as "inaccurate and wrong." The *New York Times* joined the *New Yorker* in wondering whether the persistently high-pitched coverage by the two tabloids would make a fair trial impossible. (In the end, Berkowitz was judged unfit to plead through insanity.)

Sometimes controversies arose for reasons Murdoch found baffling. It seemed there were people in New York who would seize on any small detail, any apparently inoffensive headline, and use it as evidence against him. In the summer of 1977 a major power failure in New York was followed by a night of looting in many areas. Production of the *Post* was lost for a day because of the lack of electricity, and when it returned its front-page headline was: 24 HOURS OF TERROR.

The city administration, under Mayor Abraham Beame, thought it a sensational and exaggerated account of the night's events, perhaps a subtle attempt to discredit Beame in a year when he was up for re-election. Beame's deputy mayor for economic development was Osborn Elliott, a former editor of *Newsweek,* later made Dean of Columbia University's School of Journalism. He wrote an angry open letter, published in the *New York Times,* accusing Murdoch of cheapening American journalism by importing crude Australian methods.

Murdoch, who never ducks a fight, wrote a full-page editorial equally rude about Elliott. A couple of years later the *Columbia Journalism Review,* published by the school Elliott ran, printed a startling editorial entitled: DOING THE DEVIL'S WORK. It described the *Post* "as appealing to the basest passions and appetites of the hour" and seemed to suggest some kind of protective legislation against it. It exploited social passions, terrorized the fearful and incited the wrathful. "It is no longer enough to judge the paper solely by journalistic standards.... Here we enter a moral universe in which judgments are of a different order altogether, suggesting, as they do, that the matter ought not to be allowed to rest after the press critics have pronounced their anathemas. For the *New York Post* is no longer merely a journalistic problem. It is a social problem—a force for evil."

Murdoch and Dunleavy had long ago learned to dismiss such pomposities as coming from effete martini-sipping intellectuals, too refined to soil their hands by engaging in the kind of journalism the bulk of New Yorkers actually wanted to read.

"I don't give a damn what the media critics say," Murdoch told *More* magazine.

In May 1977, three years before that *Review* editorial, he had given a cogent defense of his philosophy and of lowest-common-denominator journalism in a speech to the American Newspaper Publishers' Association in San Francisco. He accused the publishers of going above the heads of their audience, catering to an idealized market, pretending the interests of readers were as lofty as their own and their writers'. "Elitist journalism," he dubbed it, adding: "A press that fails to interest the whole community is one that will ultimately become a house organ of the elite engaged in an increasingly private conversation with a dwindling club. . . . I cannot avoid the temptation of wondering whether there is any other industry in this country which seeks to presume so completely to give the customer what he does not want."

Yet many of the *Post* reporters shared the "elitist" opinion of their paper. They saw the new brashness and brutalism infecting not just the coverage of crime but also political reporting. Many were offended by what they saw as the insensitivity of Paul Rigby, the cartoonist. They found two cartoons in the early summer particularly hard to take. The first was about Andrew Young, the suave black southerner President Carter appointed ambassador to the United Nations, where he offended traditional American conservatives by his outspoken support for the Third World. Some felt the cartoon was racist. Not long afterwards another cartoon provoked the staff to action. It was a comment on a decision by the city to introduce one-woman police cars. It showed a policewoman luring a gang of robbers into her car by showing a seductive pair of thighs. A few dozen reporters signed a petition against it, calling it "sexist and offensive." Joy Cook and Barbara Yuncker, officials of the office branch of the Newspaper Guild, the trade union for journalists and clerical workers, sent the petition to Murdoch.

He replied with a terse note: "Personally I have known Mr. Rigby and his work for many years and have never found him to be either sexist or racist. But then, perhaps I am insensitive! Mr. Rigby's cartoons add brightness and humor to the paper. It could do with more of both!" And he added this hand-written postscript: "Andy Young enjoyed the other cartoon so much he has asked for the original!"

The main political event in the city that year was the election for mayor. Beame, who had held the office for four years, was running again but faced several opponents in the September Democratic primary. Newspaper endorsements are important for candidates running for city office. Traditionally, the candidates present themselves for interviews with senior editors of all the papers and submit to questioning, as if they were applying for a job.

Early in the summer, Murdoch had been inclining towards Mario Cuomo, an Italian-American who had the support of Hugh Carey, the Governor of New York State. The *Post*'s coverage of the early campaigning reflected this preference. Murdoch was disinclined to support Beame, whom he blamed for the city's near-bankruptcy two years earlier. He thought Beame was too weak in dealing with the unions representing city workers.

When a report by the federal government on the fiscal crisis appeared that summer, the *Post* put it on the front page with the uncompromising headline: BEAME CONNED CITY. Beame responded crisply by calling Murdoch an "'Australian carpetbagger."

In the interviews with the candidates, Murdoch was unimpressed with Cuomo, but was much taken with Edward Koch, a Jewish congressman who had entered the race with little support, as measured by the opinion polls. It seemed to Murdoch that Koch shared his own pragmatism, especially his realistic attitude to the limits of the city's ability to pay for welfare and services. He seemed determined to stand up to the unions and vested interests. He was a Democrat of a conservative stamp—a category in which, at that time, Murdoch placed himself.

Koch learned he was going to get the *Post*'s endorsement at seven o'clock one morning in August. The phone rang. "Hallo, Ed, this is Rupert." For an instant Koch was at a loss. "'I don't know any Ruperts," he thought. Rupert was not a common name in his social set.

Then he recognized the Australian accent and said quickly: "Yes, Rupert?"

On hearing the news Koch said: "It's very important to me." Murdoch replied patronizingly: "All we ask is that you do a good job."

Koch was endorsed by the *News* two weeks later and believes that he would not have won the primary, nor the election itself, without the support of both. And he doubted whether he would have been backed by the *Post* had the more liberal Dolly Schiff still been in charge.

Koch and Murdoch have remained friends. The mayor admires the publisher's modesty ("He never comes with an entourage") and relishes the paper's brash, campaigning approach, especially when it is campaigning for him. "Sock, sock, sock, day after day," is how he sees it.

What many of the paper's staff objected to was that the "sock, sock, sock" was not confined to the editorial opinion column. Suddenly, with the endorsement, the extensive and generally favorable news coverage given to Cuomo was turned off and Koch replaced him as the star contender. Barbara Yuncker drafted another petition to Murdoch speaking of the "great disquiet" of the staff, and some eighty journalists signed it:

"We are dismayed," it said, "at the kind of puff journalism which has followed your endorsements. We believe that it will ultimately help neither the newspaper nor your candidates.

"You have lost good writers over this and related issues. You should be aware that editorial people of stature and integrity whom you ought to value are very unsettled and also may be lost to the paper.

"All of us signing below accept the basic premise that independent reporting produces the best results for public welfare. Journalists did not become the Fourth Estate and Thomas Jefferson did not put us ahead of courts and legislatures in anticipation that narrow partisanship would guide us.

"Political stories should be written by the best intelligence good reporters can bring to the facts—and not homogenized afterwards to fit an editorial position. Space should be even-handedly divided among viable contenders; not to do so cheapens the support for the paper's choices and destroys our credibility."

This could have been calculated to infuriate Murdoch, and it did. Pretentious twaddle. Who did these people think they were? All that nonsense about Jefferson confirmed his prejudices against American journalists. If only they would come down from the clouds and get stuck in to some proper reporting, learn to write a half-decent headline, he might be able to sell a few more papers. If they didn't like it why didn't they leave? It was all too like that irritating business with staff of the *Australian* in 1975.

But Murdoch knows too much to rant in front of his reporters. When he summoned Yuncker to discuss the petition he tried hard to remain his measured self, though clearly angry. "If anyone on the staff thinks I lack integrity, if he had any integrity himself he'd quit," he said.

Yuncker said she had signed it. Did he want her to quit? "Let's not get personal," Murdoch said. Yuncker persisted. "It's our newspaper, too," she affirmed, and at this Murdoch very nearly blew his top. "Oh no, it's not," he snarled. "When you pay the losses you can say it's your paper too. It's *my* newspaper. You just work here and don't you forget it."

Had he taken the trouble to go back over some of the old files of the paper, to remind himself how it had looked just before he took it over, Murdoch would have been able to deploy a more telling argument. For it was disingenuous of the reporters to claim that slanting and selecting news stories for political purposes was something Mrs. Schiff's *Post* never did. In the run-up to the presidential election of 1976 the paper carried several front-page headlines calculated to damage President Ford's chance of re-election. HOW FORD BLOCKED FIRST NIXON PROBE screamed one, raking over the coals of Watergate. NEW QUESTIONS ON FORD'S MONEY read another.

The anti-Ford campaign reached its climax on October 29th with a banner headline that even Murdoch would have found hard to improve: FORD AD MAN LINKED TO PORN. The story told how Michael Goldbaum, who was helping promote the Ford campaign, also made pornographic films. When the *Post* presented Goldbaum with the evidence he was fired by Ford's staff. Readers were spared no details of the pornographic films he had made: "Principal actors must perform their own fellatio and cunnilingus." And for good measure the same day's paper carried another story headlined: FORD FILES DON'T ADD UP.

The vital difference between this and the *Post*'s campaign for Koch was that most *Post* reporters were liberals who, like their paper, had supported the Democratic presidential candidate, Jimmy Carter. Not many were similarly committed to Koch.

Murdoch's defenders point out that political favoritism is nothing startlingly new in American journalism. "He's not doing anything that publishers historically in this country haven't done," says one of his editors. "At the *New York Times* Arthur Sulzberger has relations with politicians. He invites them for dinner and lunch. He wields tremendous power in this city but in a very different way. Rupert is more open about it. He's less discreet about what he's doing. The *Times* is the ultimate in this country of a discreet newspaper. You can never find their footprints."

Barbara Yuncker, as head of the Guild's office branch, saw much of Murdoch during his first two years of ownership. Towards the end of 1977 she began to hear from senior executives that he was trying to get rid of the "dead wood," including many who had signed the pre-election petition. In February 1978 he presented a list of 148 Guild members he wanted to dismiss—about a third of the membership on the paper.

On March 9th he announced: "The *Post* proposes, on a one-time basis, the right to terminate members of the staff, with appropriate severance pay, who in its judgment are incompatible with the new management's publishing concept." The shell-shocked staff dubbed it the "Auschwitz clause." Since it conflicted with the existing Guild contract, it had to be negotiated.

Discussions continued for two months, partly under the auspices of the federal mediation service in Washington. In the end, Murdoch achieved as much as he could reasonably have hoped. The 148 listed people would be asked, not forced, to leave, and attractive severance terms were offered to help persuade them. They were called in one by one and told they were no longer required. Nearly half agreed to go, and several who were not on the "hit list" took advantage of the improved terms and left of their own accord, bringing the number who left to eighty. After that, the management announced dismissal of a further eighteen employees who had been with the paper for less than two years and thus had no protection under the Guild contract. Sixteen of them went but seven were later re-engaged.

While this dispute was important for the evidence it gave of Murdoch's attitude to his journalists, it was soon overshadowed by much graver labor troubles involving all three New York papers. With new contracts due to be negotiated with the work force that year, there had been talk for months of a likely strike. The managements were known to be determined to reduce the manning levels in their pressrooms, and the unions just as determined to resist them.

A successful negotiation with the printers four years earlier had encouraged the publishers to think that this time they could solve once and for all the problems of overmanning in the pressrooms, where the newspapers are produced. The printers are the men who operate the Linotype machines and then fit the metal type into the page. When newspapers introduce the new technology of photo-composition, their role becomes redundant.

In 1974 the printing unions had agreed, without a strike, to the introduction of the new machinery. They ceded to the proprietors the right of deciding how many men were needed to operate it. In return, the publishers agreed to keep on the payroll everyone then working as a printer, even if there was virtually nothing for them to do.

This agreement did not include the men who worked the printing presses, the pressmen. They are represented by a different union. To complete their program of modernization and reducing labor costs, the proprietors sought to alter the system by which manning levels were decided. The existing system was known as "unit manning": the publishers agreed to deploy a fixed number of men to every press or unit. They wanted to go over to "room manning" where they, the publishers, would decide how many people were needed to perform the overall printing operation and would bring the staff down to whatever figure they arrived at. As with the printers, they were prepared to give lifetime job guarantees to existing employees.

The New York City proprietors argued that radical surgery was the only way they could bring their costs into line with suburban papers, operating at lower manning levels than they and competing more and more effectively for circulation and advertising on the fringes of the city.

The *Post* had not negotiated in concert with the other two papers since 1963, when Dorothy Schiff quit the Publishers' Association and made her own settlement with striking printers. There was diffidence on both sides before the three decided to make common cause in 1978. Executives of the *News* and the *Times* were suspicious of the newcomer. As for Murdoch, in a worse financial position than the other two, he feared they would make a deal with the union so expensive that he would not be able to afford it and would be forced to close down. But at a dinner with the proprietors of the two papers in the summer of 1977 he became convinced that they were determined to force manpower cuts on the pressmen and were prepared to take a strike if necessary. At the dinner they reached no firm agreement to negotiate together, but they could see they were headed in the same direction. In November that year the *Post* rejoined the Publishers' Association.

The other two papers did not give Murdoch any support, though, in his "hit list" battle with the Newspaper Guild. A long account of the 1978 strike was written for the *New Yorker* by A. H. Raskin, a veteran labor reporter. In it, he recounts how he met Arthur Ochs ("Punch") Sulzberger, publisher of the *New York Times*, during the Guild dispute at the *Post*. "The man is wild," Sulzberger said of Murdoch. "We'll support him on the things we have in common but not on the crazy kind of things he's after with the Guild."

The *Times* and the *News*, still negotiating without the *Post*, had told the pressmen's union in the summer that they would unilaterally introduce new working conditions and manning levels on August 8th unless an agreeement on cuts had been negotiated by then. This would inevitably mean a strike. Murdoch, before formally joining them, wanted to convince himself that they were committed to holding out for room manning—especially the *Times*, which had historically taken a softer line with the unions than the other two. On July 18th, 1978, he had dinner at Christ Cella with Joe Barletta of the *News* and Walter Mattson of the *Times*—the two who were to play with him the leading roles in the negotiations on the publishers' side. Barletta was a lawyer sent to New York by the Chicago Tribune Company, owners of the *News*. He came with a reputation for ruthless bargaining that made Murdoch warm to him from the beginning. Mattson was the executive vice-president and general manager of the *Times*, Sulzberger's most important adviser, and a man of a very different stamp from Murdoch and Barletta. He was taciturn and philosophical. On the comparatively rare occasions when he did speak, his voice was so quiet that it was a strain to catch what he was saying. He was not at all Murdoch's kind of person and they never got on well from the start. Almost the only factor common to the three men was their age: all were in their forties.

At the dinner they agreed to hold out for room manning, although even at that stage Murdoch was worried about Mattson's resolve. He feared he would in the end settle for slightly reduced manning but still on the unit basis. Yet when the day of the deadline came, and negotiations were still in progress, it was the *Times* that took the lead in introducing the new work rules without agreement from the union, inevitably provoking the strike that began on August 9th, 1978.

A few days later, Mattson and Barletta came up with what seemed a masterly idea to serve the twin functions of improving the public image of the proprietors and ensuring that Murdoch did not do what Mrs. Schiff had done and break away from the alliance. They invited him to become spokesman for the Publishers' Association, with the title of President. They still by no means trusted him and felt that as nominal leader he would be less likely to make a hasty exit when things looked gloomy, as from time to time they surely would. They recognized, too, that his brisk confidence went over well on television.

As with many strikes that affected people's way of life, it was important for each side to convince the public that it was being reasonable. Murdoch would prove the most persuasive spokesman of the three: and since his paper was in the worst shape financially, he could most effectively plead the case for substantial cuts.

He did not immediately accept the offer, and his decision whether or not to do so marked the introduction into the dispute—or at least on to its sidelines—of Theodore Kheel, the labor lawyer and power broker who had acted as mediator in many of New York's most notable strikes, including that of the newspapers in 1962/3.

Kheel and Murdoch had been on different sides in the *New York* magazine takeover struggle, but a few months later Murdoch accepted Kheel's help in solving a dispute with the Guild stemming from his takeover of the circulation list of the *Long Island Press,* a suburban evening newspaper that had sold 150,000 copies daily before its closure. During the dispute Murdoch had been impressed by the work of Martin Fischbein, a young assistant to Kheel, and he hired him for his own organization in April 1978.

Fischbein was the only one of Murdoch's advisers to oppose his accepting the presidency of the Publishers' Association. He thought the risks outweighed the advantages. If Murdoch was going to hold out for a tougher settlement than the other two, he would be in a stronger position if he could make them worry all the time about his breaking away from them. Fischbein telephoned Kheel, his former boss, to ask him to persuade Murdoch to refuse. The three— Murdoch, Kheel and Fischbein—agreed to meet for breakfast next morning at the Regency Hotel on Park Avenue, only a few blocks east of Murdoch's flat and the place where many powerful city people meet to start the day: the Elaine's of the breakfast hour.

Not long after the meal began it became apparent to Kheel that Murdoch had all but made up his mind to accept. He harbored a suspicion about the other two publishers similar to theirs of him, that they would leave him in the lurch and make a more expensive deal with the union than he could afford. That would be harder if he were their nominal leader. He had more personal reasons, too, connected with his *amour propre.* "It will give me international projection," he enthused to Kheel. And later he was to tell Raskin: "Aside from the temptation of flattery, I knew I'd be the lightning rod. There was a chance to be seen arguing a case other than Son of Sam or some dumb headline in the *Post.*" He formally accepted the role at a lunch at Christ Cella on August 18th.

It was not long before Fischbein's warning proved justified. After a study into the cost of moving to room manning, in terms of job guarantees that would have to be given to presently employed pressmen, the *Times* and the *News* decided to drop it from their negotiating position and move instead to substantive cuts in personnel under the existing unit-manning system.

Murdoch saw this as a weakening and was reluctant to acquiesce. Only his newly strengthened commitment to collective bargaining persuaded him to accept the change. The proposal was that the existing twelve qualified pressmen on each machine should go down to eight and there should be cuts in subsidiary operations in the pressroom, resulting in a staff reduction of some 50 percent. William Kennedy, president of the pressmen's union, responded with a plan to reduce the number at each press by only one. Negotiations trickled to a halt and the prospect of an early settlement receded. Kenneth Moffett, the mediator appointed by the Federal Arbitration Service, found himself powerless and returned to Washington.

By now three strike papers had appeared in New York to accommodate the demand from advertisers and to provide rudimentary news coverage for New Yorkers. They were professional jobs in the sense that they were staffed by journalists from the three regular papers but they were poorly produced and, because printed outside the city, had impossibly early deadlines. Each had a loose link with one of the strike-bound papers in that it was delivered to the homes of its regular subscribers through the co-operation of distributors.

The *New York Post* had teamed up with the *Daily Metro,* the best of the three strike sheets, published by Frederick Iseman, a young newspaperman and entrepreneur. Iseman used to work for the *New York Times* and had initially approached that paper for support, going to Murdoch only when he found the *Times* had made other arrangements.

Murdoch agreed to lend Iseman $100,000—two-thirds of his start-up capital. Iseman quickly discovered that was nowhere near enough: the paper was costing $70,000 a day to print and advertising revenue takes several weeks to materialize. So he went to Murdoch for more money. They agreed on a loan of nearly a million dollars and in return Murdoch took a lien on the paper, meaning that he would have first call on any outstanding revenues should it become bankrupt.

When, ten days later, Murdoch's involvement was made public, there was a staff walkout. Most of the paper's journalists came from the *New York Times* and, such was Murdoch's reputation, they did not want to be associated with a paper over which he had any authority. Murdoch then suggested to Iseman that he should get executives from the *Post* to produce the paper for him instead. Iseman said he would prefer to close the paper.

Murdoch seemed deeply offended by that attitude, but did agree to write an open letter stressing that although he had loaned money to the paper he exercized no control over it. This persuaded the protesting journalists to return to work.

Post subscribers, who were receiving the *Metro* automatically, were beginning to cancel it. Being written by *Times* journalists, it was a more serious read than they were accustomed to. This alarmed Murdoch who, through his senior *Post* executives, started urging Iseman to get a new editor. Iseman thought it highly presumptuous—though not uncharacteristic—of Murdoch to seek to fire the editor of a paper he did not even own, and refused for the second time to do his bidding. The editor stayed throughout the paper's brief life. Iseman has met Murdoch only once since, a chance encounter one weekend at the carousel in New York's Central Park, where Murdoch was taking his daughter Elisabeth for a ride. Through a friend, though, he later learned Murdoch's view of him. The two met at a London party and the friend mentioned Iseman's name. "Oh yes," Murdoch responded. "Fred has a lot to learn."

Back at the main strike negotiations, now deadlocked, Murdoch, Barletta and Mattson discussed how they could get them moving again. To bring in Kheel was one obvious way, but none of the three was keen on doing it, feeling that past settlements in which he had been involved tended to favor the unions at management's expense. Kheel was pawing the ground on the sidelines, scarcely able to believe that this major city dispute was being conducted without him.

On September 2nd, Labor Day weekend, Kheel wrote an article in the *Daily Press,* one of the strike papers, suggesting that the strike's fate might hinge ultimately on the attitude of the other printing unions not involved in it, and how long they would refuse to cross the pressmen's picket lines.

The print unions are linked in a co-ordinating body, the Allied Printing Trades Council. After the article appeared, the council president, George McDonald, invited Kheel to enter the talks as his adviser. If, as Kheel hoped, he was to act as a mediator—one with better contacts and greater depth of experience than Moffett—he had to get the approval of the still reluctant publishers. He was invited to Murdoch's apartment to meet him, Barletta and Mattson. Barletta, as he recalls it, was strongly opposed to letting Kheel play a role. "His way of settling is to give in to the unions," he told the other two, before Kheel arrived. But, again according to Barletta, Murdoch was keen to have Kheel, remembering his useful part in the earlier dispute at the *Post.* He saw the appointment as a way of getting things moving. As the owner of the most vulnerable of the papers, he needed a settlement more urgently.

Kheel passed his audition, and told the three men that he would need ten days to marshal the facts. He stressed that he would not be making any firm recommendations for a settlement, just clarifying the points at issue. Soon after his arrival on the scene the mistrust between the publishers, always dormant, almost came to a head.

Murdoch suspected that Kheel was having a secret meeting with Mattson. He had Fischbein check it by asking friends in Kheel's office. When he learned beyond doubt that it was true, Murdoch was furious. He had always feared that, despite Mattson's protestations, the real aim of the *Times* was to make a deal with the union that would be too expensive for the other papers to live with.

The secret meeting seemed to confirm it. Relations between the three publishers were never to recover fully.

Kheel's attempt was allowed to proceed, but it was not long before Murdoch regretted he had given any support to it. Kennedy was none too happy, either, knowing that Kheel had met the publishers and fearing a plot to persuade the other print unions to cross his picket lines. Mistrust abounded. Murdoch, without consulting the other two, made things tenser by appealing on television to the Allied unions to go back to work. Next day Kheel countered by making a public request to be allowed to investigate whether both sides were acting in good faith. The publishers, Murdoch especially, thought Kheel was taking too much on himself. Murdoch phoned Barletta and, repeating himself as he does when under stress, blurted: "Joe, you were right, you were right, you were right, you were right." Barletta said later: "He'd let the camel into the tent and he recognized it."

Murdoch issued a further statement, this time agreed with the other two, denouncing Kheel. But within a few days Barletta and Mattson had persuaded Murdoch—or they thought they had—that Kheel represented the best, almost the only hope for a reasonably fast solution. Their alliance was patched up and the negotiations resumed both in New York and in Washington, whence Moffett had summoned the parties in a fruitless attempt to promote some real give-and-take. In New York, Kheel finished defining the issues, but that did not seem to get anyone very far.

By now Murdoch was at the end of his patience. The strike had lasted six weeks and there was no prospect of an early deal. How could he be sure that, when he had sweated through the remaining weeks, he would not after all have been conned by Mattson, that the settlement would not be too expensive for him to bear? He was growing convinced that this was just what would happen and he found himself thinking more and more of Dorothy Schiff and the 1962/3 strike when she had broken ranks with the other publishers. They had found it despicable. Well, they would, but it had worked, hadn't it?

The *Post* had survived, while most of the other papers, those that had loyally stayed in harness, had gone out of business within a few years. For sure, the people at the *Times* and the *News* would be outraged if he left them and made a separate deal, but he was fairly certain they had a contempt for him already. And in the final reckoning, they would have more respect for a skipper who steered his ship to survival than one who let someone else take over the navigation and guide it on to the reefs.

On the morning of September 27th he called his advisers to his office and announced, according to Raskin's account: "We have to blow this up and get out of it." He phoned Barletta and arranged lunch at Windows on the World, the restaurant on the 103rd floor of the World Trade Center in Lower Manhattan, close to the federal mediation office where a round of negotiations was due to be held that afternoon. Each took his senior legal adviser. Murdoch complained about Kheel and the seeming endlessness of the dispute, although Barletta insists he gave no hint of what he was about to do.

"What's the alternative?" Barletta asked him, and within minutes he had his answer. The four men went down in the lift and walked the few blocks to the office of the mediator. As they neared the entrance Murdoch said to Howard Squadron, his lawyer: "Go on in and throw the bomb, throw the bomb." Squadron went in and told the other negotiators that in Murdoch's view Kheel's role was now too dominant: "He has become the *de facto* mediator and seems to be moving towards becoming the *de facto* arbitrator." The *Post,* he went on, could not accept that and was pulling out of the negotiations. The meeting ended in confusion.

While the other two publishers huddled to assess the damage his defection would cause them, Murdoch began that evening an attempt to make a separate deal with Kennedy and the pressmen. His withdrawal had been a gamble because he had no guarantee that they would agree to settle with him alone—indeed Kennedy had walked out of the meeting as Squadron was announcing the *Post*'s decision. What Murdoch was seeking, again drawing on the Schiff precedent, was a "me-too" agreement, under which the *Post* would resume publication quickly and eventually go along with whatever settlement was reached by the other two papers. There was, he knew, still a risk that the agreement would be more expensive than he could afford, but at least if it was he would have had a few weeks of a virtual monopoly of the New York press in the prosperous autumn advertising season.

The union leader had his doubts but in the end saw it as a useful weapon against the other two papers. It took five days to negotiate the "me-too" deal. In the small hours of the morning of Monday, October 2nd, Murdoch left Squadron's office with the agreement under his belt and said wryly: "I'll be even less popular in this town in certain quarters." It was not long before that prediction was fulfilled. "His actions are reprehensible and unconscionable," said John Thompson, a senior executive and spokesman for the *Daily News.*

On Thursday the first plump edition of the post-strike *Post* appeared, eighty-four of its 128 pages crammed with advertising. WELCOME BACK! its banner headline shouted, like a man shaking hands with himself.

"The *Post* is a piece of junk," said John Pomfret of the *New York Times* when he saw that first edition. "Just another strike paper," said Barletta.

Kheel was more personal. He called Murdoch "an immigrant heady with power." Kheel was to add later: "Rupert committed the arch-crime of collective bargaining: he walked through the publishers' own picket line . . . he may have me-tooed himself to death."

Murdoch was quick to cash in on his initiative. For the next month, before the other two settled, the *Post* printed more than a million copies a day—nearly double its former circulation. He started a Sunday edition, declaring that it would continue even after the strike at his rivals had ended—it did, but only for a few weeks. He announced plans to start a permanent daily called the *Sun* but this was scotched by the unions. They did not mind helping Murdoch make money so long as their own position did not decline, but he had declared his intention of making the *Sun* a low-budget paper with a bare minimum of staff: why should they let him thus jeopardize the future of the *News,* where so many of their members worked and where more generous staffing arrangements were in operation?

Murdoch and his people were strident in justifying what the other publishers saw as their treachery. "They made a complete fool out of me," he said, and Squadron elaborated: "They were definitely trying to do a number on Rupert. We were scared stiff. They were playing footsie with each other and we thought they might try to get on the streets before us. That would have killed us." But Murdoch was understandably chirpy. "Monopoly is a terrible thing—till you have it," he told Raskin. Kheel, meanwhile, was suspected of being the source of photocopies of a Robert Browning poem that were scattered over the room where the negotiations with the other papers were continuing:

"Just for a handful of silver he left us,
Just for a riband to stick in his coat."

Murdoch's opponents cite his abandonment of the publishers' alliance as conclusive proof of his treachery and unreliability. It is the most famous incident in his early American career, exceeding even the battle for *New York* magazine. His exact motives may be as unclear to him as to the others who took part. There are no grounds for thinking that the move was premeditated, that he joined with the *News* and *Times* simply to increase the impact of his break with them later, or that he urged them to stand firm so as to lengthen the time he could enjoy his monopoly. With Murdoch it is often best to take him at face value, to stick to the simpler explanation. He knew that, since the Felker incident, the city establishment held him in low regard, so he could justify to himself the suspicion that the other papers were bent on reaching an agreement that would damage him mortally, hoping to run him out of town. The *Times* had a history of making soft deals with the unions. There was a risk that at any moment the city's wealthiest paper might revert to type. In retrospect, it seems clear that this was not Sulzberger's intention, but with a tender, newly-acquired property to nurture, Murdoch did not want to take the chance. His experience in Australia had taught him that there are seldom good reasons for trusting anyone.

On November 6th, a month after the *Post* resumed, the *Times* and the *News* were back on the streets. The eighty-eight day strike had not produced the savings the publishers originally sought—only one fewer pressman was to be assigned to each machine, though there were more significant reductions in apprentices, maintenance men and supporting personnel. Murdoch insisted that what he feared had come to pass, that the other two had been insufficiently vigorous in their pursuit of savings; but he paid up all the same.

Meantime, as he had predicted, personal attacks on him increased. Richard Reeves, earlier among the most vociferous opponents of the *New York* takeover, wrote an article in *Esquire* (then edited by Felker) that quoted A. M. Rosenthal, the executive editor of the *New York Times,* as calling Murdoch "a bad element, practicing mean, ugly, violent journalism," adding that he hoped he would disappear from the New York scene within two years. At the

News, advertising executives instituted a "Bury Murdoch" campaign. Their salesmen were given "pallbearer" awards if they
managed to take advertising away from the *Post.* Pete Hamill, who
had been at the Elaine's celebration party when Murdoch took over
the *Post,* wrote a column in the *News* likening him to the guest who
throws up at dinner.

A few months later another article appeared in *Esquire,* by
Chris Welles. It began with a quote from Barletta. "In Murdoch's
world there are no rules. His world is amoral. I'm not going to
lecture him that what he's doing is outside the bounds of agreeable
behavior. But now that he has shown how he works, we'll do it too.
We're willing to play the game with him by his rules if that's what he
wants."

Offended, Murdoch wrote to Barletta, ostensibly to return a
book. In the covering letter he said he had just read the "amazing
statement" in *Esquire.* It was, he continued, a malicious falsehood.
"Maybe God will forgive you but I will have more difficulty."
Barletta said later: "It's a measure of the man that I don't know
whether he was joking." He replied in a friendly vein but listed a
number of incidents during the strike that in his view could have
justified his remarks. Murdoch left the letter unanswered for some
months, then wrote suggesting: "Let's have a drink some time—but
don't bring Mattson."

Murdoch was not the only person to feel wounded by the debris
of rancor that continued to rain down after the strike was over. In its
issue of January 8th, 1979, his *New York* magazine had as its cover
story a profile of Kheel by Richard Karp. It detailed deals of what
Karp called a "questionable nature" in which Kheel had been
involved. *New York* printed a long reply from Kheel together with its
reply to the reply.

Kheel sued for defamation, in a thirty-page complaint, alleging
that Murdoch had approved the hostile article partly as revenge
against Kheel for having helped settle the strike against the *Times*
and *News,* ending the *Post*'s temporary monopoly. After two years
the action was dropped after an agreed settlement in which Kheel
conceded that Murdoch had taken no part in preparing the article,
while Murdoch accepted that it had been "inappropriate," although
Karp did not associate himself with the statement.

The *Post* quickly lost most of the readers it had borrowed from
the *Times* and the *News.* After the rival papers resumed, its

circulation settled at about 650,000—not far above its level when the strike began. And the advertising position continued unhealthy. Although Murdoch sold something like 20 percent of the newspapers bought every day in New York, he had less than a 7-percent share of the advertising market. He thought this was partly to do with prejudice against him by the large department stores, persuaded by representatives of the other two papers to take a lofty, disapproving view of his defection during the strike. The same had happened to Mrs. Schiff in 1962/3, but this was something new for Murdoch. Nowhere else had he heard of commercial decisions taken for essentially sentimental reasons.

The store executives did not admit to such motives. They said their reluctance to advertise in the *Post* was based on demographics. The paper did not reach the people they wanted to attract to their stores. "Our customers are sophisticated and urbane and don't want to hear about the violence and sex the *Post* touts," one advertising executive told the *Wall Street Journal* in 1980. And *Newsday,* a year later, quoted a discussion between Murdoch and a space buyer from Bloomingdales, the most chic of the New York stores, in which the buyer was supposed to have said: "But Rupert, Rupert, your readers are my shoplifters." That remark has been much repeated, but Murdoch denies it was ever made.

Murdoch was concerned at first about the criticism that most of the *Post*'s senior staff were from Britain or Australia. For a time he tried earnestly to do something about it. After the unhappy experience with Bolwell, he was not going to oust Roger Wood, whose cheerful lack of the finer sensibilities makes him an ideal Murdoch editor. He thought the number two post on the news side, managing editor, should go to an American if at all possible. He tried several, none of whom lasted more than a few months, until, at a lunch at *New York* magazine, he sat next to John Van Doorn, a former editor of the "Week in Review" section in the Sunday edition of the *New York Times.* Van Doorn, a respected figure among the city's journalists, had gone to *New York* early in 1978. In the conversation with Murdoch he said he would like to get back into newspapers. "Why not come down to the *Post*?" Murdoch asked. It was settled at a private lunch a week later. Van Doorn was to edit the *Post*'s own weekly review section, appearing on Saturdays. And he would, he was assured, have wide powers to shape the rest of the news coverage as he saw fit.

After only a few days, as Van Doorn now recalls it, he could see that neither Murdoch nor Wood really wanted any change in the paper's essential direction. They liked the *idea* of employing American executives so long as they did not bring with them notions that would cut across Dunleavy's brand of fact-stretching journalism. It was not that the Americans were too timid or conscience-stricken to do a properly ruthless job. Sometimes it was the other way round. They had no native instinct for just how far they could go. Fleet Street has perfected a way of handling scandal and sensation that seems crude but can be subtle, and few Americans, Murdoch found, had developed sufficiently sensitive antennae to judge just where the line should be drawn. If anyone complained to Murdoch of an excess of bad taste he would often respond: "That must be one of my American editors. They try too hard." And once, standing in the news room, he told Van Doorn: "Americans don't know how to do journalism."

Friends had warned Van Doorn before he joined that it would be like this but, won over by Murdoch's persuasive enthusiasm, he had preferred to believe he would be the exception. Wood, though, ignored his ideas, changed things he had done without consulting him and progressively whittled away the space given to the Weekly Review, which was obviously continued only under sufferance. The influence of Dunleavy, who ran the news-gathering operation at key times of the day, was paramount. Murdoch and Dunleavy together were like a benevolent uncle with his nephew. If the younger man behaved outrageously, as he often did, Murdoch would humor him. "Now Steve, now Steve," he would chide playfully if Dunleavy made an especially aggressive remark to a guest at one of the lunches Murdoch gave in his private dining-room for prominent civic personalities. Dunleavy is tough and macho and Murdoch likes that.

After a few months Murdoch was as unhappy with Van Doorn as the newcomer was with his own position. In February 1979 Murdoch had lunch with the Associated Press. Afterwards, he left their headquarters in Rockefeller Centre with Craig Ammerman, head of AP's New York bureau, and they strolled along Fifth Avenue together. He had known Ammerman since acquiring the *Post,* and had been impressed with him from the start. Ammerman was a youngster of twenty-eight when he first went to see Murdoch in November 1977, a few days after the *Post* deal was announced. He wanted to discuss whether, under the new management, the paper still wanted to subscribe to the AP service.

"The one question I hoped he wouldn't ask me was how much they were paying for the service," Ammerman remembers. "He asked it before I got in the door and I thought: 'Boy, this is headed for no good.'" When Ammerman said the fee was around $12,000 a week—the same as the other papers paid—Murdoch replied: "You must mean a month." The price did not go down but the two men became friends, meeting from time to time for lunch. They drew closer during the strike, when Murdoch would phone Ammerman, sometimes more than once a day, to check what was happening.

Walking down Fifth Avenue, on that February afternoon, Ammerman told Murdoch he had been offered a job as deputy editor on the Boston *Herald American* and asked him what he thought. Murdoch said he would consider it and within a few weeks Ammerman was on the staff of the *Post* as joint managing editor. His partner, Van Doorn, was not told why the appointment had been made, and viewed it with foreboding.

Ammerman, despite being American, was much more Murdoch's kind of person. One of the first projects he masterminded was a series raking over the coals of the Chappaquiddick scandal. It was based on the allegations of a woman who said she had been Senator Edward Kennedy's mistress. She maintained that the party at Chappaquiddick in 1969, resulting in the death of Mary Jo Kopechne, was not the first he had attended there. This was the kind of journalism Murdoch liked, especially because it was conveniently timed just before Kennedy's planned campaign for the Democratic presidential nomination.

Ammerman quickly eclipsed Van Doorn, but they both left at about the same time, in mid-1980, Van Doorn to edit *Next,* a new but short-lived magazine, Ammerman to run *The Bulletin,* an afternoon paper in Philadelphia. Van Doorn received no send-off except a farewell call from Don Kummerfeld, Murdoch's chief American executive. The call was interrupted: "Rupert's on the line. I'll call you back," Kummerfeld said, but he did not. That was the last link Van Doorn had with the Murdoch empire. The pair were replaced by a New Zealander and an Englishman.

SIX

Taking to the Air

I don't think that a newspaper should own outside interests.... By owning something outside journalism you lay
yourself open for attack. And newspapers should be above that.
—Rupert Murdoch, November 1977

While trying to secure his position in New York, Murdoch was not
neglecting his interests in Britain and Australia. Early in 1977 Sir
Max Aitken, son of Lord Beaverbrook, decided that the Express
group of papers—chiefly the *Daily Express, Evening Standard* and
Sunday Express—could not survive without an injection of capital
beyond his resources. The *Express* had been brought to prosperity
by his father and in the immediate post-war period it and the *Daily
Mirror* had been the most successful popular papers in Fleet Street.
But now it was being challenged by Lord Rothermere's revived
Daily Mail, and both were being affected by the vigorous struggle
between their down-market competitors, the *Mirror* and the *Sun.*
The *Standard,* while for years the more admired of London's two
evening papers among Fleet Street opinion-formers, still lagged in
circulation behind Rothermere's *Evening News.* Both were losing
money and it was doubtful if there was any longer a sufficiently
prosperous market in London for two evening papers. Only the
Sunday Express made money consistently, but it was not enough to
cancel out the losses of the other two. The trouble was that, unlike
most of his competitors, Lord Beaverbrook had never been much
inclined to diversify outside newspapers—for instance into televi-

sion or magazines. This left the group vulnerable and in 1977 Sir Max felt it was time to seek help.

Most of the familiar cast of potential purchasers—familiar from the *Observer* struggle a few months earlier—rushed into the arena. Sir James Goldsmith was an early contender, putting together a joint bid with Tiny Rowland's Lonrho group. Rothermere would certainly have liked to buy, but would have wanted to merge the *Standard* with the *News* right away, and probably the *Express* with the *Mail* before too long. Olga Deterding again expressed interest, as did Trafalgar House, the property company that also owned Cunard shipping and hotels, including the liner *Queen Elizabeth 2*.

Early in June the *Sunday Times* reported that Murdoch was now in the hunt. At a meeting with Sir Max the previous week he had offered ten million pounds as a capital injection in return for a say in running the papers. "I am a friend of Sir Max's and want to stay so," he said. "I have told him that if at any stage there is a question of closing down the titles, and I can help in any way to avoid it, I would be happy to do so." If Sir Max reflected that it was in these terms Murdoch had come to "rescue" Sir William Carr nine years earlier he did not say so. Indeed, for a time this seemed the deal he favored, and he was urged by Murdoch's friend Lord Goodman to consider it seriously, if only as a way of keeping out Goldsmith, who then seemed the front runner.

But Murdoch's bid was opposed by Jocelyn Stevens, Beaverbrook Newspapers' flamboyant chief executive. Discretion has never been a Murdoch forte and nobody was in much doubt that among the privileges he sought in return for his ten million pounds was the right to change the management team, and that Stevens did not form a part of the future he envisaged. The two had never been friendly. Stevens had master-minded an *Express* campaign against Murdoch in 1974, attacking the role of *The Sun* and the *News of the World* in unmasking Lord Lambton's sexual peccadilloes. It was in a sense a replay of the Profumo affair, though less grave. Lambton was a junior minister in the Ministry of Defense and also a friend of Stevens: he was a contributor to the *Evening Standard* when Stevens was the paper's managing director.

This was presumably why Murdoch approached Sir Max Aitken direct with his offer of help, without consulting Stevens. He may have over-estimated the real power that Sir Max, in declining health, was able to exert.

Murdoch offered to buy Sir Max's 20 percent of the Beaverbrook shares, going so far as to send him a check for £1,400,000 with the letter in which the offer was made. But Sir Max was never to cash the check, for Stevens's ability at in-fighting won the day and Trafalgar House bought the company for £13,690,000. Murdoch had sustained another defeat but not one that hurt his pride unduly. He had more important things to worry about in America and Australia. Yet he can scarcely have resisted a smirk when Stevens was dismissed by Lord Matthews, the new chairman of the Express group, in 1981.

Discussing Murdoch's bid later, Stevens said: "He's got the appetite of a snake. He'll swallow a sheep if it's passing."

There was one respect in which Murdoch did not measure up to his Sydney rivals, Fairfax and Packer, and that was television. While he controlled more newspapers than either, they both had strong TV stations in Australia's biggest markets, Sydney and Melbourne. All Murdoch owned was Channel 9 in Adelaide and the station in Wollongong, a suburb of Sydney, that he acquired in 1963 hoping— vainly as it turned out—to compete with the central Sydney stations. Apart from the (not insignificant) question of prestige, the ownership of two small stations gave him no muscle when it came to buying programs and, by extension, deciding what Australians should watch. The bulk of programs on Australian television are bought from America. Since Sydney and Melbourne are the wealthiest markets, companies with stations in both centers gener-ally buy all the Australian rights to suitable American material and resell them to stations in smaller cities. Murdoch's 1963 coup, when he bought all the best programs as part of his battle with Packer, had been strictly a one-time aberration.

With only three privately owned channels in both major cities, the chance for an outsider to break in was limited. In 1962 his bid for Channel 10 in Sydney was rejected. Since then, the closest Murdoch had come to getting his foot in the door was in 1972 when it looked as though Ansett, the internal airline that owned Channel 0 (later Channel 10) in Melbourne, might be taken over by Thomas Nationwide Transport (TNT). If that happened Murdoch was confident that TNT would sell off the TV interest to him; but in the event the deal did not take place.

Sydney's third channel, also Channel 10, was owned by United Telecasters Ltd., a public company headed by Sir Kenneth Humphreys in which no single group had a controlling interest. Early in 1979 two of the major shareholders indicated a desire to sell their holdings, totalling 22 percent. Sir Kenneth was worried that another existing large shareholder would buy the extra shares and put itself in a position where it could take control.

To thwart this, he acted rather as Sir William Carr had done. He phoned Murdoch and asked whether he would like to bid for some of the available shares. Murdoch, through his Wollongong station, already owned slightly less than 5 percent of United Telecasters. Humphreys' plan was to let him buy another 16 percent and sell the remaining 6 percent of the available stock to the existing largest shareholder, Amalgamated Wireless Australia (AWA). This would have left AWA with about 25 percent and Murdoch with 21 percent, allowing neither to take full control.

This cozy arrangement was not quite what Murdoch had in mind. He began a classic takeover move on the Sydney exchange, seeking as many shares as possible on the open market. When AWA put in a better bid, Murdoch raised his again and after making a private deal with the owner of one of the large blocks on offer, he was able to announce that he had 46.6 percent—effectively a controlling interest.

To satisfy broadcasting rules he had to sell his interest in Wollongong, for nobody is allowed to hold more than 5 percent in more than two television stations. He also had to have his ownership approved by the Australian Broadcasting Tribunal, where he was opposed by the Labour Party, still bitter over the performance of Murdoch's papers in the 1975 election, and by Fairfax, by now so obsessed with Murdoch that they dreaded any extension of his empire.

Before the tribunal, Murdoch gave a plausible performance of high dudgeon, affecting shock and horror that his motives or record should be impugned. It is a role that, after years of practice, he plays to perfection. He said Fairfax were "trying to paint me as a crazed tycoon who cannot be trusted with a TV company." He maintained

Murdoch's parents, Sir
Keith Murdoch and Dame
Elizabeth *(Melbourne
Herald* and *Keystone Press)*

Murdoch and Anna Torv on
their wedding day, Sydney,
1967 *(John Fairfax and Sons
Ltd)*

In 1960, Murdoch breaks into Sydney journalism when he buys
the *Daily Mirror (Keystone Press)*

On a visit to Washington in 1962, Murdoch and Zell Rabin (left),
editor of the Sydney *Daily Mirror*, meet President Kennedy
(Keystone Press)

Threatened with takeover by Robert Maxwell, the Carr family,
owners of the *News of the World*, show solidarity by having a
group photograph taken *(The Press Association)*

On January 2nd, 1969, Sir William Carr and Rupert Murdoch
congratulate each other on Maxwell's defeat. Sir William had less
to smile about a few months later *(The Press Association)*

Frost assuming the role of prosecutor on his show in 1969, when he interviewed Murdoch about the *News of the World*'s serialisation of Christine Keeler's memoirs (*London Weekend Television*)

After a row over the Keeler memoirs, Murdoch restores his image as a family man by posing with his wife Anna and fourteen-month-old daughter Elizabeth at their London home in October 1969 (*Keystone Press*)

November 1969: Rupert Murdoch with the first issue of the *Sun* under his ownership (*The Press Association*)

At a luncheon in September 1969, Murdoch is photographed with Denis Hamilton (left) and Lord Thompson of *Times* Newspapers and Sir Eric Clayson (right) of the *Birmingham Post and Mail*. Hamilton was to play a key role in Murdoch's acquisition of *The Times* eleven years later, after Thomson's death (*The Press Association*)

When Murdoch bought the *New York Post* and *New York* magazine in the space of a few weeks, the American press started taking him seriously. On January 17th, 1977, he appeared on the front cover of both *Time* and *Newsweek* (*Popperfoto*)

Below: Clay Felker, who felt betrayed by Murdoch's takeover of his magazines, *New York* and the *Village Voice* (*Associated Press*)

Below right: Larry Lamb, Murdoch's first editor of the *Sun*, wearing the insignia of his knighthood, awarded in 1980 (*Popperfoto*)

Above: Kenneth Thomson (*Central Press Photos*)

Above right: Gordon Brunton (*International Thomson Organisation*)

Murdoch with Harold Evans, editor of the *Sunday Times*, and William Rees-Mogg of *The Times*, at the announcement of his purchase of the two papers in February 1981 (*Associated Press*)

Above: Harold Evans puts on a brave face to interviewers outside *The Times* building during his fight to keep the editorship in March 1982 (*Express Newspapers*)

Above right: Charles Douglas-Home, who succeeded Evans as editor (*Popperfoto*)

Rupert Murdoch meeting Marshall Field V at a news conference, November 1st, 1983, after Murdoch's purchase of the *Chicago Sun Times* (*Popperfoto*)

the Fairfax papers had run "a gutter campaign" of misleading and insulting articles about him, alleging that the policy of his papers was motivated by personal political ambition. He had, he said, been fighting the Fairfax monopoly since he was twenty-three. And he defended himself against charges that because he spent so much time abroad he was not really an Australian.

"Because I love this country, because my wife and children do, I bring them here as often as I can," he said. "Who else has risked everything to start a national newspaper which goes across the length and breadth of this country? Who employs more than 15,000 people with opportunities to work throughout the world? I started the *Australian* fifteen years ago as a dream. Nearly thirteen million dollars has gone into making that dream a reality."

He was asked whether he would make any changes in management if he acquired the station and he was firm in his denial. Sir Kenneth Humphreys, he vouchsafed, had performed "a magnificent job in steering the company through difficult waters." Moreover, "it would seem from the results of the company, the ratings, the service it is giving the public that it would be madness to contemplate any changes at all.... I wish to give an assurance to the tribunal that no change is contemplated." He did not let it stop there. Channel 10, he insisted "will continue exactly as it is today." And he concluded: "There has been so much industry hearsay that I am about to march in and fire everybody, which I hope I have laid to rest today.... It will remain totally independent.... We will not be interfering."

Unambiguous words, yet two weeks after the tribunal decided in his favor, Channel 10's general manager, Ian Kennon, was dismissed and replaced by Brian Morris, a director of News Ltd. with a background in advertising and no experience in television. Two months later Sir Kenneth Humphreys resigned as chairman, no doubt reflecting, like many Murdoch victims before and since, that he had brought it all on himself.

Gossips speculated that as soon as he won control of a Sydney channel, Murdoch would go for a Melbourne station to complete his network, but at the tribunal he denied it. "I do not see why I should give up a very profitable station in Adelaide for a loser in Melbourne," he said.

Three months later he could see why very clearly. Sydney–Melbourne was the proper axis for a network, not Sydney–Adelaide. Together, Australia's two largest cities account for 60 percent of the country's advertising revenue. Of the three Melbourne stations, one was owned by the Packer organization and effectively impregnable. The second belonged to the Herald and Weekly Times, the group Sir Keith Murdoch had built up that now controlled more than half Australia's newspapers. It was in the hands of a large number of shareholders and possibly vulnerable to a takeover bid. But the most likely target was Channel 10, owned by Ansett—the one Murdoch had made a pass at seven years earlier.

The market in Ansett shares had been volatile through most of 1979, because of the enforced liquidation of a finance company the airline group had only recently acquired. The shares had fallen in value and that made them attractive to ambitious speculators. One of the rising stars of Australian finance was Robert Holmes à Court, who, at forty-two, ran the Bell Group, a diversified conglomerate based in Perth, Western Australia, with important interests in transport and some in television. Holmes à Court, born in South Africa, is a lean, canny, soft-spoken man with a distinctly different business style from Murdoch. While Murdoch is an opportunist, Holmes à Court takes the long view. He plans ahead and is prepared to wait years for his aims to be accomplished. That is an unfamiliar technique in Australia, where the outback tradition of the huckster and the fast deal remains a powerful influence. That is why Holmes à Court has been regarded as something of a dilettante in Australian business and why for a long time he was not taken too seriously— that, and because, as Murdoch had discovered when he moved to Sydney nineteen years earlier, it is not in the nature of competitors to make life easy for the *arriviste*.

Holmes à Court began buying Ansett shares on the market and by May he had acquired about 5 percent of the company, paying little more than one dollar a share on average. Thomas Nationwide Transport, run by Sir Peter Abeles, had a 15 percent holding left from their abortive 1972 bid, but there was an agreement between Sir Peter and Sir Reginald Ansett that Ansett would have first option on them. But he could not afford to take up his option. Holmes à Court sought to buy the TNT shares, bringing him up to 20 percent—a sound base for a long-term assault on the company. Abeles agreed to sell and Sir Reginald, who trusted Holmes à Court, would have given permission.

Murdoch was temporarily rich in cash after selling his bauxite holdings in Western Australia for more than fifty million dollars. (Throughout his career he had been excited by the potential of Australian minerals and had made useful profits from investments in that area.) He approached Holmes à Court and Abeles and indicated his intention of buying 5 percent of the Ansett shares. When control changed hands, he said, he would like to be allowed to run the TV station, or at least to enroll it in a network with his Sydney station.

At this point Ampol, the Australian oil company, made a swift market raid and mopped up 20 percent of Ansett shares. Abeles decided to defer his deal with Holmes à Court, who instead bought on the open market and brought his holding up to 15 percent. By the end of October he and Abeles had 15 percent each, Ampol 20 percent and Murdoch had gone beyond his intention and bought about 9 percent.

Sir Reginald Ansett, at seventy-one, had a reputation as a dictatorial and tough businessman. But with only 1 percent holding in the company himself he could see the danger of being crushed in the scramble for control. Seeking a survival route, he telephoned Holmes à Court. "Are you just playing with my shares or are you genuinely interested?" he demanded gruffly. When Holmes à Court said he was serious, and that he would run the company personally if he won, Sir Reginald agreed to back him. Now an old though still vigorous man, Sir Reginald viewed business largely in terms of personal relations. He disliked Sir Peter Abeles and was keen that, whatever happened to the company, Sir Peter should be kept away from it.

Holmes à Court then phoned Murdoch and suggested that, to break the log-jam, one of the four contending parties should take control, with the agreement of the others. The necessary share transfers would be made at a mutually negotiated price. Murdoch invited Holmes à Court and Sir Peter Abeles to Cavan for the last weekend in October.

It was mainly a social weekend, for it took the trio less than an hour, after the two guests arrived mid-morning on the Saturday, to conclude their business. Sitting in Murdoch's study, they agreed that it was in nobody's interest to let things drift. Holmes à Court strengthened his case by saying that if he took charge he would have the support of Sir Reginald Ansett. The other two quickly agreed to sell their shares to him and he in return undertook that if he was not able to go through with his bid he would sell back to them at the same price. Murdoch phoned Sir Reginald Ansett during the meeting to confirm that Holmes à Court was his favored candidate. When the old tycoon concurred, Murdoch arranged a meeting between the four men in Sir Reginald's Melbourne office the following Tuesday to complete the deal.

Their business done, the three men were able to enjoy the rest of the Cavan weekend. Over a late barbecue lunch, cooked by Murdoch, they listened to a commentary on the Cox Plate in Melbourne, in which Holmes à Court's horse Lawman came a creditable third. They inspected the ranch and the livestock. Next morning Murdoch was chef again at breakfast. His two guests left before lunch on Sunday.

At the Tuesday meeting with Sir Reginald they were joined by Ted Harris, of Ampol. Murdoch, although the smallest shareholder of the four contenders, took the initiative. He told Sir Reginald the others would sell to Holmes à Court and stressed that he, Murdoch, wanted the television station. Holmes à Court said he could probably have it but gave no firm commitment. Sir Reginald agreed, with some relief. For months he had felt beleaguered, like a dying man encircled by wolves, any of which could have turned and chewed him up. Now he had seen off three of the wolves and the one that remained seemed the least hungry and dangerous. At any event, it was not the hated Abeles or the disconcerting Murdoch. He could handle young Holmes à Court; Sir Reginald was sure of that.

With the pressure off, Sir Reginald reverted to delaying tactics. He saw no need, he said, to announce the result of the summit meeting there and then. They could draw up a considered statement and release it to the press in a few days. Murdoch, with some amusement, told him that newspapers did not work like that. They would want to know tonight. At that moment a woman from the outer office informed them that three reporters had arrived, from the *Australian,* the *Mirror* and the *Telegraph.* The announcement was made that night, and the following day Sir Reginald held a press conference, giving a glowing account of Holmes à Court's honesty and straight dealing. The engagement was confirmed, the father of the bride was delighted and there seemed no obstacle to the solemnization of the marriage.

But losing a daughter is never easy, even to so personable a suitor as Robert Holmes à Court. In the succeeding days Sir Reginald began to have his doubts. Now that the immediate threat was cleared, he wondered whether he might be able to save everything for himself. The press were saying that, at seventy-one, he had lost his touch, the old fox had been outsmarted at last, and by someone little more than half his age. This hurt. He questioned Holmes à Court why his giant company should be taken over by his comparatively puny outfit from Perth. Should it not be the other way round? And he asked himself why he couldn't do what he had always done, play one party off against the other, and so stay in charge?

In little ways, Sir Reginald's irritation became clear. There had been a well-publicized dispute not long before about his refusal to hire a qualified woman pilot. A newspaper reporter telephoned Holmes à Court's wife and sought her view on the matter. She said she and Robert had been travelling in the Soviet Union recently and had found the female pilots for Aeroflot perfectly competent. Sir Reginald was furious. He phoned Holmes à Court and said: "You tell your wife from me that those Russian women pilots have got balls."

Murdoch was getting impatient. By mid-November, thinking that Sir Reginald might succeed in delaying things indefinitely, he decided to embark on a quite different tack to attain his Melbourne television outlet.

Sir Keith Macpherson had been with the Melbourne Herald and Weekly Times group for forty-three years, since he was sixteen. He had joined as an office boy: one of his first jobs had been to clean Sir Keith Murdoch's fountain pens. He had worked his way up to be chairman and chief executive of the group; a plump, mild, comfortable man.

Normally he arrived in his office on Flinders Street—the same panelled and polished office Sir Keith Murdoch had worked in—at nine sharp. But on Tuesday, November 20th, 1979, Macpherson was about half an hour late, because he had returned only the night before from a trip out of town. On arrival he was told Rupert

Murdoch had just phoned to say he was in Melbourne and would stop by at about twenty to ten, hoping to catch him in. He would be bringing with him his chief lieutenant, Ken May, chairman of News Ltd., and nobody had to tell him the way, for he used to visit his father and worked briefly there as a cadet reporter during the holidays.

Macpherson guessed it would be something more than a social call. The pleasantries were short: the two men inquired after each other's health and Macpherson asked Murdoch to what Melbourne owed the pleasure of this, one of his infrequent visits. Murdoch told him. He was going to make a bid for the Herald and Weekly Times group. There was no rancorous argument. Macpherson told Murdoch he had no hope of winning control and Murdoch politely disagreed.

"We'd want you to stay on," Murdoch said.

"Oh yes," May concurred. "We'd want you to do that" —the only words he spoke during the brief encounter.

"What?" rejoined Macpherson. "Like all those other gentlemen who have been sacked so frequently from everything you've taken over?"

"Oh, they were no good," Murdoch declared. "You would have sacked them, too."

"Well, I don't know about that," Macpherson replied. "If I'd already given an undertaking not to, I doubt that I would have."

From the *Herald* office, Murdoch and May went to the Melbourne stock exchange and formally delivered a letter setting out the terms of their bid. It amounted to $126 million for just over half the HWT shares, valuing the company at $250 million. Murdoch's News group was itself valued at only $150 million. As with Holmes à Court and Ansett, the smaller beast was seeking to gobble up the larger. Or, as Jocelyn Stevens would have put it, the snake was swallowing the sheep.

It was not just for that reason that Murdoch's bid for HWT was the epitome of cheek. He could not possibly have expected that it would go unchallenged, for if it succeeded he would control something like three-quarters of the Australian media and wield unprecedented influence. He enjoyed particularly the historical neatness of the attempt. For this was the group that his father had built up—the father who had never been confident that his son had inherited his flair for journalism and business. And Rupert had always felt in some way cheated by the HWT directors. He believed it was they—particularly Sir Keith's successor Sir John Williams— who had so maneuvered things after his father's death that the *Courier-Mail* in Brisbane had fallen out of family ownership. If he were to succeed now in buying the company, the injury would be avenged.

As soon as his two visitors had left, Macpherson telephoned Robert Falkingham, the chief executive of Fairfax in Sydney. A horrified Falkingham summoned a hurried meeting with his colleagues on the board, who agreed that urgent action had to be taken. Again, the irony was exquisite. Nineteen years earlier it was Fairfax who had launched Murdoch into the big time by favoring him as the buyer of the *Daily Mirror,* in order that the HWT group should not get a foothold in Sydney. What Murdoch was now proposing was not just a foothold, but a giant step under which Fairfax could, they feared, be crushed.

One of the most alarming prospects for Falkingham and his colleagues was that if Murdoch bought HWT he would become a partner of Fairfax in Australian Newsprint Mills and the news agency Australian Associated Press, both controlled jointly by Fairfax and HWT. How could they trust him as a partner? After a telephone talk with Sir Warwick Fairfax, visiting London, Falkingham decided that Fairfax would have to go into the market and buy HWT shares to thwart Murdoch. The shares stood at $2.74 when Murdoch put in his offer of $4. Before long they had gone substantially above the offer price.

News of the bid was reported in Murdoch's *Australian* on a scale usually reserved for war or disaster. The front page carried a photograph of the proprietor across three columns and some eight inches deep, accompanied by an idolatrous interview by the paper's star columnist, Buzz Kennedy.

"Rupert Murdoch is a forty-eight-year-old groupie—a newspaper groupie," Kennedy twittered. "He has had a lifelong love affair with newspapers." Then he broke off to make some sort of apology for the nature of the piece:

"Sympathetic readers who have made a study of the art of walking on eggshells will appreciate that conducting last night's interview had its problems, not all of them to do with having the subject of the interview continually breaking off to make and answer phone calls, issue instructions and display an eager elation and energy which belied an enormously strenuous day—and days—before."

There was a desultory attempt to give a thumbnail sketch of Murdoch, his style of administration— "What I do is delegate, then interfere" —and his personal foibles: "I inherited a Presbyterian conscience. My family calls it stinginess." And Murdoch declared, for the benefit of people who shared the Broadcasting Tribunal's doubts about his being an authentic Australian: "Even before the idea of the Herald offer came, my wife and I decided we would make our base in Australia. The children will go to school here— although they haven't been told that yet. We will be back here, whatever comes of the Herald affair." Like many of Murdoch's publicly stated intentions, that was not to be.

The takeover bid for the Herald group lasted just two hectic days. Faced with the determination of Fairfax to deny him control, and a threatened intervention by the Trade Practices Commission, there was little Murdoch could do. Fairfax spent $52,300,000 to buy a 15 percent stake in the group. While they achieved their object of thwarting Murdoch, it was an expensive maneuver, for as soon as Murdoch withdrew, the value of their holding fell by some twenty million dollars—and they were still saddled with the interest on the borrowed capital. It is a measure of their paranoia about Murdoch that they felt it was money well spent. Murdoch, although he failed to gain control, came away with a handy profit of some three million dollars on his shares and was so pleased with his cleverness that he allowed the *Australian,* next day, to describe in detail how he had managed to retreat in such good order, even if the ethics of the operation were questionable.

Murdoch knew that once the word spread that he was pulling out, the share price would drop from its level then of $5.52. To mislead the market—and Fairfax in particular—he worked through two brokers. To sell his shares he used May and Mellor, a broker not previously associated with him, while his regular broker, J. B. Were, pretended to be still in the market as a buyer. Thus when the new broker put the shares on sale at $5.52 and Fairfax's broker tried to push the price down, the second Murdoch broker would express an interest at just below that price, forcing a still desperate Fairfax to pay the full sum. In the first hour of trading on November 22nd,

Murdoch unloaded the 3,500,000 shares he had acquired during the previous two days. Then he announced his withdrawal from the contest and the share price fell to $3.45. Not a man to let such a coup go by without pressing home a propaganda advantage, Murdoch called the Fairfax rescue of the Herald "two incompetent managements throwing themselves into each other's arms at the expense of their shareholders."

A week later Murdoch was back on the Ansett trail as the deal between Sir Reginald and Holmes à Court collapsed. Part of the agreement had been that, when the Bell Group bought Ansett, Bell's transport operations in Perth should in turn be sold to the airline. After stalling for a month, Sir Reginald and the Ansett board decided not to go through with that part of it and announced that decision, without first telling Holmes à Court. Hearing the news on television in his hotel room, Holmes à Court rushed angrily to Sir Reginald's office and told him the whole deal was off. Sir Reginald did not believe him. "The deal's still on," he said. "Cool down. Things will look better in the morning." Holmes à Court replied: "By morning I'll have sold my shares and I'll be back in Perth."

He returned to his hotel and phoned Murdoch, tracing him to a tennis court where he was playing with former Wimbledon champion John Newcombe. He offered him his Ansett shares on the same terms Murdoch had given him—$2.50, half down, the balance in twelve months. "How long have I got?" Murdoch asked. "'The duration of this call," was the reply. At the end of the call, Holmes à Court told the press that the deal was made. It was announced on the evening television news. A flabbergasted Sir Reginald made repeated telephone calls to Holmes à Court trying to get him to change his decision, but it was too late.

With Holmes à Court's shares, Murdoch had 20 percent. Then he arranged to buy the Ampol shares, which gave him 40 percent, and he kept on buying in the market. Abeles had 15 percent, so between them they had control. Holmes à Court came away with a profit of eleven million dollars on the shares and was given a standing ovation by shareholders at his annual general meeting. He said later: "After I withdrew I had a long philosophical discussion with Rupert about winning."

Murdoch had not quite won yet, for Sir Reginald Ansett mounted a rearguard action. He told Murdoch he would not agree to the registration of his new shares. "Good luck to you," Murdoch replied, and predicted a long battle in the courts. Then Sir Reginald appealed to the Broadcasting Tribunal to veto the deal because it would mean Murdoch had violated the law by owning more than 5 percent of four TV stations—double the maximum allowable. But Murdoch had already assured the tribunal that he would sell Ansett's station in Brisbane and his own in Adelaide once he gained control, and his assurance was accepted. When Sir Reginald discovered he would get no government help in warding off Murdoch—who had, after all, made it his business to cultivate Malcolm Fraser—he capitulated. Murdoch then agreed that Thomas Nationwide Transport should increase its stake in the company and Sir Peter Abeles become joint chief executive of Ansett with Murdoch—the one outcome Sir Reginald had striven so hard to avoid.

Sir Reginald stayed on for a while as chairman but, like Sir William Carr ten years earlier, he found that this position gave him no share of power. His impotence was symbolized right away, when Murdoch decided that Sir Reginald's personal helicopter, in which he was accustomed to commute to Melbourne the thirty miles from his home in Mount Eliza, could be better used by the television station for fast-breaking news and traffic reports. In theory Sir Reginald was still entitled to use it, but in practice it was always engaged on other business. He commented: "Of recent times I don't take any notice of what anybody says. I have never had that experience with people like I am dealing with at the present time. I have always been able to make my verbal arrangements. My word's been my bond and I have expected it to be with people I am dealing with. That sort of attitude and principle in business today has gone right out the door."

Early in 1980 Sir Reginald left with a payoff of five million dollars and bought a company farm to retire to. The following year he died.

Before he could cement his control of Channel 10 in Melbourne, Murdoch had to endure another long series of hearings and once again was forced to listen to complaints by the Australian Journalists' Association, the Labour Party and others who felt that the overt political partisanship of his newspapers disqualified him from owning a TV station. The journalists' strike of 1975 was brought up again, as was the question whether or not he was a true

Australian. And this time there were new charges that, since his acquisition of Ansett, Murdoch's papers had given the airline unduly favorable publicity at the expense of the government-owned competitor, Trans-Australia Airlines (TAA).

The Broadcasting Tribunal at first rejected him as the proprietor of Channel 10 on grounds of public interest. Then the government obligingly amended the Broadcasting Act to circumscribe the power of the tribunal. They decreed that the only criteria as to a person's suitability to own a TV station should be financial and technical competence and moral fitness. It was hard to believe that this was not done as a specific favor to Murdoch in return for his past support. The new legislation made it inevitable that, on appeal, the tribunal's decision was reversed. Murdoch had his national television network at last—and an airline to go with it.

One unforeseen result of the Ansett purchase was to embroil Murdoch in the suspicion of a scandal involving President Jimmy Carter. In the end, a Senate inquiry and several newspaper investigations could find no evidence that either had behaved improperly; but the story sheds an intriguing light on Murdoch's astute business methods. He exposed the limitations as negotiators of the supposed financial wizards in one of the most important government agencies in Washington.

Ansett and TAA had for years operated a cozy pact that imposed clear limits on the extent of their competition. They used the same kind of aircraft and flew them on almost exactly the same schedule between the major Australian cities. This meant that they split the market fifty-fifty and both could make a reasonable profit. That kind of arrangement is anathema to someone of Murdoch's competitive spirit. He was determined to enter into battle with TAA. If he could win 60 percent of the traffic he would count it a success. The risk that he would end up with 40 percent was one he was prepared to take.

In November 1979, when Murdoch acquired Ansett, both airlines were in the process of renewing their fleet of jet passenger planes. On December 7th TAA ordered four wide-bodied Airbus A300B4s, made by a consortium of European countries, and took an option on another eight. If past practice was to be followed,

Ansett would be expected to put in a similar order, and Airbus had promised that they could expect delivery of the first aircraft almost simultaneously with TAA, on the same favorable financing terms.

Murdoch was disinclined to accept an Airbus order as a *fait accompli* and wondered whether there was an alternative. The most advanced American competitor to the European jet was the Boeing 767, so new it was not yet in service. Murdoch decided it was the one he wanted, provided he could get financing on at least as good terms as those Airbus offered.

The Export-Import Bank exists to foster American exports by offering low-interest credit to overseas buyers of American goods. In its modern headquarters, a short walk from the White House in Washington, are often to be found lobbyists for the larger industrial concerns, pleading the case for generous loans to their customers. One of the most frequent visitors was Jack Pierce, the treasurer of the Boeing Aircraft Company, based in Seattle. The country's largest manufacturer of airplanes, much of Boeing's business was done with foreign airlines. In January 1980 Pierce started to sound out officials at the bank about how much help they could give his company, in terms of a low-rate loan to Ansett, if the airline should decide it wanted Boeings.

The American consulate in Melbourne and the embassy in Canberra had raised the prospect of an Ansett/Boeing deal in cables to the State Department in December. They said Ansett favored the more economical Boeing 767 but might be forced to go along with TAA in buying the Airbus because of the earlier delivery dates and the generous financing terms. A team of officials from the Export-Import Bank went to Australia at the end of January. At a meeting with Ansett officials on February 15th they were told that the airline had all but decided to buy Boeings. The late delivery dates of the 767s compared with those of the Airbuses would be offset by buying additional narrow-bodied 727 and 737 planes and using increased frequencies as a marketing weapon against TAA's newer and bigger jets. The bank team expected a formal loan application to be made while they were in Australia, but by the time they left on February 22nd Ansett had still not decided finally what combination of planes they wanted to order.

The president of the Export-Import Bank was John Moore, an affable, distinguished southern lawyer, one of the many old Georgia associates Carter appointed to federal positions when he became President. (The senior among them was Bert Lance, the banker, who had had to resign as head of the Office of Management and Budget because of questions about loans his banks had made to members of his family.) During the transition period before Carter took office, Moore was given the job of screening potential government appointees for any conflict of interest. He had earlier served on the Georgia mental health commission with Carter's wife Rosalynn.

The senior partner in Moore's Atlanta law firm was Phillip Alston, an even closer associate of Carter. Alston, born in 1911, was eighteen years older than Moore. "I sort of feel like I helped raise Mr. Moore," he told the Senate Banking Committee during their hearings into the Ansett loan affair. He had a similar paternal relationship with Carter who, on becoming President, asked Alston to be his ambassador in Australia.

One of the most important duties of American ambassadors is to foster trade between their own country and the one to which they are accredited. That is why the embassy in Canberra had alerted the State Department in December about the possibility of a Boeing purchase by Ansett. Yet despite his friendship with Moore, Alston, according to his evidence before the committee, did not personally get involved in the transaction until late in February. At two earlier meetings (one of them quite fortuitous) with principals in the case, the subject, he said, did not come up.

On January 27th Ambassador Alston flew to America to help prepare for a forthcoming visit to Washington by Malcolm Fraser, the Australian Prime Minister. By chance, as he was leaving the VIP room at Sydney airport, he noticed Murdoch, whom he had met once or twice socially in Canberra. They waved to each other. Murdoch went to sit in the upstairs portion of the plane's first-class section. About half an hour after take-off Alston climbed the stairs to say hello and they exchanged pleasantries for less than a minute, according to the ambassador's estimate. Murdoch was on his way to Seattle to see Boeing and got off at Los Angeles. From there he would go to see Moore in Washington, but the subject of the proposed loan did not come up in this airborne talk, Alston said. And neither, he affirmed, was it discussed when he met Moore and his wife, and another of their former Georgia law partners and his wife, for dinner at the Metropolitan Club in Washington on February 4th.

Alston, then, went back to Australia apparently without having discussed the Ansett aircraft purchase with anyone. Murdoch, when he had completed his visit to Seattle, flew east, where he had two important engagements.

Since the autumn of 1979 the people running Carter's re-election campaign in New York had been anxious to arrange a meeting between Murdoch and the President. If Carter was to beat Senator Edward Kennedy in the Democratic primary in New York, it was important, they thought, that he should get the endorsement of the *New York Post*. Joel McCleary, a former White House aide, was head of Carter's New York campaign. He worked to arrange a meeting through Howard Rubenstein, who did public relations work for Murdoch. Dates had been arranged in November and December but Murdoch had cried off from both because he had to be out of the country. At the end of January a third date was agreed: February 19th.

In Seattle the people at Boeing had told Murdoch it would help him get a favorable loan from the bank if he went and put his case personally to Moore and his fellow officials. Murdoch told Pierce, the treasurer, about his date with Carter and suggested that, to get maximum value from his visit to Washington, the Eximbank meeting should be fixed for the 19th also. Pierce telephoned Moore on the 12th and made the appointment for 11:15 a.m. He pointed out that Murdoch, because of his arrangement to see the President, would not be able to join them for lunch afterwards.

Moore had an appointment outside the office on the morning of the 19th and returned a bit late to find the Ansett and Boeing party being received in the lobby by Charles Houston, vice-president of the bank's Asian division. Moore had left the memo with Murdoch's name on it on his desk in the office. He has a poor memory for names and at first could not remember who Murdoch was, but he plunged in to join the party, forced to mumble when the time came to address his guests directly. During the meeting, everyone's identity was clarified.

Murdoch felt himself in a reasonably strong position to drive a hard bargain. He had in his pocket a firm offer of financing for four Airbus planes that he was sure would be extended to the full twelve envisaged. The loan was to be in a "basket" of currencies—40 percent French francs at an interest rate of 8.75 percent, 40 percent German marks at 6.5 percent, and 20 percent U.S. dollars at 9.25 percent. This worked out at a blended rate of a shade under 8 percent. Though the Eximbank loan would all be in U.S. dollars, Murdoch insisted that the interest rate should not exceed that 8 percent.

Commercial interest rates were then running at around 17 percent but the bank customarily offers much better terms to overseas customers buying American products. However, the bank's recent rate for aircraft sales had seldom gone below 8.5 percent. And when talking in terms of $657 million, the amount of the original loan request, the extra half percent means a difference of more than three million dollars a year in repayments.

There was also the question of the differential rates between currencies. Although it was impossible to predict precisely how exchange rates would move during the term of the loan, the conventional wisdom among financiers was that in the long term the mark and franc would increase in value against the dollar. That was why interest rates on the dollar loans were higher than those for the other two currencies. On this assumption, the interest rate on a dollar loan by Eximbank to Ansett could have been higher than 7.95 percent but still competitive with the Airbus package.

When Moore made this point at the meeting, Murdoch contested the reasoning. He used the peculiar argument that he was not worried about taking on obligations in francs and marks because he was confident of the strength of the *Australian* dollar against other currencies, due to the country's healthy gas reserves, mineral resources and other bull points. Yet the strength of the Australian currency was not in question—the argument hinged on the future performance of the *American* dollar vis-à-vis the franc and the mark. But Murdoch insisted on his point and repeated it strongly in a follow-up letter to Moore the next day, stressing also that to match the Airbus offer the repayment of the loan would have to be over twelve years, although documents showed the Airbus term for repayment was ten years.

Murdoch and Pierce were negotiating with every trick they knew. They were adamant that a decision on the loan had to be made by February 29th, just nine days after the meeting, because that was when Murdoch's option on the first four Airbus A300 aircraft would run out; if he did not confirm the order by then but decided later to go ahead with the Airbus purchase, he would get his planes later than TAA.

At 12:30 Murdoch left the bank for his lunch appointment with President Carter. The lunch, timed as it was in the middle of the loan negotiations, gave rise to the subsequent suspicions and the Banking Committee's investigation. When press reporters got wind of the meeting, they could scarely be blamed for suspecting that Murdoch was asking Carter to intervene with the bank to ensure that he got the best possible terms for the loan—and that in return Murdoch was offering the *New York Post*'s support for Carter in the Democratic primary. Exhaustive official and unofficial inquiries eventually turned up no evidence of such a link. Three days after the lunch the *Post* announced its support for Carter but the decision had been made some weeks earlier, at a meeting attended by Murdoch, Wood, Rothwell, Ammerman and other senior executives at the paper.

Towards the end of 1979 most of the candidates for both parties' nominations had been to see Murdoch, going to his New York apartment rather than his office, to ensure secrecy. He told friends that he had been far from impressed with Jerry Brown, the governor of California, whose outspoken liberalism was calculated to infuriate him. He had enjoyed meeting Governor John Connally of Texas but thought he had little chance of nomination. As for Senator Edward Kennedy, Murdoch had been surprised to find their meeting enjoyable and rewarding. He had been especially struck by the fact that the senator had come by himself, whereas Brown was accompanied by aides and bodyguards, giving the meeting a stiff formality.

This did not mean that Murdoch was going to support Kennedy, whose politics were also too liberal for his taste. In truth, he was not taken with any of the Democratic contenders, but found Carter less objectionable than the others. Murdoch told the president at lunch that he would not commit himself to endorsing the Democratic candidate, whoever it was, when the actual election came in November. Carter was displeased at the news. The loan, according to Murdoch's evidence before the committee, was not mentioned. And he told friends he had been surprised at the humble menu: hamburgers.

Drawing on his rich experience of negotiations of all kinds, Murdoch could see that he had reached the point at which he should apply the most extreme pressure on the Export-Import Bank. He penned his cordial but no-nonsense letter to Moore. And he telephoned Boeing in Seattle to restate what he called his minimum conditions. The loan would have to be for 7.9 percent over twelve years. "Our deal is dead unless it's 8 percent or less," wrote Clarence Wilde, the Boeing executive who took Murdoch's call, in an internal memorandum.

At the same time, Boeing's representative in Australia was working on Alston to see if the ambassador could put pressure on the bank. Alston telephoned Moore in Washington to stress his concern that the loan should be made, in the interests of trading relations between the two countries. Both men insist they did not relate the question of the loan to Murdoch's publishing interests, his visit to the White House, or their old friend Carter's re-election prospects.

If Murdoch's deadline was to be met, the bank would have to move fast. Their procedure for approving large loans like this was that, following a preliminary request, officials would draw up a report on the loan and its background and this would be given to the bank's directors for a decision at their weekly meeting on Tuesdays. They would normally receive papers relating to the cases on the Friday before the meeting, so that they would have the weekend to look them over. Only two of the bank's four directors (not counting Moore) were available for the meeting on Tuesday, February 26th. They were Thibault de St. Phalle, an expert in international finance, and Mrs. Margaret Kahliff, who had been an independent businesswoman. No papers relating to the Ansett negotiations were handed to them on the previous Friday, and neither of them knew of the visit Murdoch had made to the bank earlier that week.

It was the custom for the directors to meet early—shortly after eight a.m.—before their Tuesday meetings. Under the so-called "sunshine laws" applying to the conduct of public bodies like the Eximbank, they are not allowed to engage in substantive discussion of forthcoming cases at these preliminary get-togethers. That has to be done in a properly convened session where a record is taken. The early meetings are to discuss "housekeeping" matters relating to the conduct of the bank; if any of the directors tries to raise an issue of substance about a loan, he or she is normally slapped down by the others. At the early meeting on February 26th, Moore came close to putting himself out of bounds when he told the other two that the Ansett case they were going to discuss that morning was especially interesting; they should give it particular attention.

De St. Phalle and Mrs. Kahliff were puzzled; neither was aware of any Ansett case, because the documents had not been among those they took home on Friday. Both hurried back to their offices and found the relevant file on their desks. It had been placed there the previous afternoon. They had less than half an hour to digest the outline of the case before their main meeting began.

Everything had been rushed. Dave Peacock, a loan officer at the bank, apologized for any "rough spots" in his memorandum about the loan. "We had to put it together in about twenty-four hours," he said. And he expressed reservations about the plan. The bank was being "put to the wall on a competitive deal." Referring to the haste, he added: "I think the negotiating tactics of Ansett and Boeing should make us very wary of this deal."

Moore, following his conversation with his old friend Alston, was now thoroughly committed to the loan and rounded on Peacock for being unfair, bearing in mind that Ansett had been involved in a take-over battle the previous year that had delayed the conclusion of plans for new aircraft. "I really do think it's important not to hold any hard feelings against either Boeing or Ansett," he said.

Because of the short time for preparation, discussion at the meeting was highly confused. There were two main points of argument: the interest rate and the number of planes that should be covered by the low-interest loan. Although the terms offered by Airbus were initially only for four planes, it was assumed that they would be extended to cover the other eight that would eventually be needed. But against that, as de St. Phalle pointed out forcefully, Boeing and Ansett were asking for a loan of below 8 percent to cover twenty-five planes—twelve would be the 767s that competed directly with Airbus, the others the smaller 727s and 737s, needed to increase capacity during the period that TAA had wide-bodied planes and Ansett had not.

De St. Phalle did not see why they should get the smaller planes, which did not have serious European competition, at 8 percent, but Moore was at first adamant. "I'm convinced that whether we like it or not it's an all or nothing situation," he said. "We cover this whole thing, 85 percent cover at 8 percent, or there's just no decision."

But de St. Phalle persevered. He suggested financing a lower portion of the purchase price of the smaller planes—around 40 percent—and increasing the rate on them to something like 8.5 percent, closer to the bank's recent average for aircraft. Of course, he pointed out, Murdoch would say it was all or nothing, because that was the way he negotiated. Thinking back to that quarrelsome dinner party where they last met, de St. Phalle said: "Murdoch is one of the brightest ment that I have ever come across.... Murdoch is a really shrewd negotiator and I don't blame him for doing that, but I think that we ought to exercise control."

Mrs. Kahliff concurred with the judgment on Murdoch. "I think that he is very, very aggressive," she commented.

Several aspects of the deal troubled de St. Phalle. He was puzzled by the last-minute nature of the documentation. Murdoch had visited the bank, he now learned, the previous Tuesday, so there was no reason why the staff should not have been able to make most of the background documents available by the Friday. Nobody seemed certain about the details of the rival offer from Airbus—how many planes it covered, how long the repayment term was, and so forth. Finally there was Moore's unusual decision to go personally to see officials at the Treasury and Federal Reserve Bank, who have to approve the bank's loans. It was presumably a bid to pre-empt likely objections on the grounds of extravagance. In most cases Moore would contact these two officials by telephone or written memorandum.

By the time the board met again two days later, some of the questions had been resolved. The Airbus offer was for only four wide-bodied aircraft and there was no written commitment from them to finance any more on the same terms, although there could have been a verbal understanding. The term of the loan was ten years. All this confirmed de St. Phalle's mistrust of Murdoch as a negotiator, and others at that second board meeting agreed with him. John Lange of the Treasury observed that "the decision maker in this case is playing Mexican standoff with us," a phrase meaning roughly that he was playing hard to get. And George Heidrich, deputy vice-president for Asia at the bank, said: "It seems to me that the fellow that talks about an 8 percent dollar rate is either financially naive or thinks we are," to which Moore replied: "The latter."

In the end, though, the result of all this impressive wizardry in negotiation was much less satisfactory for Murdoch than the deal he originally sought—a point overlooked in most of the critical and suggestive articles written afterwards. He won his 8 percent rate all right, but only on five aircraft instead of the twenty-five in the package. These were five 767s, broadly equivalent in seating capacity to the four Airbus A300s for which he had the rival financing commitment. The loan for the five was just over $200 million, less than a third of the original request. It represented 85 percent of the cost of the aircraft. Loans for the 727s and 737s, amounting to some eighty-nine million dollars, were at around 8.4 percent, covering 50 percent and 40 percent of the purchase price only. The offer was finalized just before the February 27th deadline—which Airbus promptly extended, as most had assumed they would.

Moore had one more try at improving the deal. He drafted a letter to Murdoch saying that future purchases of 767s up to twelve would be financed at the same favorable rate. De St. Phalle saw it before it went out and had it altered to read that terms for later loans would be discussed in the light of circumstances prevailing at the time. Murdoch, despite his uncompromising earlier posture, accepted the bank's terms.

Looking back at the affair later, de St. Phalle remains puzzled. "I just don't understand the transaction," he says. "I don't know how to explain this. I don't know why the board wasn't given the time to consider the transaction. I don't know why this rush was on that particular day. I don't know why there wasn't an extension of time. I don't know why the people who reported seemed to know so little about the transaction. I don't know why they hadn't made the usual checks with the French. I don't know why Mr. Moore thought it important to go personally and check with the Treasury Department or with the Federal Reserve." But he stresses that he knows nothing to suggest Moore had any political motive. "I consider Mr. Moore to be an extraordinarily bright individual and a very honorable person and I just can't conceive of his doing anything in a given deal because it had political implications."

It took a little less than three weeks for the press to begin to question the deal. It began with an article in the *New York Times* on March 18th—the day after Murdoch formally announced the Boeing purchase at a Melbourne press conference. The article stressed doubts among officials at the Bank and Treasury about the low interest rate give on the 767s, and the apparent lack of financial logic in equating the rate for a dollar loan with the rate for the basket of currencies. And it raised the possibility of a link with the *New York Post*'s endorsement of Carter. Other papers soon started to run follow-up stories.

The Senate Committee on Banking, Housing and Urban Affairs is charged with overseeing the Export-Import Bank. Its chairman is Senator William Proxmire of Wisconsin, who has made a reputation as a rigorous watchdog against waste in public spending. Three days after the first *New York Times* article appeared, he wrote to Moore raising questions about the loan. He pointed out that the *New York Post*'s endorsement of President Carter so soon after the bank gave its preliminary approval for the deal "gives an appearance of impropriety and leaves the impression that a key government agency may have been politicized to further the President's re-election."

He wrote also to the Treasury Department and the Federal Reserve Bank. The Treasury, in reply, sent a copy of an internal memorandum criticizing the loan as one which "fritters away bank resources" by offering over-generous terms. And the equation of interest on a dollar loan with that on a mixed-currency loan was described as "interest rate illusion at its most galling."

After considering these replies, the committee held hearings on the question on May 12th and 13th, in their hearing room on the fifth floor of the Dirksen Building next to the Capitol. It is a modern, fairly anonymous building, used mainly as offices for senators. The hearing room seats about eighty people. On the afternoon of the 13th, when Murdoch was due to give evidence, there were almost double that number of spectators, many of them reporters. They stood leaning against the walls. The press table was jammed full and television cameras were everywhere. Members of the committee sat round a horseshoe-shaped table and the witnesses faced them.

They had no power to make Murdoch attend but he agreed to do so. He was the last witness, accompanied by Donald Kummerfeld, his most important American executive, and Howard Squadron, his New York lawyer. Murdoch's evidence was fluent, given in a kind of aggrieved tone suggesting that he was always being maligned unfairly, but it was something he had learned to live with.

"No matter what your approach is to interest and cost computation, the Exim loan proposal cannot be regarded as more favorable than the Airbus loan offer. Even after the Exim commitment was received, it was a very close question for Ansett.... Nobody at Ansett, myself included, ever regarded the Exim loan proposal as containing unusually favorable terms.... The Exim loan application was not made until after the last luncheon appointment (February 19th) had already been scheduled. Neither at the luncheon nor at any other time—with the President or anybody else connected with the White House or the President's campaign—did I or anybody else representing Ansett discuss the purchase of Boeing aircraft or the Exim loan." And he ended his prepared statement with a pious homily: "I publish newspapers and have been subject to misleading publicity in the past so I am personally able to keep this situation in perspective. It would be most unfortunate if other potential foreign purchasers from American companies that compete with aggressive and successful foreign producers like Airbus were to receive a signal that American financing is unavailable or unnecessarily difficult to obtain."

Under questioning, Murdoch began truculently. When he was read a passage critical of him from an article by William Safire in the *New York Times* he responded: "He works for other people who have other barrels to roll." But he did admit to an error of judgment in going to meet Moore at the bank on the day he went for lunch at the White House. "I'm sorry I agreed to do that.... I'm sorry we had this meeting with Eximbank and it could have been misinterpreted in this way. We have always been extremely careful to keep our duties as publishers quite separate from any other business interest, although we behaved in the most responsible way as businessmen and all behavior involves a public duty."

Senator Donald Riegle of Michigan was bemused by all this self-righteousness. "Everyone comes in and says 'not me.' ...Maybe what we have here is a series of innocent parties who were involved in a situation that certainly has a disturbing appearance." Riegle did manage to catch Murdoch out on a claim that his attacks on Senator Edward Kennedy had been made before he bought Ansett. The Senator brandished a March edition with the headline DESPERATE TED STORMS NEW YORK and in January TED KENNEDY'S SECRET PARTIES.

"The *Post* really worked Senator Kennedy over," Riegle said. "This may be the norm in other places or in other countries. It's certainly not the norm here.... If somebody did want to get a good reception here in Washington from the administration, it just might occur to somebody that this might be one way to do it."

Murdoch said: "I see my papers. I don't write them."

Senator Riegle went on: "If you had been running the equivalent pieces on President Carter, you wouldn't have been invited to lunch. I think that's one way not to get invited to lunch."

Murdoch picked that up with characteristic bravado. "On the contrary, sir, we ran in another newspaper with five times the circulation of that, an extremely embarrassing article about President Carter's family on page one."

"Which paper would that have occurred in?"

"The *Star,* which has a circulation of 3.5 million. That was about President Carter...."

"I am not a regular reader. I have heard of it."

"Well, you're missing something."

"I may be glad I am missing it. I am not sure."

The session ended with pointed questions from Senator Proxmire. Murdoch replied that Ansett and the loan were not mentioned in the lunchtime discussion. It was about political issues including the Iran hostages and New York City's finances. "Nobody even knew that I had an investment in an airline, no knowledge at all.... I just told President Carter that we expected to be endorsing him in the primary, although we hadn't made up our mind about the general election, which he didn't seem very pleased with."

It was clear that Murdoch had made a good impression on the committee and Senator Proxmire was patronizing enough to say so:

"You are a remarkable man, Mr. Murdoch. We have had a lot of witnesses before this committee but I was especially impressed with what a quick study you are. You seem to know a whale of a lot about an industry which you've just gotten into. You are very refreshing, intelligent and an effective witness, and responsive."

"Thank you, sir."

"You are also able to win your way with the Export-Import Bank."

Nine days after the hearing, Proxmire wrote to Moore to inform him of the committee's conclusions. The letter criticized bank officials for being "sloppy" because of their "failure to question the factual assertions and bargaining tactics of Mr. Rupert Murdoch of Ansett Airlines and Mr. Jack Pierce of the Boeing Company." It said the loan offer was too generous, resulting in a waste of public money. It added that the bank seemed to devote too great a proportion of its resources to loans for aircraft purchases and concluded: "Bank lending at interest rates several percentage points below the U.S. Government's cost of borrowing constitutes an extraordinary subsidy and, if continued, could erode the financial soundness of the bank."

Proxmire's letter did not mention the allegations of collusion between Murdoch and President Carter, and the hearings had uncovered no solid evidence to substantiate the charges. In the wake of Watergate, questing reporters seek conspiracy everywhere and some who examined the affair remain convinced that the full story has not been uncovered. Yet the theory seems palpably improbable. It was never conceivable that the *New York Post,* vehemently critical of Senator Kennedy's advocacy of improved welfare services and his liberal philosophy, would support the senator in the primary, and Carter's staff were aware of this. So a promise to back Carter was scarcely credible as a bargaining chip. A pledge to support him in the election proper in November would have been of real value but in the event the *Post* plumped for Reagan. An alternative theory is that the political implications of lending federal money to an influential newspaper proprietor occurred independently to Carter's old Georgia chums, Alston and Moore, with no prompting from the White House. Yet they deny it and there is no evidence to suggest they are not telling the truth.

The incident is significant chiefly for the reason Proxmire suggested as he thanked Murdoch for his appearance as a witness, and later in his letter to Moore. It shows Murdoch as a ruthless and single-minded negotiator, firm and even self-righteous in going after the best possible deal and not too squeamish to bend the facts a bit to attain it; yet flexible enough to settle quickly for less when he sees he is not going to get all he wants. For the clinching fact is that the loan he was finally granted was less than a third of the amount originally envisaged and only part of it was at the 8 percent rate. If Carter had intervened as was suggested, he would surely have done a bit better for Murdoch.

SEVEN

Showdown at Gray's Inn Road

To buy *The Times* would be a highly irresponsible thing to do
for your shareholders.
—Rupert Murdoch, November 1979

A man who has known Murdoch longer than most is Richard
Searby, a Melbourne lawyer who was at school and university with
him and has been an important business adviser for years. He is now
chairman of the News Corporation Ltd. and Deputy Chairman of
Times Newspapers. In Simon Regan's book on Murdoch, Searby
was quoted as being responsible for possibly the most useful—if
scarcely profound—characterization of him: "Fundamentally,
Rupert's a fidget." In a letter to the the London *Times* in 1983
Searby denied ever having said it, but in any case it does support an
impression others have of him. Robert Holmes à Court put it a bit
differently: "Rupert loves the macro-deal." And when one macro-
deal is in the bag, he cannot wait to get started on the next.

By the middle of 1980 his Sydney-Melbourne television network was formed and he had bought the expensive new jets for his
airline. What else was there to do? For sure, he could always slip
down to the stone and write a headline or two, fire one of his editors
or deal with any of the hundreds of details a tycoon can involve
himself in. Indeed, there were few things he enjoyed more than
keeping his executives on their toes with a pointed question about
budgets and operating procedures.

170

"How come you're paying so much for newsprint?" he would bark down the phone at a manager of one of his smaller papers, after a quick study of the accounts. "I can get it at a much better price." As one editor said: "He comes into town and he makes sure that on every single property he owns, the person responsible knows he's watching. And while he's there, they're better papers for it." But even that kind of power begins to pall after a while. Where was the next really big challenge to come from?

Throughout his career, Murdoch had repeatedly been asked whether he would like to own *The Times* of London. Often the question would be put almost satirically, for *The Times,* though with an insignificant circulation and scarcely ever profitable, was still Britain's most famous paper, a symbol of access to the upper echelons of power. It represented everything in Britain he disliked— subservience to authority based on tradition rather than on merit, a toffee-nosed morality and a general air of tedium. Even when it did resort to light relief—in its letters page and sometimes its Diary column—it was of a whimsical variety that Murdoch found unappealing. His answers to the oft-put question would generally be discouraging.

In an Australian television interview in 1971 he was asked about speculation that he was interested in *The Times* of London and that he planned to own the *New York Times* within ten years. He replied: "I think you can certainly discount the latter. As for the former, you can discount that, too. Without any disrespect, I think Lord Thomson might be persuaded to make a gift of the London *Times.* We have other ideas there." More recently, in November 1979, he had said: "To buy *The Times* would be a highly irresponsible thing to do for your shareholders."

Indeed it would have been, for that was the point at which *The Times* and the *Sunday Times* were just struggling back to life after a debilitating year of non-publication, during which their survival was many times called into question. Not many papers would have appeared again after so long a break. That they did was in large measure due to the unique position *The Times* holds in British life. Even people who do not read it regularly find it hard to imagine the nation doing without it over the long term.

The dispute that caused the suspension was partly over new printing technology—an issue that has plagued the paper throughout its 200-year history. When John Walter founded it as the *Daily Universal Register* in 1785, he did so to advertise a new printing process in which type was bunched into logograms of several letters instead of being set letter by letter. It proved no cheaper or quicker than the conventional single-letter setting and by the time the name of the paper had been changed to *The Times,* in 1788, the process had been abandoned.

Walter became more interested in what went into his newspaper than in how it was produced, and on March 25th, 1788, he published a long, self-important manifesto of its ideals and virtues. *The Times,* employed "correspondents of the first literary abilities which this country can boast." Parliamentary debates would be reported impartially, "our reporters being of the first class, equally incapable of perverting the language of debate to serve the purposes of faction, or to support the popularity of administration." Arrangements had been made to get the earliest foreign news as well; and finally "to indecent language or double entendre, no place shall be given in *The Times,* nor shall it contain any passage capable of insulting the eye, or ear, or modesty, or suffusing the cheeks of innocence with a blush."

Despite that hype, as it would nowadays be called, the paper lived up to some of its promises. It had the best and earliest reports of the French Revolution in 1789, and soon reached a healthy circulation of some 5,000.

It was under Walter's son, John Walter II, that *The Times* first rose to a position of great influence. By 1803, at the age of only twenty-seven, the younger Walter was both editor and manager of the paper. His refusal to enter into corrupt deals with postal officials to receive journals from abroad forced him to create his own foreign news service—the first London paper to have one. Amongst early scoops were the death of Nelson in 1805, and the capture of the Dutch port of Flushing in 1809, of which *The Times* had news before the government. The nickname "The Thunderer" dates from this period, provoked by the outspoken editorials of Edward Sterling and John Stoddart, who edited the paper briefly before he fell out with Walter and was replaced by the redoubtable Thomas Barnes, editor for twenty-four years until 1841.

Barnes died in office and was succeeded by another long-serving editor, John Delane, only twenty-three when he assumed the chair. During his thirty-six years as editor the paper gained an international reputation and its circulation climbed steadily. By 1855 it was selling 60,000 copies, nearly three times the total sale of all five of its rivals in London.

During the Crimean War, sales went up to 70,000, largely because of the vividly searing despatches of William Howard Russell, who some regard as the first-ever war correspondent. When Russell went to cover the American Civil War in 1861, President Lincoln told him: *"The Times* is the most powerful thing in the world, except, perhaps, the Mississippi."* And he regretted that it was using its power to back the southern states, reflecting the opinion of most of its readers.

Towards the end of the nineteenth century the paper's fortune began to wane. New titles, using more modern printing methods than *The Times* and catering to a less elite audience, were mopping up the readers. The paper was ailing and in 1907 the courts, at the request of some of the smaller partners in ownership, ordered that it should be sold.

This opened the door to the first of the disreputable proprietors of *The Times,* Lord Northcliffe. I do not use the word in any personal denigratory sense but to convey that Northcliffe—like Roy Thomson and Rupert Murdoch later—had made his fortune in newspapers of a racier, more popular nature. There would be nothing very harmful in that were it not that *The Times,* as a result of its excellence in the middle years of the nineteenth century, had come to be regarded as a national institution. Northcliffe, who as Alfred Harmsworth had created the immensely successful *Daily Mail,* agreed, as Thomson and Murdoch would have to do in time, to leave the editorial policy of the paper strictly in the hands of the editor.

When Northcliffe bought it, *The Times* sold about 30,000 copies a day at three pence. By 1914 he had taken the price down to a penny and the circulation was up to 150,000. During the First World War it jumped again to 278,000. But it was not in Northcliffe's nature to leave the editorial side to its own devices and his pledge to do so soon fell by the wayside. By the time he died, circulation had fallen to a little over 100,000. The paper had also lost its reputation for judicious even-handedness. All the same, there was no shortage of potential purchasers when it was put up for sale. John Jacob Astor, from one of Britain's and America's wealthiest families, joined forces with John Walter IV, a descendant of the founder, to buy the paper for £1,350,000—a high price, given its lack of commercial success.

To prevent, as they hoped, any further unsuitable transfer of power, Walter and Astor established an ex-officio committee of five worthies to ensure that any future change of ownership would be to someone within the paper's tradition. They were the Warden of All Souls, the Governor of the Bank of England, the Lord Chief Justice, the President of the Royal Society and the President of the Institute of Chartered Accountants. The innovation strengthened the concept of *The Times* as a national institution that should rise above squalid commercial considerations. One reason it was never for long able to increase its circulation to much above 300,000 may have been the unstated implication that readers who are not from the privileged class are in some way interlopers—voyeurs, in a sense, of rites in which they are not allowed to take part and do not fully understand. The high-minded letters to the editor, the opaque announcements of the new term arrangements at exclusive but insignificant fee-paying schools—what is it all supposed to mean? Is it some kind of elaborate joke? The 1958 slogan that "Top People take *The Times*" seemed to suggest that unless you were a top person by *The Times*'s own reckoning, you were not wanted as a reader.

Things have not changed much. Even today, committees of great men are set up to safeguard the nebulous concept of "the national interest" in the administration of the paper. Its writers still congratulate themselves on the quality and probity of their detailed reports of parliamentary debates and intricate law cases, the weight and importance of the leading articles, the elegance and occasional waspishness of the obituaries, the appeal of the crossword and even of the personal advertisement columns, which remained on the front page until 1966, far beyond the time when reason and modern practice suggested they should have been banished elsewhere. No attempt was made early enough to explore the market and see whether these virtues might not be exploited to appeal to a wider audience. The writers enjoyed the feeling that they were communicating with an elite, "important" readership; but sadly that readership was unable to sustain the paper economically. Specifically, it was not a large enough market to attract big national advertisers.

By the mid-1960s it became clear that something decisive would have to be attempted if *The Times* was not to wither and die along with the dwindling class to which it was addressing itself. The ediitor, Sir William Haley, and the management devised a series of editorial changes. The most visible element was the card they had been thinking of playing for years: putting news on the front page.

In terms of circulation, the changes were a success. An extra 10,000 readers were added almost immediately and the graph continued to rise. But the innovations cost money and it had become increasingly apparent that the Astor family would not much longer be able to subsidize the paper from their own resources. An injection of capital was badly needed and a search for investors was begun.

Roy Thomson was Britain's newest press tycoon. The son of a Toronto barber, he had tried his hand at a number of ventures, including ranching and selling motor supplies, before falling by accident into the communications business. In 1928, when he was already thirty-four and had failed twice in commerce, he moved to North Bay in northern Ontario to sell radios and other modern goods. The trouble was that there was no radio station in the vicinity, so his sets were useless. His remedy was to start a station himself, then a second one in Timmins farther north.

It was there, at the age of forty, that Thomson bought his first newspaper, *The Press*. It thrived and in the 1930s and 1940s he steadily acquired more Canadian papers and radio stations. In 1952, after failing in a bid to enter politics, he bought a paper in Florida. The following year he founded his British empire by purchasing the *Scotsman* in Edinburgh, and a few years later took a controlling stake in Scottish Television, making his celebrated remark that a commercial TV station was a license to print money. Later, through his Scottish interests, he was able to acquire a valuable investment in North Sea oil.

His largest British press involvement came in 1959 when he bought the Kemsley group of papers, including the *Sunday Times,* then unconnected with *The Times*. He made his first pass at *The*

Times in 1963, with an offer for the 10 percent shareholding of the Walter family. Gavin Astor bought the shares instead, to bolster his family's control. Two years later, hearing rumors that the paper was now in serious need of funds, Thomson asked Denis Hamilton, editor of the *Sunday Times,* to sniff around.

Hamilton lunched with executives of *The Times* to sound out possibilities. The proposition did not at first seem attractive to them, and not just because, in Thomson's own words, he was a "rough-neck Canadian." Less than fifty years earlier the paper had only with difficulty extricated itself from the grasp of a newspaper magnate, and although Thomson's *Sunday Times* was a different proposition from Northcliffe's *Mail,* it did not seem an ideal solution. Yet balanced against that were the obvious economies that could be made by a closer link between *The Times* and the *Sunday Times,* the latter making a profit of over one million pounds a year.

The deal had to pass through several hoops before it was approved. Recognizing that to own a newspaper in a democracy is a conduit to great power and influence, the British have instituted elaborate safeguards and procedures designed to prevent them falling into unsuitable hands. It is surprising how often they prove ineffective.

To win the consent of the Monopolies Commission, Thomson had to agree to play no role in running the paper. Sir William Haley would be chairman for three years and would be succeeded by Thomson's son Kenneth—who, being separated by a generation from his father's humble origins, was found more acceptable. And the old 1922 plan of roping in representatives of the great and the good to safeguard the national interest was revised. Four "national directors" were appointed to the board—two each nominated by the main political parties.

Despite such seeming indignities, Thomson was as pleased as punch about his acquisition. "This deal was the greatest thing I have ever done," he wrote in his book *After I Was Sixty.* "It was the summit of a lifetime's work. I had had to agree to keep out of the running of the paper; at least my son would be there sharing fully in the management." And he pledged his and his successors' private fortunes to continuing *The Times* and the *Sunday Times* "as quality papers edited in the national interest." He affirmed: "This undertaking will continue for twenty-one years and will be binding on our successors and assigns." (It did not and was not.)

Hamilton was appointed editor-in-chief of the newly merged papers. As editor of *The Times* he chose William Rees-Mogg, thirty-eight years old, deputy editor of the *Sunday Times*, whose father came from a line of country gentry and whose mother was an American actress. A tall intellectual with a high voice, a product of Oxford University and an exclusive private school, he slipped naturally into the role of a *Times* editor.

Harold Evans, the new editor of the *Sunday Times*, was a complete contrast. Small, wiry and dynamic, a keen motorcyclist, he had been editor of a regional daily paper in the north of England when Hamilton brought him to London as his deputy on the *Sunday Times*. The son of a railroad engineer, he had taken a late degree at the University of Durham, an old provincial institution without the cachet of Oxford and Cambridge.

Despite the fact that Rees-Mogg was patently one of them, dedicated *Times* men were apprehensive about what would become of their paper under the new ownership. There were changes that went right against the grain. Headlines were made larger and so was the body type, meaning that wordy writers had their work cut back. They received another shock when a circular came round urging them to write shorter sentences.

Yet although not universally approved, the changes were having a healthy effect on circulation. By the end of 1967 it was up to 364,193, an increase of nearly a hundred thousand in a year, and there were signs that Rees-Mogg's head was being turned. In a radio interview in March 1968 he predicted that within ten years sales would be up to 900,000. By late 1969 it had reached 450,000 but it fell after a penny price increase and profitability was still a distant prospect. The Thomson management were willing to fund initial losses but had not regarded their purchase of the papers as an open-ended commitment to a limitless subsidy. The new readers, they discovered, were costing them money, because they had been acquired largely through an expensive and gimmicky advertising campaign. Moreover, to appeal to this broader group *The Times* was fast alienating its traditional readers. It was a fundamental commercial miscalculation.

A pull-back by management was inevitable and when Denis Hamilton wrote to the staff sounding the financial alarm, the old guard at *The Times,* who had never really reconciled themselves to the innovations, thought it time to win back some lost ground. A group of thirty senior journalists met at the White Swan, a pub in Farringdon Street, and drafted a list of grievances concerning the editorial direction of the paper. Authority, independence, accuracy, discrimination and seriousness were among the qualities they perceived to have been diluted.

The mutineers drew up a document, among whose signatories the most senior was Teddy Hodgkin, the foreign editor. Others included Charles Douglas-Home, Brian MacArthur, Hugh Stephenson, Patrick Brogan and Geoffrey Smith, young journalists who were all to be involved in a more public melodrama twelve years later. *Times* editors are never serious enough for their staff—the men Lord Northcliffe used to call the "Black Friars of Printing House Square."

Later that year substantial changes were made to the layout and character of the paper that answered many of the old guard's complaints. Headlines and bylines were made smaller. Although it was never announced in unambiguous terms to the staff, the drive for higher circulation through popularization had been abandoned as too expensive in relation to the likely financial benefit. The old guard were exultant. The paper had switched back into its role as a low-circulation journal for the knowing elite, a "paper of record." And in another move that was to have a profound long-term effect, Marmaduke "Duke" Hussey, an executive with a possibly undeserved reputation for ruthlessness, was recruited from the *Daily Mail* group to become managing-director of Times Newspapers.

One of the early Thomson decisions that was not revoked was to move *The Times* into a new building next to the *Sunday Times* in Gray's Inn Road, where both papers would be printed on the same presses. Many had reservations about this. *The Times* had been printed on its site hard by Blackfriars Bridge ever since its inception. Must it really move? More practically, there were fears, later borne out, that the merging of the two printing staffs would cause industrial unrest: each would want to share the fringe benefits of the other, without giving up any of its own privileges. Sunday papers were traditionally hardest hit by the labor-intensive "Spanish customs" of hiring more people than were actually needed to carry out a task. Yet Thomson's would not reverse the decision and the move was made in the summer of 1975.

It was botched, and one whole day's run of *The Times* was lost. Few of the anticipated economies came to pass. Even the libraries of *The Times* and the *Sunday Times* remained separate. Confidence in the efficacy of the management was further reduced when it was revealed that the valuable Henry Moore sundial, made specially for *The Times* only a few years earlier, had been included inadvertently in the sale of the old Printing House Square and thus could not be moved north with the paper. Instead, a tiny replica was made for the lobby of the new building.

The two qualities needed for the effective conduct of labor relations are flexibility and conviction. Rupert Murdoch can deploy both, and he has as well a reliable sense of which to stress at any given time. Thus, although he has endured his share of labor disputes, they have generally been settled before any lasting damage is done. Sometimes he has sacrificed his short-term aims for a quick peace, but overall he has not conceded more than he calculates he can afford. And he has never been too rigid or haughty to bargain.

The Thomson management at *The Times* and *Sunday Times* were, by comparison, maladroit. They were of the school that believes firmness to be paramount: that if you stand fast behind what you believe to be right, the work force will respect you for it and finally accept your terms. From time to time that tough approach has been effective, despite the fact that it conflicts with the notion of collective bargaining. What it requires, however, is to be linked to credible sanctions that will be deployed if agreement is not reached.

Labor relations on the two papers deteriorated rapidly after *The Times* moved to Gray's Inn Road. There were frequent unofficial work stoppages, mostly affecting distribution of the *Sunday Times,* which was thus unable to make sufficient profits to cover the losses of the daily paper.

These disruptions and their cost were chronicled by "Duke" Hussey, the managing director, in an increasingly lugubrious series of notes to the workers. Hussey is a genial aristocrat, a bear-like man with an artificial leg replacing one lost in the Second World

War. His wife, Lady Susan Hussey, has for years been a lady-in-waiting to the Queen. A press commentator called him "one of the most engaging characters in Fleet Street," and so he is. Yet he and his colleagues crucially lacked the ability to forge cordial day-to-day relationships with the representatives of their work force.

On April 10th, 1978, he wrote to the staff reporting the loss of two million pounds in revenue because of work stoppages. Management had to restore their right to manage. Some executives, said Hussey, were spending ninety percent of their time dealing with disputes as they arose. Something had to be done. It had to stop. Meetings would be held over the next few days. Decisions of weight would be reached and communicated to the staff.

There is no reason to doubt that Hussey was accurately conveying the frustration of the management in London and Toronto over their growing problems with the newspapers. The old Lord Thomson had died in 1976 and his son Kenneth was much less tolerant of Fleet Street's peculiarities. He had been inordinately fond of his father but did not completely share his excitement at being the owner of *The Times*. He was in truth more comfortable at home in Toronto, surrounded by his fine paintings, than on the international press circuit where such as Roy Thomson and Rupert Murdoch thrived. He felt himself a Canadian essentially; although he had inherited his father's peerage, he preferred not to use the title, and liked to leave the running of things in London to Hussey and Gordon Brunton, chief executive of the Thomson Organization in Britain. In 1978 the headquarters of the Thomson group was moved from London to Toronto. Though prepared to continue his father's commitment to the papers, the new Lord Thomson did not want it to be a permanent drain on his organization's resources, however extensive these had lately become as a result of investment in North Sea oil.

In fact *The Times* had made a modest profit in 1977, although circulation had by mid-1978 sunk to below 300,000, largely because of a 50 percent price rise, from ten pence to fifteen pence since 1976. It was partly this indication that they could make money from their papers if only they could solve their production difficulties that persuaded the Thomson directors to go for what came to be called the "big bang" solution. In essence, they were warning the unions that unless they could reach agreements for the uninterrupted production of the two papers and the three *Times* supplements, and for the smooth introduction of labor-saving technological advances, management would suspend production of the newspapers until such agreements were reached. Nowhere in Fleet Street had the new technology been introduced, although it was common in the United States and elsewhere. It was partly apprehension about their long-term job prospects in the face of this modern wizardry that had provoked the print unions into the disruption Hussey was complaining about.

On April 13th, 1978, Hussey and other directors met leaders of the print unions and outlined to them the ultimatum they were about to issue. It came in a memorandum to staff, signed by Hussey, announcing that a series of new agreements on working conditions, staffing, restricting unofficial strikes and introducing modern technology would be proposed. If agreement on all points was not reached by November 30, 1978, publication of *The Times,* the *Sunday Times* and the supplements would be suspended.

It would be a short, sharp shock, and many on the board were convinced that such tactics would quickly bring unions "to their senses." Authority would be reasserted. Others, though, had their doubts, and there was no sign of any backing-down in the unions' response to the threat. Accusations flew.

The *Times* management, inexplicably, had no detailed proposals to present to the unions until the end of the summer. It seemed that the management was for a time overawed by its own threat, representing as it did such a break with traditional labor relations; the act of steeling themselves for the confrontation had quite exhausted their stock of initiatives. In the event, when the suspension had lasted nearly a year and the prospect of permanent closure loomed, it was the management that gave way. Publication of the papers was resumed in mid-November 1979, fifty weeks after the administration of the short, sharp shock. Both sides, as is customary on such occasions, claimed victory, but although the management had achieved some concessions on manning and work practices, they could nowhere near justify the thirty-nine million pounds of Thomson money that Hussey had spent on leading his troops to the firing line and then negotiating the retreat. And many of the agreements on which the return to work was based—notably the one that committed the unions to completing negotiations within a year on the introduction of new technology—were never to be fulfilled.

Less than a mile south of the Gray's Inn Road headquarters of Times Newspapers, at his offices in the *Sun* building in Bouverie Street, Rupert Murdoch watched it all with eyebrows raised quizzically, wondering how any newspaper executive could allow this to happen—and wondering, as always, whether there might in the long run be anything in it for him.

During the exciting weeks leading to the resumption of *The Times* in November 1979, its reporters and correspondents were told that the aim was to make it seem as though the paper had never been away. All should be as it was when they had stopped work fifty weeks earlier. The idea was to convince themselves and readers that 1979 was a bad dream, a year that, due to circumstances beyond their control, had not taken place.

So far as readers were concerned, that strategy appeared to work. Circulation of the *Sunday Times* quickly regained its former level of 1,500,000 and *The Times* actually increased by a substantial 40,000 to over 320,000—benefiting in those first weeks from the publicity generated by the closure. The snag was that not only journalists and readers regarded 1979 as The Year That Never Was: the print unions did as well. It was soon clear that they saw the return-to-work agreements not as final and immutable but simply as a basis for further apparently endless negotiation. The disputes that were supposed to have been ruled out by the agreements continued much as before. The essential problems remained and grew worse. *The Times*'s circulation in June dipped below 300,000 for the first time since the resumption, partly because production delays had led to missed trains, meaning that papers outside London were delivered late. Rees-Mogg, briefing assistant editors, said that while he and his fellow directors had not expected the unions to honor all agreements, they were surprised and distressed to discover that hardly any were being complied with.

By the middle of the year it became clear that the deficit of the two papers in 1980 would amount to something like thirteen million pounds. Rees-Mogg told colleagues that Lord Thomson's morale was at rock bottom. Then, in early August, came the blow that was to prove fatal: the company's statisticians did their sums and produced projections for 1981 that made it clear that the loss would be at least as heavy that year as in 1980. Almost simultaneously, journalists on *The Times* went on strike over pay.

It was only a five-day strike but its effect was far-reaching. Lord Thomson, in his bleak mood, had said that the only consideration persuading him to keep the papers going was the loyalty of the staff, especially the journalists. So as not to jeopardize this he had—effectively from his own pocket, as he saw it—kept paying them for the year when they had produced nothing. Now they had repaid that generosity by stopping the paper again in a dispute over a mere two percent on an already high pay offer. Was there really any point in battling on?

The London board of the Thomson Organization met and decided the time had come to disconnect the life-support machine. They telephoned Thomson and told him that in their view the papers should be sold forthwith. Thomson had been moving towards such a decision since the spring but it was none the less traumatic for him. He believed he still had a heavy responsibility to his father's aspirations for *The Times*. He was swayed by John Tory, the hard-headed chief executive of his Toronto organization, who told him the paper was draining his resources at a rate beyond that which he could afford. Reluctantly, he agreed that it and its stable companion should be sold.

In early September Thomson went to London to discuss details of the sale, travelling via New York in order to catch the supersonic Concorde flight. Concorde passengers have access to an exclusive lounge in the British Airways terminal at Kennedy Airport, with comfortable settees and armchairs, trays of canapés with caviar and a running champagne bar, even desks with typewriters for executives who need to take executive action before they board the plane for their three-and-a-half-hour dash across the Atlantic.

Thomson was not much interested in the champagne or the typewriters but he did take notice when he spotted Rupert Murdoch on one of the settees. They exchanged cordial greetings, one newspaper tycoon to another. For the few minutes before takeoff, they spoke earnestly.

Murdoch, whose intelligence service is the best in Fleet Street, was aware of the bleak mood of the Thomson management in the wake of the continuing problems of the two papers. The possibility that they might soon be for sale had occurred to him. On the face of it they did not seem an attractive proposition, yet his business success had been based largely on doing the unexpected, on seeing opportunities in situations from which others would shy away. That was how he had built an international empire from the meager inheritance from his father.

"So how are things going?" he asked the Canadian, with his casual familiarity.

"Not too well," Thomson replied, never diffident about sharing his burdens with a fellow. "In fact, it's a mess."

Later, Thomson and Brunton were anxious to play down the significance of the encounter and those remarks. "It's always a mess," Thomson would explain. "It's what I would say to anyone who asked." But to Murdoch, at least, it was more than a routine bout of venting steam against a hostile world.

"The conversation was pretty general," he told the *Sunday Times* the following February, after his purchase of the papers had been finalized. "All about what a mess England was in and how dreadful the unions were. But I sensed he was getting sick of it and wanted out."

It took Brunton and his colleagues two months to work out the mechanics of the sale and announce it formally. After the scarcely veiled tip given to Murdoch by Thomson in the Concorde lounge, a Concorde was to be setting for the next stage in Murdoch's gradual conviction that he should become the next proprietor of *The Times*. Flying to Bahrein in October for a meeting of the directors of Reuters news agency, he sat for a while next to Sir Denis Hamilton, who had been in charge of travel arrangements for the meeting and had deliberately put himself and the Australian on the same flight, although he claims no ulterior motive.

"I had to be pretty Delphic in everything I said," Hamilton told the *Sunday Times* later. All the same, from that and the earlier meeting with Thomson, Murdoch had no doubt that Times Newspapers would be for sale before long. And he had now reached a tentative clarification of his position: that while the *Sunday Times* would make a profitable addition to his newspaper collection, *The Times* was chronically unviable, despite the obvious prestige to be gained from owning it.

Brunton announced the plan to sell on October 22nd, adding that if a suitable buyer was not found by March 1981 the papers would close. He stressed that the sale would be conducted with the highest degree of probity. Hamilton, Harold Evans, Rees-Mogg and the national directors would advise on a set of criteria for proposed purchasers. He concluded: "We believe that it is very much in the public interest that matters affecting the future of great national newspapers should be conducted in an open and responsible way."

Next morning the *Financial Times* ran through the list of possible buyers. The only one to express an interest at that stage was the inevitable Robert Maxwell. Tiny Rowland, chief executive of Lonrho, who controlled the *Glasgow Herald* and was later to buy the *Observer* from Atlantic Richfield, said: "No interest will be expressed and that should not be surprising. They are loss-makers." Rupert Murdoch said a bid from him was unlikely. "We've got our hands pretty full," he mused. "I doubt whether there will be any buyers." And he added a glimpse of the obvious when he stated that, from an industrial relations viewpoint, Times Newspapers was a "snake pit."

In his statement, Brunton appeared to leave open the question whether the papers would be sold as one company or separately. In fact he had already made up his mind to sell them as a unit if he could, and in the two months between the decision to sell and the announcement he and his colleagues had been devising a procedure for the sale that would offer the best chance of such an outcome.

When he came to make a list of those who might want to buy the newspapers and who fulfilled his criteria he could find only a handful. At the top of his list were Rupert Murdoch and Lord Rothermere of Associated Newspapers. Having reached the conclusion that these were the most desirable purchasers, Brunton then had to frame conditions for the sale that would attract them. He decided to institute a strict timetable for every stage in the purchase. To begin with, Warburg's, Thomson's bankers, would prepare a prospectus on the commercial condition of Times Newspapers. Anyone with a plausible interest in making a bid would be given a copy on condition they signed a pledge of confidentiality. This was a useful primary filter, for Thomson's could simply decline to give a prospectus to bidders they thought manifestly unsuitable from the outset.

The prospectus appeared in November. It was a remarkably optimistic document. Thomson's private projections for 1981, before the sale had been decided upon, were that losses would be at least as great as in 1980—13 million pounds. In the document, though, they had been whittled down to £4,295,000. The two papers were seen as making an 8-million-pound profit in 1982 and double that in 1983.

Potential buyers had little time to ponder these dazzling predictions, for bids had to be in by the end of December. Bids were invited for both the whole company and the papers separately, on the understanding that a good bid for the company as a whole would take precedence over the others. By adhering rigidly to the December 23rd deadline, Brunton ensured that nobody seriously interested could afford to wait and see what the others were doing— the way Murdoch for one preferred to do business. It minimized the chance of a buyer coming in at the end and picking up the papers for almost nothing as a bidder of last resort, as Murdoch had done with the *Sun.*

Brunton left ten weeks for negotiation after the closing of bids. The most important result of this was virtually to rule out any reference to the Monopolies Commission—which usually takes about three months—unless there were to be a break in publication. This was important because neither Murdoch nor Rothermere, with their important Fleet Street holdings, could expect an easy time from the Commission. In all, the procedure for the sale amounted to an expert piece of stage management.

Sudden shocks often make people act out of character, sparking responses that surprise even themselves. Allowing for that, though, Rees-Mogg's reaction to Brunton's announcement was altogether remarkable. During the last few months his colleagues had noted that the suspension of the paper and the troubled year since had left the editor with an ineffable weariness, persuading some that he was losing interest in his job and in the paper. But its impending closure concentrated his mind wonderfully, almost miraculously.

By philosophy and emotion, Rees-Mogg had always been opposed to the collective ethic, thundering against it in the leader columns of *The Times.* Yet what he proposed, when he called the staff together on the afternoon of the Thomson statement, was a new form of ownership for *The Times,* a modified co-operative of journalists and managers, financed by outside capital.

When he told this to his stunned staff—their second shock following the announcement of the sale—Rees-Mogg adopted a revivalist tone. "I do not myself think we should wait for the arrival of a new proprietor on a white horse," he cried. "If we are to secure the future of the paper we must do it ourselves....I have already begun working on trying to put these ideas together....We now have two choices: we can leave it to other people to save us or we can work to save ourselves." He added that he was going to Canada and America on the weekend to fulfil a longstanding engagement and would take the opportunity to speak to Lord Thomson about his plan and sound out prospects for American investment in the consortium.

Armed with his new alliance, Rees-Mogg headed for America to shake the dollar tree, but found it for the most part unshakable. It was not suprising, when you thought about it, for in his editorials about the suspension and the sale of the paper, he had given vent to his most dire musings about the appalling state of Fleet Street's industrial relations: hardly an effective lure for a prospective backer. And most Americans thought the idea of a workers' cooperative, however hard Rees-Mogg tried to avoid using the word, was...well, a bit flaky. He saw Katharine Graham at the *Washington Post* and the senior executives at *Time* magazine. He also went down to the office of the *New York Post* to talk to Rupert Murdoch.

Although it was only a few days since Murdoch had seemed to declare his lack of interest, Rees-Mogg received the impression that he would bid for the *Sunday Times* if it could be separated from *The Times*. Murdoch spent some time praising Harold Evans in the most effusive manner, describing him—as he was to do publicly a few months later—as the greatest editor in the world. If this appeared an impolite observation to make to a man who might think *he* was in the runing for that accolade, Rees-Mogg did not seem to notice. Indeed, like many after their first meeting with the mature Murdoch, he went away with a much more favorable impression than he had anticipated. Basing his expectation on what he had read in his own and other newspapers, he had been prepared to meet an uncouth ogre with a rough accent, but was instead surprised at the tycoon's smoothness and refined manners. What gave Rees-Mogg more pleasure than anything was to be served a thoroughly English cup of tea (not normally encountered in Manhattan offices). It came on traditional blue and white china, in gracious comfortable surroundings. As he sipped and clinked cup on saucer, Rees-Mogg reflected that it is the *detail* that is so important on occasions of this kind, and Murdoch had the detail just right. Could he, surreptitiously, be a gentleman after all?

Back in London, Rees-Mogg telephoned Harold Evans to tell him about his meeting with Murdoch and to report that the Australian seemed interested in the *Sunday Times,* especially in its editor. "Why don't you phone him?" Rees-Mogg suggested, but Evans did not. He had long been under the impression that Murdoch did not much like him—a belief based on previous brief encounters and on reports from colleagues. For his own part, while he could admire Murdoch's energy and skills in tabloid journalism, he had no reason to think they could, work profitably together. Rees-Mogg's report of how Murdoch had sung his praises only made Evans wary, for he was now engaged in consortium-building himself. At his right hand was Bernard Donoughue, an economist who had been an adviser to former Prime Minister Harold Wilson and a close friend of Evans since then. Donoughue had long been convinced that the only future for national newspapers lay in their workers having a real stake in their success, discouraging the strikes and go-slows that constantly hampered production. With Evans, he devised a formula under which journalists would have the chance of buying £1,000 worth of shares each and the production unions could also invest in the company.

The main capital would have to come from outside and, given that the paper had made a profit in seventeen of the last twenty years, it was not too. hard to raise. American investors *were* interested in the *Sunday Times.* Charter Oil of Pennsylvania, owners of the Philadelphia *Bulletin,* pledged support and in Britain there was backing from the Scottish Widows Insurance Company. Addressing a meeting of his staff, Evans stressed that his scheme would be a lot preferable to being owned by any of the "seven dwarfs" who tended to sniff around whenever papers were for sale. (He was referring to Rupert Murdoch, Robert Maxwell, Lord Rothermere, Sir James Goldsmith, Tiny Rowland, Lord Matthews of the Express group and Lord Barnetson of United Newspapers.) Most of his listeners agreed.

As December wore on, Brunton waited in some trepidation for expressions of interest to come in and, rather to his surprise, several did, mounting to as high as fifty before the deadline was reached. When Brunton and Thomson thought of Times Newspapers the only figures dancing in their heads were in red ink, or were images of obstructive printers and undelivered newspapers. Yet to many people the idea of owning one or two such famous titles was inordinately seductive. To own *The Times:* wouldn't that be a passport to the top tables, the most influential circles in the land? And wouldn't that be something worth having? For fifty hopefuls, it would.

Murdoch's instinct would have been to wait until after the December deadline on the assumption that there would by then have been no acceptable bid and he could have picked up the company— or the *Sunday Times* part of it at least—at a bargain basement price. But when he heard rumors of the other buyers in the field he decided he must make his move within the specified time if he was to stand a chance. He also realized that, because other bidders had expressed interest in the two papers and the supplements as a package, he must do the same if his bid was to be considered. Brunton's tactics had worked and had brought Murdoch to the point of decision. Did he really want to saddle himself with *The Times*? Was the undoubted prestige worth the equally undoubted strife? Well, yes, in the end it was. The shark, despite having declared himself a convert to vegetarianism, could not, when it came to it, resist the smell of blood. Addiction is never really cured.

In early December Murdoch telephoned Brunton from New York. "I want to put in a bid," he said. "Rupert, you'd better come over," Brunton replied. "We'll talk." Murdoch went to Warburg's to pick up the prospectus and quickly decided it was over-optimistic. All the same, he met Brunton at the London flat of Lord Catto, Murdoch's London banker, and the negotiations were under way.

What helped convince Brunton that Murdoch was the most serious and thus the most suitable potential purchaser was the fact that he oversaw the negotiations personally and was constantly on the phone to Brunton or one of his executives questioning this or that figure in the Warburg prospectus. No other bidder took such an interest. Moreover, from what Brunton knew of Murdoch—mainly from contacts in the Newspaper Publishers' Association—he was a straight-dealing man who would stick to a bargain and knew how to skirt Fleet Street's industrial booby-traps. Maybe his existing British papers would make curious bedfellows for *The Times* and the *Sunday Times* but at least they were competently run, which more than anything was what Times Newspapers needed. Murdoch was not the ideal owner for *The Times,* but then neither was Lord Thomson fourteen years earlier. You had to settle for the best available.

Before bids closed in December, Brunton had decided that he wanted Murdoch to buy the papers. His resolve was strengthened the following month when he called in the leaders of the print unions and asked them which of a list of potential purchasers they preferred. They strongly favored Murdoch, on the grounds that they knew him, found him a tough but fair bargainer and because he had rescued the *Sun*—and with it many of their members' jobs. (More surprisingly, when Harold Evans took a similar poll among some *Sunday Times* journalists, he found the same majority opinion.)

Brunton recognized that Murdoch's initial bid of a million pounds was a sighting shot, a declaration of interest that would be improved upon. The final price of twelve million pounds was not the highest offer Brunton received. Associated Newspapers put in two bids—twenty million pounds for the company as a whole or twenty-five million for the *Sunday Times* alone. Rothermere badly wanted a Sunday paper to maximize the use of his *Daily Mail* presses, but Brunton was not convinced that his intentions towards *The Times* were motivated by an equal fervor.

Brunton's conviction that Murdoch was the right man was not in itself enough to ensure that he would be chosen, for to establish the purity of their intentions Thomson's had devised a "vetting" procedure under which the selected candidate had to submit himself to a committee comprising Hamilton, the two editors and the four national directors—now Lord Robens, the veteran politician, Lord Dacre, still better known as historian Hugh Trevor-Roper, former rail union leader Lord (Sid) Greene and the economist Lord Roll, chairman of Warburg's, whose dual role in the affair gave rise to suggestions in Parliament of conflict of interest. They met on January 21st at Thomson House—a solid Regency terraced house in Stratford Place, to the north of Oxford Street.

Robens was abroad and unable to attend. The other six, as they sat waiting for Murdoch to appear before them, felt uncomfortable. They were, in effect, a court of last resort, custodians of the public interest, the final obstacle to a consummation which, only months earlier, most of them would have regarded as unthinkable. Both editors had published articles condemning Murdoch and the style of journalism he personified. He was one of Harold Evans's "seven dwarfs."

In September, at the express insistence of Rees-Mogg, I had written an article from New York about the poor repute in which Murdoch was held in some circles there. I wrote of "the journalism of the lowest common denominator" and "the breathless, grubby vision of the world inherent in the Murdoch style." The editor, pleased with my work, had given the article unusual prominence, illustrated with a front page of the *New York Post* bearing the headline: PREGNANT MOM IN 911 TERROR.

Now Rees-Mogg was being asked to approve this man as the proprietor of the paper he had nurtured during the last fourteen years, and the others had equally painful adjustments to make. Hamilton wryly recalled his leading part in condemning Murdoch over the Keeler memoirs but, drawing as he often did on his wartime experience, he comforted himself with the thought that the Australians had been the best fighters on either side—the least disciplined but tremendous in a scrap. In the current condition of Fleet Street, this was a quality that would be needed above all. When asked by Lord Dacre whether any undertakings Murdoch gave could be relied upon, Hamilton had to admit that what the Australian actually did was not always consistent with what he said he was going to do. But he recommended approval none the less, stressing that the new owner should be made to put on paper specific pledges which the Trade Minister, whose approval of the deal was necessary, could give the force of legislation. Realistically, despite their serious reservations, that was all the vetting committee could do.

Upstairs, the negotiations between Murdoch and Brunton were reaching their final stages. There was a hiccup when Murdoch angrily accused the Thomson team, in the person of Scottish accountant Ian Clubb, of misleading him over the valuation of the company's assets. Brunton leapt to his colleague's defense: "Rupert, you bloody well don't talk to my people like that," he shouted. "This deal is off as of now, but before you walk out of this room, bloody well apologize to him." That seemed to calm Murdoch. Clubb explained the disputed point again and Searby, who accompanied Murdoch throughout the discussions, said he now understood it.

Both principals made much of that tiff in describing the deal later, with the aim of convincing people that they had negotiated toughly to the limit. Brunton used it as the basis for saying there had been "blood on the walls" at Thomson House and Murdoch told the *Sunday Times* that he had been shaking when he went up to meet the national directors. "These dignified gentlemen probably thought I was quaking with fear," he said. In fact, the dignified gentlemen noticed nothing untoward.

In his book *Good Times, Bad Times,* Harold Evans describes how Murdoch entered "like someone visiting a friend in hospital, walking quietly, speaking softly." Hamilton seemed almost apologetic at having to ask such intrusive questions about his intentions. He stressed the tradition of editorial independence on the two papers and Murdoch gave ringing assurances that he intended to respect it. And he accepted that editors could be appointed and dismissed only with the agreement of the national directors. At least one member of the committee thought he had given the pledges a little too readily. "One got the feeling that even if we'd asked for a different set of assurances he'd have given them equally easily," he said. "It wasn't too reassuring—very Australian." As well as promising to give the national directors the right to veto his choice of editor, Murdoch undertook to augment them by two. The national directors voted to approve Murdoch and, around midnight, Brunton opened the celebratory drinks.

The deal for Murdoch to buy Times Newspapers was conditional on his agreeing with staff unions about economies, but when it was announced the following day everyone assumed it would go ahead. "I have operated and launched newspapers all over the world," said a jubilant Murdoch at a press conference at the Portman Hotel in London. "This new undertaking I regard as the most exciting challenge of my life."

The day after the announcement, Murdoch trotted excitedly round the Gray's Inn Road offices of his two new properties. "Who are you?" he would ask random people at desks. "Are you important?" He would not wait for reply, but his patent enthusiasm for the most exciting challenge of his life was to lead him into an error that might easily have damaged his prospect of being confirmed as owner. He had two hurdles to clear yet—his negotiations with the unions and the possibility of a referral to the Monopolies Commission, which would have delayed matters beyond the Thomson deadline for closure. Yet he could scarcely contain himself. On his first Saturday visit to the *Sunday Times* office, he noticed the paper was running an editorial headlined "Rupert Murdoch" and asked to see a proof. Written by Evans, it gave an enthusiastic welcome to the new proprietor. "He is certainly now preferred to any of the other would-be corporate purchasers," Evans wrote, "because of his energy, his directness, his publishing flair and, above all, the commitments he has given on editorial independence."

The argument of the editorial was that the Murdoch purchase ought not to be referred to the Monopolies Commission because the delay might jeopardize the papers' future. In support of his case, Evans listed the newspaper titles owned by other Fleet Street groups; but in his listing for Express Newspapers he omitted the *Daily Star.* Murdoch noticed the omission, made a mark on the proof and sent it to Evans suggesting it should be altered. In later editions, it was. Neither man saw it as an especially significant intervention—the simple correction of a fact. Critics, though, interpreted it as the first instance of the new proprietor intervening to promote his self-interest.

While negotiations with the unions on manning cuts went ahead rapidly, the issue of the Monopolies Commission looked more menacing. The legal position was that any deal involving a change of ownership of a newspaper selling more than half a million copies had automatically to be referred to the commission unless the Government were satisfied that the papers were losing money and that the delay (generally about three months) might prove fatal. Murdoch, whose existing British newspapers were enthusiastic in their support of Margaret Thatcher, felt the Government owed him a favor and there was skilled and discreet lobbying in Westminster by Denis Hamilton. Persuaded, Trade Minister John Biffen issued a White Paper declaring that, since both papers were in the red, the purchase would not be referred to the commission. Murdoch had made it clear from the beginning that if the deal was referred he might not go through with it, summing up his attitude in this snap answer when he appeared before the House of Commons Education Committee: "People seem to think they are doing me a favor in allowing me to take something that is losing thirteen million pounds a year."

A group of journalists on the *Sunday Times,* hoping that the favor might still be undone, decided to fight Biffen's ruling. While nobody could deny that *The Times* was losing money, the *Sunday Times,* according to the Warburg prospectus, was viable. The journalists suspected sharp practice with the figures and decided to institute legal action against Biffen to force him to refer the deal. They became dismayed, though, to discover that the cost of taking legal action could be hundreds of pounds for each of them, and most were thus quite relieved when Murdoch offered a compromise: if they dropped the action he would further strengthen the guarantees of editorial freedom and agree to the appointment of two journalists to the board of Times Newspapers.

Those most fervently opposed to Murdoch were disappointed that they received no support from Harold Evans, who now seemed by his actions and his editorials to be committed firmly to Murdoch. (When his book was published in 1983, Evans sought to reopen the question of a Monopolies Commission reference, asserting that subsequent research proved that Biffen was working on falsified figures when he declared the *Sunday Times* unviable. Had he supported that proposition when made by his staff 2½ years earlier, he might have prevented Murdoch's acquisition of the papers.) Some suspected that Evans had been won over at a quite early stage by a promise that he could edit *The Times,* but both men have denied this.

On Monday, January 26th, five days after his positive vetting, Murdoch addressed the editorial staff of *The Times* in a crowded news room. One questioner told him that not all the staff were convinced by the guarantees of editorial independence. "A lot of us are in two minds yet as to whether or not this is in fact the best thing or whether we should be satisfied," he agonized. "Could you say anything further?"

Murdoch's answer was modest to the point of bleakness. "I can sell myself to you as the least of the alternative evils," he said. "As regards the guarantees themselves...I think I have locked myself in, particularly with the power I have given (to the national directors) of absolute right of hiring and firing of editors and given them the right to be a self-perpetuating body.... What if I found a way of tearing up all those guarantees and fired an editor? The answer is there would be a terrible public stink and it would destroy the paper.... I get on with these people or I get out. Otherwise I would destroy what I am attempting to buy."

The journalists were sufficiently impressed for a group of them to draft a statement announcing that they now approved of the Murdoch purchase. An explanation for this new attitude had been made to foreign correspondents a few days earlier by Leslie Plommer, an astute young Canadian woman who worked on the foreign desk. In a circular to overseas bureaus, she wrote: "Most journalists seem in the throes of what we in the Pentagon siege-psychology section like to call Self Induced Mind Reversal, in which the subject seeks to persuade himself that the object of fear and loathing is not so bad, and even likely to be quite beneficial."

In Toronto Lord Thomson could scarcely contain his relief at having shed the dreadful burden, although he was able to muster a few decent words of regret. "It's a sadness to know that we are no longer associated with these wonderful newspapers," he said. "But we have committed the papers to the hands of someone who has the ability to make them work. Rupert Murdoch is a good newspaper-man and businessman. I know that he has the desire to show the world that he can produce good newspapers as well as sensational ones."

EIGHT

The Trouble with Harry

Harold Evans...I regard as one of the world's great editors.
—Rupert Murdoch, January 1981

He wanted to be loved by everybody. But he ended up being loved by nobody.
—Murdoch on Evans, November 1983

Three weeks after the installation of a new administration is a busy and fruitful time for the hundreds of correspondents from all over the world whose job is to report and interpret the word from Washington. There are new government appointments to be reported and speculated about, straws to be plucked from the wind to see if they offer hints as to how sincerely campaign pledges will be fulfilled. New contacts are to be sought, phone numbers noted, dates made for lunch.

On February 12th, 1981, twenty-three days into the Reagan era, Patrick Brogan, the lean, grey Washington correspondent of *The Times,* would have expected to be engrossed in just such concerns. He had been nearly eight years in the capital, first as deputy chief correspondent and for the last four years as the chief. He had arrived as the Watergate drama was reaching its climax and this was his third presidential inauguration. He had seen Gerald Ford take the oath as the man who would heal the nation's wounds, then reported the single and in some respects singular term of Jimmy Carter. At the start of the new conservative era this talented correspondent, whose father Denis Brogan had been one of the most vivid of all British writers about America, was ideally equipped to interpret for his readers just what it all meant.

Yet on this wintry Washington Thursday he was in no mood to do any such thing and his readers would, for the most part, have taken only a passing interest if he had tried. He and they were preoccupied with a matter that affected them in a more personal way. Entering *The Times*'s spartan fifth-floor office in the National Press Building at his usual gentlemanly hour of 10 a.m., Brogan walked right over to the Telex machine and perused a one-line message that had arrived a few moments earlier. It was terse and contained news that for weeks he had been dreading, though he had known there was no real chance of averting it:

IT'S THE DIGGER: OFFICIAL.

As Brogan stood and read in silence, the machine burst into life with a second cable, fuller than the first and unsigned. The indications were that it had been composed by one of the Telex operators in the wire-room at Gray's Inn Road, keen to have his say and impart the news to the largely faceless folk across the Atlantic with whom he was in daily communication:

THE DIGGER NOW HAS OUR TITLES FIRMLY IN HIS POUCH.
SIGNING OF THE WALLABY DEAL 1500 GMT.
COVER YOUR PRIVATE PARTS.
NICE DAY IN LONDON AFTER OVERNIGHT FROST.
SUN SHINING OUTSIDE.
LONG LIVE THE TIMES.

Brogan smiled thinly at the line about private parts. It referred to a message he had sent to London four weeks earlier, when he had first, to his horror and amazement, heard that the negotiations with Murdoch were advanced and likely to succeed. Brogan, although only in his early forties, was an archetypal old *Times* man who had cared enough about the traditional standards of the paper to sign the White Swan letter in 1970. Murdoch, he was convinced, would destroy what little remained of those standards, not right away—even he was too subtle—but gradually, as he saw prospects for commercial success by the old route slip away. So a month ago, getting the first whiff of the change, Brogan had rattled out a feature about Murdoch's image in America, about how he had altered the *New York Post,* spicing his article with the hint of suspected scandal over the loan from the Export-Import Bank.

He had cabled the piece to London but, scarcely surprisingly in the circumstances, it had not been printed. Next day he sent off an uncharacteristically fierce enquiry, asking:

WHY WASN'T MY MURDOCH PIECE USED? OR RATHER, WHOSE PUSILLANIMITY PREVAILED?

I AM TOLD THAT HE IS GOING AROUND TELLING HIS COBBERS THAT HE IS ABSOLUTELY DETERMINED TO BUY TNL., IGNORING COUNSELS OF CAUTION FROM SAID COBBERS. THEN HE WILL CUT ALL YOUR BALLS OFF, IF YOU HAVE ANY.

He had followed up that démarche with an exchange of telex messages with Rees-Mogg. "Mr. Murdoch runs very many, very bad newspapers," he wrote, comparing him with Northcliffe. "I believe that Brunton, James Evans and the rest of them are betraying all the promises Roy Thomson made in 1966 and repeated frequently afterwards. . . . When Thomson's intention to sell *The Times* was announced, you wrote that *The Times* would fight for her own survival and that you would join the fight. I hope you will continue to do so."

Rees-Mogg replied briefly, assuring Brogan that he took his message seriously but rejecting the comparison of Murdoch with Northcliffe. "I believe *The Times* will benefit from a stronger commercial drive, that he will not appoint an editor who is not worthy of the paper and that any editor who is worthy of the paper will, under the system of guarantees, be able to maintain his independence." He thought the Murdoch purchase was the only way of avoiding at least a temporary closure of the paper.

Brogan thought of that message, and of his career with *The Times,* as he walked to his desk with the two "digger" telexes. He considered, then rejected, the notion that perhaps Rees-Mogg saw all this as sweet revenge for his humiliation by the White Swan rebels. In the end, Brogan and those who thought like him had been able to ensure that the Thomsons kept the paper in something like the condition in which they had found it. He was not at all convinced that this was why they had failed to sustain it.

Their management had, it was clear, been woefully inadequate. When they had screwed up their courage to get tough with the unions it had scarcely been a convincing performance. Murdoch would doubtless avoid those errors, indeed labor negotiations seemed to be among his strengths. Yet there was nothing in his record to suggest that he would want to nourish those qualities of rectitude, tolerance and moderation that had so impressed Brogan and others of his generation that they were proud to work for *The Times*. The Washington correspondent began composing in his mind a letter of resignation. He never wrote it, but before the end of the year he had left.

There were the familiar last-minute alarms before Murdoch's purchase of Times Newspapers was finalized. He had not achieved the full cost savings he had hoped in his negotiations with the unions, and before the year was out he was to regret not having been tougher. He did reach agreement for the gradual introduction of new technology, but the unions claimed it was on the same terms Thomson's had been offered but rejected. The staff of over 4,000 would be reduced by some twenty percent. Announcing the agreements, Murdoch warned that if there were further industrial trouble at Gray's Inn Road, "I will close the place down."

His other preoccupation in the days leading up to the agreement had been the appoinment of a new editor for *The Times*. Rees-Mogg had made it known for some time earlier that he would want to step down as soon as was decent after the new owner took command, and had he not done so voluntarily, it is likely that Murdoch would have found a way of persuading him to go, since he thought that, after fourteen years, a change was due. The identity of the new editor would be a crucial guide to the validity of his pledges about editorial freedom, for they would ring hollow if he were to bring in someone from his own stable.

Among the Murdoch men rumored to be in contention were the Australian Bruce Rothwell, the editorial page editor of the *New York Post,* and even Sir Larry Lamb of the London *Sun,* who was after all the senior editor in the group. It always seemed more likely that

Murdoch would consider it politic to appoint an editor from inside the paper, or at least from inside Times Newspapers.

The forty-four-year-old deputy editor Charles Douglas-Home was the candidate favored by the old Thomson regime of Rees-Mogg, Hussey and Hamilton. An Old Etonian, an officer in the Royal Scots Greys and briefly an aide-de-camp to one of the last colonial governors of Kenya, he is the nephew of Lord Home, the former Conservative Prime Minister. Somewhat ascetic—he does not smoke, drink or eat meat—he nevertheless enjoys traditional country pursuits such as hunting, though he is prone to falling off horses and hurting himself. He was Diplomatic Correspondent of the *Daily Express* until shortly before Lord Thomson bought *The Times,* when he was recruited as Defense Correspondent.

He rose through a number of executive positions with a smoothness marred by only one setback, when it was discovered that he was keeping intimate personal dossiers on members of the reporting staff. Someone broke into his office and peeped at the documents. Douglas-Home was obliged to make a grovelling apology and undertook to discontinue the practice. In the six years or so since then, he had largely restored his reputation, and it was clear he saw himself as a potential editor, if not necessarily the next one.

There were, however, persistent rumors that Murdoch's choice was Harold Evans—and they had not been stilled by Evans's announcement only the previous week that he intended to stay with the *Sunday Times.* He had edited the Sunday paper for fourteen years and colleagues believed he was getting stale. *The Times* seemed a logical move for him, although he insists Murdoch did not raise the question until their second meeting after Thomson's announcement that the Australian was the favored purchaser.

After that, Evans and his fiancée Tina Brown—then editor of *The Tatler* and later of *Vanity Fair* in New York—went to dinner at Murdoch's Belgravia flat, but Evans says the offer of *The Times* editorship was not made until a lunch the following week. He did not accept finally until after the appointment had been approved by the board, when Murdoch took him to lunch at the Savoy Grill. On returning to the office to tell his *Sunday Times* colleagues, he dissolved into tears.

For Murdoch, Evans seemed the ideal choice, a man within the organization he had bought but not identified with the paper on which radical changes would have to be made. But not everyone agreed that the talents that had blossomed on the *Sunday Times* would stand Evans in good stead on the daily paper.

There are two basic techniques of *Sunday Times* journalism, as created by Hamilton and Evans. One is to make accessible the difficult but important stories of the day—finance, industry, politics and foreign affairs—by dramatizing them and bringing out the personalities involved. The complementary skill is to use hard reporting methods on essentially soft stories—probes into antique dealers' price-fixing rings and phoney wine labelling. By contrast *The Times* has traditionally treated serious events seriously and trivial news trivially.

Murdoch took a more straightforward view. Evans was reputed to be the best journalist in Britain, and that was whom he wanted for *The Times*. First he had to convince the board, especially the national directors, to whom he had ceded the power of veto over the selection of editor. They were one below strength, Lord McGregor having rejected the invitation to be one of the two new ones Murdoch promised to appoint. Casting round for a replacement, Murdoch thought back to the man who had taught him much of what he knew about popular journalism—Sir Edward Pickering, his mentor at the *Daily Express* nearly thirty years earlier. Though sixty-eight and in retirement, Pickering was still active in the Commonwealth Press Union and the Press Council. He had bumped into Murdoch now and again through the years, but he was surprised to get a phone call one day in February, with Murdoch asking a characteristic question: "Are you free to have a bite to eat?" He was, and he accepted the directorship.

There had been no time to inform the other national directors of this addition to their strength before the February 17th board meeting at which the editor was to be chosen. The meeting was to begin in late morning and continue through lunch into the afternoon. Lord Dacre had warned Murdoch and the others that he would have to leave at 3:30 p.m. sharp, when a car would be waiting to drive him to Oxford to give a lecture. Dacre arrived a little early and went to see Denis Hamilton.

"Pickering's going to be there," Hamilton told him. "He's the new national director."

Dacre was horrified. The high-handed action by the new proprietor seemed to confirm all the fears he had expressed at the Thomson House meeting in January. "We can't have it," he said. "We are supposed to approve new national directors." When Pickering arrived it was agreed he should stand in the corridor until his appointment had been confirmed.

Murdoch was abjectly contrite, pleading a new boy's ignorance of the rules. "I didn't know it was wrong," he maintained. "I'll tell him to go away if you like." The national directors approved Pickering's appointment, Dacre abstaining from the vote.

Murdoch was keen to get Pickering on the board right away because he anticipated difficulty in having Evans's appointment as editor approved by the other national directors and was sure Pickering would accept his choice. The delay meant that they did not start talking about the editorship until after lunch.

Hamilton and Dacre agreed with Rees-Mogg that Douglas-Home was a better choice. Dacre delivered some cautious personal criticism of Evans, and said the *Sunday Times* under his editorship was a tasteless paper. At first it seemed that the collective view of the national directors was in accord with Dacre's. Hamilton weighed in. He felt that his protégé Evans, while a tremendous editor of a Sunday paper, had the opposite qualities from those needed to edit *The Times*. He was emotional, inconsistent, brilliant in flashes. He did not have the required backbone, the gravitas, the solid worth.

By the time Dacre had to leave for his drive to Oxford, he was sure that the mood of the meeting was for him, that Evans would be rejected and Murdoch be forced to nominate Douglas-Home. "I presume Lord Dacre is voting against," said Murdoch as he left the room. He was, but in the end his was the only negative vote, for Murdoch then made an eloquent plea for Evans, saying he desperately needed the services of the most able journalist in the land if he were to carry out his aim of reviving *The Times*.

The choice for the *Sunday Times* had been more difficult—though less publicly contentious—than *The Times*. The two main candidates from inside the paper were Ron Hall, editor of the color magazine, and Hugo Young, the brainy political editor. Hall had been on the paper longer than Evans and the two were friends. Evans recommended him. Hamilton, though, plumped for Young, who would bring less technical expertise but greater political insight. Hall was notoriously uninterested in all run-of-the-mill politics. Faced with these conflicting recommendations, Murdoch took a characteristic way out: he appointed Frank Giles, the sleek deputy editor, who at sixty-two was regarded by most as too old to be considered. Murdoch's idea was that the two younger men should fight it out for the top job and he would then see who was the better at asserting himself. "He expected us to behave like Australians," one of them complained a few months later, when the ruse had clearly gone wrong.

Apart from masterminding the choice of editor, Murdoch was prevented from imposing changes in editorial personnel by the conditions of his purchase. He had agreed with the journalists' union that no journalist would be dismissed, though he sought thirty voluntary severances. One hand thus tied, he decided to make a virtual clean sweep on the commercial side of the paper, where no such restraint applied. He made his intention plain from the beginning. On the day of his first visit to the paper's offices he went to see Bryan Todd, the bluff, portly advertisement and marketing director for *The Times*. On his office wall were photographs of recent promotional campaigns. Murdoch was patently unimpressed. "What circulation have we put on as a result of these campaigns?" he asked Todd, who thought it impolite to tell his new proprietor that he thought the question simplistic, that with *The Times* it was not straight numbers that were significant but the quality of circulation, the proportion of high-income readers.

Todd could see changes were coming, but like many of his colleagues, he clung as long as possible to the belief that he would survive them, as in battle the soldier thinks, until the very moment the bullet strikes home, that he will be the one to dodge it. Soon he discovered that one of the bullets did have his name on it. A day or two after Murdoch's takeover was formalized, Todd was summoned to see Gerald Long, the newly-appointed managing director of Times Newspapers. A former foreign correspondent, Long had run Reuters new agency for nearly two decades with a vision and efficiency that had impressed both Murdoch and Hamilton. He had a reputation for being difficult with subordinates, but that had never been regarded by Murdoch as a disability; nor did he mind his lack of experience in running newspapers. Long had shown at Reuters an aptitude for managing a business profitably, which recommended him not just to Murdoch but also to the commercial people at Times Newspapers. Todd felt well disposed towards him.

Long, a gaunt man with a droopy mustache, had just moved into his new office, furnished with a shaggy white carpet and little else. He perched on a card table. "I know nothing about advertising," he began, and Todd guessed what was coming. When people say they know nothing about a subject they are about to deliver their opinion on it. "I can only tell you," Long went on, "that *The Times*'s promotional advertising is the worst in the world. Furthermore we pay huge sums of money for it. You've seen the note. We don't have marketing here any more. So perhaps you'd like to go and see Tudor Hopkins [personnel director] and arrange your redundancy [severance]."

The note Long referred to was one that had been sent round the previous day, announcing that the new regime had abolished marketing as a word and as a concept. Murdoch thought it effete and over-elaborate. He did not accept the argument of the Thomson marketing people that because *The Times* could not be sold to advertisers as value for money in terms of total readership it was a question of burnishing its image as the sort of paper that enhanced the goods and services advertised in it. "If we get the product right—and we will—then we don't need to sell on special situations, special editions, that sort of thing," Murdoch told Sheila Black in an interview for *Media World*. "Advertising is something you earn and, if you've got the product, you go out and do a hard sell on it."

Others went just as quickly as Todd. Gary Thorne, advertising and marketing director for the whole group, decided to form his own agency. Andrew Shanks, marketing manager of the *Sunday Times,* had already accepted another job and was told not to go back to his office except to clear his desk. Donald Barrett, Thorne's grey, precise deputy, had been asked by Mike Ruda, the new advertising director, to draw up some proposals for increasing advertising revenue. At nine o'clock the following Thursday morning Ruda asked to see him. Scarcely had Barrett begun to present his thoughts when Ruda cut him short. "Let's approach this from a different angle," he said. "Let's not muck about. There's not going to be room here for the two of us." Barrett trotted to see Hopkins to arrange severance terms and was told: "Don't come back on Monday." He took his son to the office on Saturday to clear away his things—a sudden end to twenty-six years with the Kemsley and Thomson groups.

Panic and confusion gripped the advertising and marketing staff as Ruda began to scythe through them from the top downwards. Until the blow was actually dealt, nearly all, like Todd, thought it could not possibly happen to them. For a few weeks, something close to hysteria reigned. By the middle of the year, scarcely any of the old people remained.

On the editorial side, it was widely conceded that, like all organizations, *The Times* had some dead wood. Murdoch and Evans went further: they thought the tree was rotten through and through and could be saved only by cutting off as many branches as possible and grafting on new shoots. So Evans took with him from the *Sunday Times* a layer of senior people that he would impose on the old structure, calculating correctly that those who could not bear the new order would take advantage of Murdoch's offer of voluntary severance, leaving him extra gaps that he could fill from his stable of favorites. Edwin Taylor and Oscar Turnill, experts in layout, were brought in to pep up the design. Anthony Holden, the young author of a successful biography of Prince Charles, became features editor. Peter Watson, who used to edit the *Sunday Times* Spectrum pages, took over the Diary. Brian MacArthur, news editor of *The Times* before going to the *Evening Standard* and then the *Sunday Times*, moved back to take charge of the daily at night. Bernard Donoughue, Evans's guru, became assistant editor for policy, a kind of one-man think tank. Adrian Hamilton, Sir Denis's son, was recruited from the *Observer* to edit the Business News section.

One appointment, essentially a by-product of the new influx, provides an illustration of Murdoch's wholesale and indiscriminate approach to the news business. MacArthur's new position made Michael Hamlyn, the previous night editor, effectively redundant and something had to be found for him to do. Between them, Murdoch and Evans decided to make room for MacArthur by appointing Hamlyn as New York bureau chief for all Murdoch's

British and Australian publications. The one bureau would serve the needs of *The Times* and the *Sun,* as well as the *Daily Mirror* and the *Australian* in Sydney, the women's magazines—everything. When it was put to him that the peculiar requirements of *The Times* might need rather more individual attention, Hamlyn would shrug and say, apparently quoting Murdoch, "a story is a story is a story." Unfamiliar Australian bylines began appearing in *The Times*. The move was, in addition, an example of Murdoch's theory of creative tension, of deliberately placing his senior people in positions where conflict with colleagues is inevitable. The Australian papers already had a head of bureau, Ross Waby, whose executive function Hamlyn was to take over—and it was left to Hamlyn himself to break the news to a distraught Waby when he visited New York to cast an eye over his new empire. The man in charge of the New York office of Times Newspapers was Old Etonian Robert Ducas, formerly president of the American subsidiary. While he had no journalistic function, some of his administrative tasks would be reassigned to Hamlyn. Ducas had been invaluable to Evans, an old friend, in organizing American financing for his proposed *Sunday Times* consortium and did receive the courtesy of a telephone call from Evans warning him of Hamlyn's impending arrival and asking him not to make waves.

That day Ducas went to see Murdoch in his office at the *New York Post.* Was it, he ventured, realistic to expect the same New York reporter to be filing for the *Sunday Times* and the *News of the World?* "You know what journos are like," Murdoch replied, "particularly journos overseas. They're bone idle—live off their expenses. I'm not having three people from my group going to cover the landing of the space shuttle: it's absurd." A few weeks later, after raising the question of his reduced status, Ducas was dismissed. A Telex message, with Murdoch's name at its foot, instructed him to vacate his office within forty-eight hours.

Ducas's departure was involuntary; but soon many decided to take the offered severance money—a month's pay for every year of service. The target of thirty was eventually reached, but the offer was kept open and over fifty members of the editorial staff left within the first year.

Evans was conscious of the danger of a rift between the old and new people but did not truly see what he could do to prevent it if he was to change the paper as he wanted. His actions indicated a conviction that hardly any of the old *Times* people were any good at all at journalism as he understood it. Only those he had brought with him were admitted to his confidence.

Evans equates good journalism with energy and bustle. He believes the quality and thoroughness of a piece of reporting are related directly to the amount of chivvying and prodding that has been carried out by him on its authors, and by them on their sources. The technique—he calls it maximum irritation—had worked spectacularly on the string of investigative reports he presided over at the *Sunday Times*. He believes the validity of the technique to be self-evident and is convinced that anyone who winces at it can be motivated only by idleness. But the many old *Times* people who *did* wince admitted to no such motive. They thought—as they had thought of the Thomson changes in the late 1960s—that it was all very silly, not at all what *The Times* ought to be doing, a great deal of energy expended for something that in the end they would prefer not to see in the paper. That dread word "authority" was being muttered darkly again. Often the irritation would get out of hand, as Evans tried to adapt to a paper that appeared daily a technique developed on one that came out once a week. "The trouble with Harry," said one disgruntled staffer, "is not that he won't come to a decision but that he comes to six different decisions on the same subject."

Like all zealots, the newcomers were amazed that the transparent rightness of their concept of journalism was not immediately recognized by the old-timers. They failed to realize that if you come into an organization and tell those in it that what they have been doing for the last umpteen years is quite worthless, a product of a lazy, old-fashioned and pedantic approach, the view is likely to be resisted.

The split widened. At the depressingly frequent farewell parties for departing staff, the new recruits would huddle together, not mixing with the old timers. Evans scarcely discouraged the division. After he had been editor for a few weeks he arranged a boardroom lunch at which Murdoch could meet key journalists, mainly his new people. It produce one telling moment. The conversation had turned to American politics and someone said that, following the defeat of President Carter, the country might be in for a series of one-term presidents. "Then that gives Harry four years," piped up Peter Watson, jocularly. When the chuckles had died down

Murdoch allowed a second or two of silence before rasping: "At the outside!" The laughs this time were hollow and edgy.

On March 11th, 1981, Murdoch was fifty. Anna organized a party at the Cavan ranch, mainly for members of the family. It was an overnight affair and motel rooms were booked for those who could not be put up in the house. It began on the Saturday evening with dancing to a group of country musicians to set the mood; then came an elaborate dinner, followed by twenty minutes of fireworks organized by two Vietnamese refugees Anna had discovered living in the vicinity. The evening ended with a film Anna had organized, made up of clips from newsreels and television profiles, illustrating highlights of Murdoch's life. Next day a small plane flew overhead pulling a streamer that read: HAPPY BIRTHDAY, RUPERT. Sky divers dropped from it and landed on the lawn, to the delight of the young family members. Anna announced her special surprise present—a commission for a portrait of Rupert to be done by his favorite Australian artist, Fred Williams. But for most guests the highlight of the weekend came on the Saturday night, after dinner and before the film, when the birthday cake was brought in for Rupert to cut. It was iced to resemble the front page of *The Times*. Everyone laughed and cheered. *Bon appétit.*

Evans made some cosmetic changes to the paper right away. He began using larger pictures and the layout became clearer and better thought out. A story he could really get his teeth into occurred on March 30th: President Reagan was shot and wounded as he left a Washington hotel after lunch. Evans stayed in the office supervising the development of the story as edition followed edition. By the time of the last edition, the one sold on the streets in London, the front page had been given over entirely to Reagan in a layout of astounding impact. The headline went across all eight columns. Across six columns, just below it, were three pictures, one on top of the other, simulating newsreel clips of the actual shooting. The main report was set across two columns all down the left of the page with articles on other aspects of the shooting lower down on the right, continuing on an inside page. It was all in larger body type than is customary, for extra drama.

The most puzzling and disappointing aspect of the first few months for Evans and Murdoch was that, despite their radical surgery, circulation was scarcely improving. After three months it was still well under 300,000, up only by 13,000 from the figure when they took over. Murdoch gave increasingly gloomy reports to the board at their meetings during the spring and summer. In April he said that losses so far were around two million pounds for Times Newspapers as a whole, but by June the rate of loss was twelve million a year. Advertising was poor, partly because of the reorganization of the department and partly because advertisers had been reluctant to book space ahead during the recent uncertain period. A five pence price rise for the *Sunday Times,* to thirty-five pence, had taken 30,000 off the weekly sale.

He was still confident, though, that the money Evans was spending on editorial changes at *The Times* would eventually be translated into increased circulation and revenue. When, at the April board meeting, he let slip the figure of 500,000 as a target, he was taken to task by alarmed directors who foresaw a replay of the Thomson attempt to popularize the paper in the late 1960s. He hurriedly assured the doubters that half a million was "a distant objective" and there was no intention of moving down market to achieve it.

In September he was still pessimistic. "There have been few bright moments since the purchase by News International," he told directors. All over Fleet Street advertising volume was down. Circulation of both papers was improving only slowly while the three supplements were dipping. The most alarming figure was the circulation of *The Times*, which in July 1981 was less than 4,000 higher than in July 1980, despite the greatly increased editorial expenditure.

The day President Sadat of Egypt was assassinated by members of his army was pivotal not just in the history of the Middle East but also in the history of *The Times*. It happened on October 6th, 1981, the week after the paper's September crisis. Evans took charge in the news room, determined that this should be an even more impressive *tour de force* than the Reagan shooting coverage. Now he had been running the paper for seven months; this time he would show Fleet Street exactly how such big occasions should be handled.

Rushing, shouting, frenzied telephone calls, wild ideas put up and shot down—such signs of incipient panic intensified throughout the late afternoon. Evans and his chief advisers gathered in groups by the foreign desk, the back bench, the features department, all trying to talk at once. Then Evans would march away, leaving a half-formed idea in his wake, and a clutch of people would follow him, waving pieces of paper. As the time for the first edition approached, nobody was at all clear how the front page was to look. The first edition, by general consent, was a disaster—and a late disaster at that. High on the front page was a pointless little story about some relatives of Sadat's in Britain, but it lacked any kind of coherent account of the shooting itself. By the final edition it looked a bit more orderly, with the main story running up and down five columns, a couple of unexciting pictures and a diagram showing the position of Sadat relative to his assassins at the moment of the attack. The whole of pages two and three were given to related stories, with a strip of pictures illustrating Sadat's life across the top of both. That worked well, as did the five-column obituary on the court page. There were two articles about Sadat on the feature page and a long editorial.

In terms of quantity the event had been done justice, but the vital front page contained all the signs of the confusion that had reigned at its creation. In the rush to print the first edition Murdoch took himself down to the stone. "How's it going?" he asked, and was told the news page would be late. "No good producing the best paper in Fleet Street if you can't get it printed on time," Murdoch grumbled. Disillusion with his brilliant but disorganized editor was starting to grow.

Until that night Murdoch's doubts about Evans had been concerned not with his competence but his over-spending. By the end of 1981, fifty-three people had left under the voluntary severance scheme. This was a burden on the bank balance but a one-time burden only. The trouble was that Evans had hired fifty-six new people in their place, nearly all at higher salaries. Murdoch had initially agreed with Evans that it was essential to clear away the dead wood among the staff and introduce new blood. But the essential weakness in all such schemes is that the very deadest wood, the people with scant hope of finding employment elsewhere, cling on stubbornly. Those with marketable abilities pick up their tax-free checks and move on. Thus Murdoch was committed to higher salaries and fat payoffs, with no commensurate increase in the quality of his staff.

During the last months of 1981 relations between the old guard and the new guard grew worse. Evans worked longer and longer hours and became less and less accessible to those old *Times* people who remained. His health was patently deteriorating. In the summer he had married Tina Brown in a well-publicized private ceremony at the Long Island holiday home of his friend Ben Bradlee, editor of the *Washington Post*. But for a newly married couple they saw precious little of each other. He was under pressure from his proprietor above and an increasingly discontented staff below. The stress was barely tolerable.

Evans's distraction during this period is a possible explanation of his acquiescence in a curious maneuver by Murdoch. At a board meeting on December 16th, attended by both Harold Evans and Frank Giles, Murdoch announced that he proposed to remove the titles of their two papers from the ownership of Times Newspapers and vest them in the parent company, News International. The two editors failed to see the possible significance of this move and they raised no objection. The national directors did not attend the meeting and were not informed of the change, finalized five days later at a meeting of only four directors, including Long and Murdoch.

The switch meant that if Murdoch were to put Times Newspapers into liquidation, the titles would not be among the assets available to the receiver. This would prevent a rival publisher from buying them and starting the papers up again. It also appeared to violate the pledges Murdoch had given to Biffen—undertakings that had the force of law—in return for being exempted from examination by the Monopolies Commission. One of the pledges stated that there would be no change in the ownership of the newspapers or any interest in them without consulting the national directors.

The switch did not emerge until Times Newspapers was well into a new labor crisis. On February 8th Murdoch wrote to all the staff saying that unless the unions would agree to six hundred job losses "within days rather than weeks," the papers would close. The alternative, wrote Murdoch, "is no work for anyone and only the statutory minimum payoff." The group stood to lose fifteen million pounds in 1982. "The most dramatic contribution to our loss comes from the fact that we are employing far more people than our competitors." Before leaving for New York on Concorde, Murdoch said he would want negotiations completed within ten days or a fortnight.

The unions at first resisted the measures but within a couple of days attention was temporarily diverted from the industrial difficulties when rumors of the switch of the newspaper titles began to circulate. On February 10th Long was asked separately by journalists at *The Times* and *Sunday Times* who owned the titles, and he said he would have to check—despite having been at the meeting where they were shifted to News International.

It was William Rees-Mogg who initiated the public outcry. He had no formal status in the matter, but as one of the vetting committee who had cleared the way for Murdoch's proprietorship he felt some residual responsibility and was unwilling to let the maneuver slip past as a *fait accompli,* as Murdoch may have hoped. On February 13th he wrote to John Biffen, the Trade Secretary, declaring the transfer of the titles to be unlawful because the national directors had not been consulted. In an interview with the *Observer,* Rees-Mogg said: "What Rupert wants is to liquidate the present company and keep the titles to himself. That is clearly his intention." If it was, he was thwarted, for in the face of criticism Murdoch retreated swiftly. He accepted that the matter was a legitimate one for the national directors and when they did not agree to the move it was reversed.

In other matters, though, he was getting his own way. His decision to brazen it out with the unions coincided with his conviction that editorial changes were needed on both papers. The *Sunday Times* had predictably lost much of its bounce since Evans's departure. Ron Hall and Hugo Young were not, as he had hoped, vying with each other to displace Frank Giles. Young had none of the practical expertise to replace Evans's flair for layout and presentation, and he did not try. Murdoch, in any case, did not warm to him: too cerebral, the kind of person, he suspected, who was saying clever, superior things about him behind his back, to politicians and the like. As for Hall, although skilled in those technical areas where Giles and Young were weakest, he was disinclined to get involved in running the paper. Murdoch was egging him on to "use your elbows" against Giles. "How are those elbows going, Ron?" he would ask when they met, with a wink and the hint of a leer. The truth was that Hall was keeping them closely tucked to his sides. Convinced Giles's editorship would fail, he wanted to distance himself from it rather than try to redeem it. Murdoch became impatient.

While nobody expected Giles to be as forceful an editor as Evans, it was a surprise that *The Times,* too, should be suffering from lack of leadership. Evans was away from the office for a period after Christmas, recovering from an injury sustained when putting up decorations at his house. Douglas-Home was taking a month-long sabbatical, leaving Brian MacArthur in charge. When Murdoch phoned from Australia or New York he would be connected to MacArthur and was impressed with his competence. Perhaps here was a man with elbows sharp enough to nudge Giles into producing a better paper. Using the pretext of dispute over a new women's section in the magazine, Murdoch had Giles dismiss Hall and appoint MacArthur as deputy editor, leapfrogging Young, who was relegated to number three in the hierarchy to the dismay of his colleagues, who tried to get Biffen to intervene here, too. Young scowled and bore it.

Murdoch's demand to the unions for manning cuts was made in the most dramatic way possible. He sent his hectoring letter to each staff member and to union leaders and, as he climbed aboard Concorde, announced: *"The Times* is not for sale. We will just close it if we don't have agreement." Owen O'Brien, the general secretary of NATSOPA, pointed to the difference, as he saw it, between this warning and those periodically issued by Thomson's. "The trouble is that Mr. Murdoch is not someone who usually cries wolf. Our experience is that when he says something he usually seems to mean it." Barry Fitzpatrick, head of the clerical chapel on the *Sunday Times,* was blunter. He said Murdoch's plans amounted to a "straightforward mugging." John Mitchell, secretary of the London machine branch of NATSOPA, said: "We can conclude that Mr. Murdoch is trying to put a facade over his real desires, which seem to be to let *The Times* and the *Sunday Times* go."

The talks continued in Murdoch's absence and little progress was made. On February 18th the company announced that the number of applications for voluntary severance had fallen short of the 600 needed. Two days later Murdoch, now back in London, said: "The state of negotiations remains bleak. If the deadlock is not broken we shall have to close the two papers. There are no plans to reopen them."

Deadlines were made and extended. Murdoch was now playing a more personal role in the talks and figured in one incident that immediately became part of trade union lore, enhancing his reputation among workers. The leader of the machine-room chapel at the *Sunday Times* was Roy (Ginger) Wilson, a strapping Cockney, more than six feet tall, noted for his colorful use of language. After working the Saturday night shift at the *Sunday Times,* he was asked to go back to the office at 10 a.m. on Sunday for talks with Murdoch. He did so, but the day wore on and he was not summoned. His patience snapped and he stormed into Murdoch's office, with Owen O'Brien trailing behind. Murdoch, who had been sitting pensively behind his large desk, put out a hand and said: "Good to see you."

"Good to see me?" stormed Wilson, using an abusive oath. "Good to see me? I've been working all night making your [expletive] profits and you [expletive] keep me hanging about here. Good to see me?"

Murdoch grinned broadly. "Sit down," he said. "You're just the kind of man I can do business with."

It was mid-March before the business was completed and Murdoch was able to announce that the future of the papers was secure, with 70 percent of his proposed reductions agreed. This meant 430 jobs and more than 400 shifts abolished, for a cut of some eight million pounds in the annual wage bill.

By this time a new drama was under way, more gripping than the battle with the unions because it was a personal struggle between Murdoch and his star editor, Harold Evans. In *The Times* of March 12th the report of the successful outcome of the labor negotiations carried this cryptic paragraph at its foot: "Mr. Harold Evans, the editor of *The Times,* said he had no comment to make on reports circulating about his future as editor. He was on duty last night as usual."

The reports referred to had been circulating for a month. They began in February with hints in the *Daily Express* and the fornightly satirical magazine *Private Eye.* The *Private Eye* story said Murdoch had already informed the board that he was thinking of removing Evans. Murdoch was persuaded to respond swiftly and unambiguously, calling the rumors "malicious, self-serving and wrong," and adding: "Mr. Evans's outstanding qualities and journalistic skills are recognized throughout the world, as are his improvements to *The Times* over the past twelve months."

Indeed they were, in particular by the Granada Television program *What the Papers Say*. In Granada's annual awards, announced the following week, Evans was named Editor of the Year. No such award can ever have been less opportune. In his acceptance speech Evans felt obliged to refer both to the rumors about his departure and Murdoch's threat to close the papers. Returning to the office, he addressed a mass meeting of the staff, stressing that the award was really for them rather than him, and handing his medal round for the journalists to touch. They were less than impressed, preferring to quiz Evans on his role in the attempted transfer of the titles. The mood was sullen, not festive.

The breach between Evans and the majority of his staff had now become more open and more personal than that between Rees-Mogg and the White Swan group twelve years earlier. The issue was the same, but the White Swan people had not aimed their anger directly at the editor, whom they saw was not himself wholly committed to the Thomson strategy. Evans, though, *was* the new strategy, the man whose idea, shared with the proprietor, was to make *The Times* attractive to readers of the *Daily Telegraph* and the Sunday color supplements by introducing features that could have served equally well in the *Telegraph* or the supplements themselves.

Since Christmas, Holden and Donoughue, Evans's closest allies, had become convinced of a plot to have Evans dismissed, and they suspected that Douglas-Home, his deputy, was part of it. They detected a more abrasive, less co-operative attitude from him when he returned from his sabbatical in mid-January. Donoughue summoned Douglas-Home and put to him directly the suggestion that he was working to undermine Evans.

Douglas-Home became angry. He not only denied the allegation but avowed in strong terms that he would never edit a paper for Murdoch, whom he believed to be a "monster" and the cause of most of the disruption at *The Times* and *Sunday Times*. Murdoch's technique, as he saw it, was to break up useful combinations and alliances in his companies, in case they should ever become a threat to him. Douglas-Home repeated his assurance to Evans and, at a second meeting with Donoughue, said he was finding things so difficult he was thinking of resigning.

Evans would have had nothing to fear from Douglas-Home or anyone had he been able to rely on the loyalty of his patron. That he could not depend on Murdoch's backing was the crucial weakness in his position. Evans's allies were right to detect a move against him, but the instigator was his proprietor rather than his deputy. By the end of the year, Murdoch had become convinced that Evans was not the man to produce the low-cost, higher-circulation paper he wanted. However sincerely they had persuaded themselves and each other, in the heady days of the previous winter, that their views on quality journalism were essentially the same, it was now apparent that they were sharply and fatally at variance.

Murdoch has, at root, a conviction that although readers of serious newspapers may want them packaged soberly, in essence they are no different from readers of his tabloids, looking to their daily paper for entertainment. Hence his emphasis on improving sports and features coverage. Evans is at heart a serious journalist who believes the press can play a beneficial role in society by exposing injustices and conscientiously reporting the truth, unbiased by political preconceptions. In Murdoch's view, an expanding readership is the only yardstick of success in a newspaper and it is arrogant of journalists to suggest otherwise. Evans, although skilled at producing papers that are readable and popular as well as important, does not shrink from making intellectual demands on readers if he believes that is what the story requires.

At the beginning, they concealed this contradiction by reminding each other of the points on which they did agree. They both admired clear, simple reporting, and thus could mutually decry "fancy writing." They both thought journalism a matter of energy and therefore could denounce those staff members they saw as lazy. But gradually the differences began to show. Evans recalls in his book how he was proud of a long story in *The Times* about Poland and pointed it out to the proprietor.

Murdoch sneered and showed him three paragraphs on the same subject in *The Sun,* saying that in his view that was enough space to devote to it.

In February, with their relationship visibly deteriorating, Evans tried to retrieve the situation by sending Murdoch a long and self-congratulatory report on his achievements in his first year, which included persuading three well-known journalists to leave. The trio were, he wrote, "all bone idle." Murdoch, in a terse reply, said he was "frankly disturbed" by the decision of the three to quit. "They are names long associated with *The Times* and they should not be lost without a great deal of thought."

It was evident that Murdoch was looking for a pretext to pounce. He found it when John Grant, the managing editor, demoralized by his rows with Evans and Long over money, decided to apply for his payoff. Grant confided his intention to Douglas-Home, who found this further erosion of the core of the old guard more than he could bear. He told Grant that he too would quit if Grant went through with his plan, but first he decided to talk to Murdoch, who saw this as the opening he needed. Told that both the deputy editor and managing editor wanted to resign, he advised Douglas-Home to defer a final decision. There might, he said, be a change in the offing.

Murdoch asked for Evans's resignation on March 9th, 1982. "Why?" Evans asked. "The place is in chaos. You can't see the wood for the trees and the senior staff are in turmoil," Murdoch replied. Evans, by now quite unnerved, made a pathetic attempt to retrieve the situation two days later when he sent a memorandum to Murdoch and the board telling them that the Chancellor of the Exchequer, Sir Geoffrey Howe, had praised the paper's coverage of his annual budget statement, which had "restored *The Times* as a newspaper of record for the first time for many years."

Murdoch was not going to be swayed by Evans's protestations of his brilliance, and it became clear that the editor would have to go. He declined to go quietly and pointed out that if he was dismissed he would expect a substantial golden handshake.

Murdoch's initial offer was £25,000, half his annual salary. Evans wanted nearly ten times that; but as news of the attempt to dislodge him spread, he and his allies insisted that the dispute was not over money but over Murdoch's right to dismiss him so summarily. Should the national directors not be brought into it?

Murdoch had taken the precaution of giving the directors advance warning of his intention. "I have to admit that Lord Dacre

was right and I was wrong," he told them. "Mea culpa, mea culpa."
The directors agreed that a resignation was a matter between the
editor and the proprietor. If the editor felt improper pressure had
been exerted on him, it was up to him to complain to the national
directors and they would take it from there. Evans did raise the issue
informally with Lord Robens. Spurred by Donoughue, he ensured
his departure was played out publicly. Anthony Holden, emerging
as Evans's spokesman, said there had been political pressure. He
claimed that Murdoch had expressed his dismay at Evans's and
Donoughue's apparent support for the new Social Democratic Party,
and at the liberal tone of editorials on racial matters and foreign
affairs, specifically Poland and El Salvador.

Donoughue claimed to have heard on his shadowy "network"
of contacts that Margaret Thatcher, the Prime Minister, had expressed displeasure at this centrist drift, and that Murdoch had
promised her that *The Times* would be firmly in her camp by Easter.
In his book, Evans maintains that she had been thinking of offering
him the chairmanship of the Sports Council to get him away from
Gray's Inn Road.

Evans's terminal negotiations with Murdoch were acrimonious.
When Holden dropped into the editor's office he found Richard
Searby, Murdoch's urbane, long-time friend and lawyer, ordering
Evans in unambiguous and abusive terms to vacate his chair for
Douglas-Home. The outspoken Searby has a special place in the
demonology of the Evans camp, based partly on his once having
told Tina Brown that the paper her husband edited was "a smelly
rag." (Searby denied making the remark in a letter to *The Times* in
1983, but Evans repeats the assertion in his book *Good Times, Bad
Times.*)

The drama was gaining increasing public attention. Radio and
television teams and reporters from rival papers were constant
visitors to Gray's Inn Road, and cameras were placed almost
permanently outside. On that same Friday, Evans was intercepted on
his way to the office by a radio reporter and managed to sustain a
chirpy mood. "I am editing *The Times* and I'm going to do that
now," he said. "And as Mark Twain said, rumors of my death have
been greatly exaggerated."

Next day, the right-hand column of the front page was headed
"The Times and its editorship." It began: "A day of speculation

about the editorship of *The Times* ended inconclusively last night."
Murdoch was reported as saying that terms had been agreed for
Evans's departure, but the editor continued to deny it, saying: "It is
and has been an argument about principle and the constitution of *The
Times* as agreed in the articles of association laid before Parliament." Anthony Holden said there had been a series of policy
disagreements between Evans and Murdoch but Murdoch denied
this: "At no point has there been any difference, stated or otherwise,
between Mr. Evans and myself about the policy of the paper," he
said.

Next day the Sunday papers carried articles based on the
assumption that Evans was about to go. The lunchtime radio
program, "The World This Weekend," contained a long segment on
the dispute. Among those interviewed was Lord Robens, who gave
the first public explanation of the position of the national directors.
If Evans felt he was being unfairly pressed to resign, he asserted, he
could approach them, but he had not done so and "it is not possible
for the national directors, on rumors that he may have resigned, to
take any action at all.... The initiative, if Harold Evans thinks he is
being pressurized or persecuted, is certainly with Harold
Evans.... He is the most protected editor in the world. He can't be
forced to resign if he thinks it's improper pressure."

It was not true that Evans had made no approach to the national
directors. By now he had discussed the matter with all of them
except Pickering. But despite his fury he could see the wisdom of
the advice Lord Robens and others were giving him: that it was
futile to fight to keep a job where he would constantly be at
loggerheads with his proprietor.

The next person interviewed in the program was Geoffrey
Smith, a leader writer, a pillar of the old guard and a committee
member of JOTT, the organization of *Times* journalists that on
Saturday had taken the unusual step of issuing a statement urging
their editor to resign and make way for Douglas-Home. "Our
concern is that the gradual erosion of editorial standards from within
might leave us with no paper worth saving," they wrote. "The way
the paper is laid out and run has changed so frequently that stability
has been destroyed."

Smith, quivering with self-righteousness, had something more
gripping than that to read to Sunday radio listeners. "I have here,"

he began, echoing Neville Chamberlain, "a copy of a memo sent by Harold Evans to the chairman Mr. Rupert Murdoch on February 24th this year. It concerns the coverage of the Budget in *The Times* this year." Evans was asking Murdoch his views on how the Budget should be reported in *The Times* and it was soon clear that Smith's motive was to combat Holden's claim that Murdoch's reason for wanting to be rid of Evans was political.

"Here is the editor," Smith raged, "going to the proprietor for his guidance on what are matters of editorial decision. I do not believe it is possible to say that the man who wrote that letter is the man who must remain as editor if the editorial independence of the paper is to continue." The next extract was tamer. Evans was asking Murdoch's opinion of an idea for a series of articles and concluded: "If you like the idea, I'll take it further."

Said Smith: "That does not sound to me like an editor eager to preserve the independence of his office.... It doesn't sound to me like an editor behaving like an independent person in the way that is traditional with the holding of that office." The explanation for the memos was not as sinister as that; indeed it was a bit pathetic. Because Evans was finding it harder and harder to get Murdoch to talk to him on the telephone, he was forced to consult him by memorandum—a form of communication Murdoch dislikes and seldom uses. All the same, the introduction of secret documents gave the affair a conspiratorial flavor, recalling Watergate.

By the following day Evans had still not confirmed his resignation, though Douglas-Home was effectively editing the paper. Smith's reading of the editor's memoranda on the radio had heightened the atmosphere of suspicion and unreality. In his book, Evans maintains that his private secretary was suborned by Douglas-Home and was giving detailed reports about the people who had been to see him and his telephone callers.

The first edition of *The Times* that night carried an announcement to the effect that Evans was still editor, but by the time the paper appeared that was no longer true. He had alerted Independent Television News to be ready for a statement at 9 p.m., in time for their News at Ten. The cameras were in place outside his office when he left it. "The differences between me and Mr. Murdoch should not be prolonged," he told the nation. "I am, therefore, resigning tonight as editor of *The Times*. I have enormously enjoyed my fifteen years as editor of the *Sunday Times* and *The Times,* and I look forward to a future as exciting and interesting."

Back home in Pimlico, South London, Evans's wife Tina had organized a party to keep everyone's spirits up. Apart from professional colleagues like Donoughue, Holden and Ron Hall, the guests included Melvyn Bragg, the novelist, and John Mortimer, the playwright and lawyer. A little after 9:30 p.m. Evans arrived clutching a piece of paper and everyone went quiet. "I have just made this statement to ITN," he announced gravely, and then read it out again. Someone turned on the television and after a few minutes the guests saw the scene re-enacted. They noticed that the cameras had lighted on one of Evans's secretaries, sobbing quietly.

Murdoch might have been weeping as well: he had to pay Evans a six-figure sum in compensation. But the proprietor said nothing in public. Certainly, it was a while since he had last described Evans as the greatest editor in Fleet Street. Murdoch had proved that an editor can only be as great as his proprietor allows him to be. It was an expensive way to make a point.

Within weeks the most important of the men Evans brought with him had left. Holden resigned in sympathy, with no payoff, while Donoughue was asked to leave because he had not informed the paper in time for the first edition that Evans planned to quit. Peter Watson, who had been in New York only a few weeks, was told his job no longer existed. Adrian Hamilton gave up the editorship of Business News.

In the week of Evans's resignation, Holden and Murdoch confronted each other at a cocktail party where the Queen and Prince Philip were the chief guests. Holden approached Murdoch pugnaciously and said he was "a deeply misguided man" for having ditched Evans. "You will never work for me again," Murdoch fumed, and stalked away. Holden rushed off to tell the story of the encounter to a circle that included Prince Philip, with whom he had become acquainted while writing his book about Prince Charles. Philip was enthralled at Holden's tale of derring-do, of bearding the fearsome beast. "Hmm," he told the assembled company inscrutably, "I used to know Murdoch's father."

As for *The Times,* it had fended off one more attempt to compromise its character. An old *Times* man, an aristocrat to boot, was now in charge, and his supporters claimed their rewards. John

Grant spent his last nine months on the paper as deputy editor, with the promise that after he retired he could edit the crossword. The counter-revolution was complete.

Evans's book, *Good Times, Bad Times,* published in October 1983, provoked no formal response from Murdoch, despite the monstrous picture Evans painted of his former proprietor. He was, however, persuaded to comment by Terry McCrann in an interview in the Melbourne *Age.* Murdoch asserted that Evans would go into his office, gesticulate and rattle off a series of half-finished and meaningless sentences: "You've done all this and what can we do...you don't know...what are we..." Then Evans would say: "You must come here more often. It's wonderful to have you here." Murdoch imitated Evans returning to his own office, holding his head in his hands and saying: "My God, the *pressure* I'm under. You don't know."

This was the same interview in which Murdoch made a remarkable attack on Mrs. Thatcher—whom Evans had accused of complicity in his dismissal. Murdoch was bewildered by her failure to support President Reagan over the American landing on the Caribbean island of Grenada. "She's gone out of her mind," Murdoch said. "I don't know what she's about. I just think she's very overtired. I know it sounds silly but I think it is a very human thing.... She's run out of puff. She's not listening to any of her friends."

With friends like Rupert...

NINE

Westward with Wingo

The problem with American journalism is that they simply
don't know how to compete. They all go to journalism school
and listen to failed editors dressed up as professors.
—*Rupert Murdoch interviewed in the Melbourne* Age,
November 1983

Scarcely had Murdoch wiped away the blood from the Evans
skirmish than he was in the thick of another battle in New York. The
circulation struggle between the *Post* and the *News* had intensified in
the second half of 1980 and been at a high pitch since. It was, on the
face of it, an unbalanced and an unlikely contest. On one side was
the powerful *News*, long established as a monopoly in the morning
tabloid field, owned by the mighty *Chicago Tribune* and boasting
the largest daily circulation in the country excepting the *Wall Street
Journal*. Against it, the *Post*, had scarcely half its sales and,
proportionately, even less advertising. Yet the *News* management
were worried by the *Post*, almost to the point of obsession.

Part of this was due to what they saw as Murdoch's blatant
treachery over the 1978 strike, but mostly it was a product of his
fearsome reputation, embellished by tall tales told in journalists'
bars and by his own boasting. "We will bleed them to death in five
years," he said of the *Daily News* in 1981, an echo of the boast his
father made—and made good—in Melbourne some fifty years
earlier.

The *News* people could not blame Murdoch entirely, or even chiefly, for their horrific plunge in circulation in the 1970s. The paper began the decade selling more than two million copies a day and three million on Sundays. By 1981 the daily circulation had gone down by 600,000 and on Sunday by a full million. Not all the lost readers had switched to the *Post*. What was really hurting the *News* was the changing population pattern of New York. Working-class readers were leaving the declining outer boroughs as fast as they could afford to. They moved to Long Island, Westchester and New Jersey, where they switched to thriving papers like Long Island's *Newsday*. As the old readers died their college-educated children subscribed to the *Times* or the *Wall Street Journal,* papers that served their interests better.

But Murdoch is a great tease. Colleagues recall how he used to chivvy Lord Ryder of the *Mirror* at meetings of the Newspaper Publishers' Association in London. Now he lost no opportunity in sniping at the *News* in public, mocking it for going over the head of its audience, boasting of his aim to drive his rival out of business, or even buy it himself.

Since Murdoch's abortive attempt to start a morning paper during the strike, executives at the *News* had convinced themselves he would try again or that he intended, by progressively advancing the printing time of his first edition, to turn the *Post* into a twenty-four hour newspaper. In the summer of 1980 they decided to make a preemptive assault. They announced that the *Daily News* would start an evening edition, called *Tonight*. It would seek to be everything they felt the *Post* was not—lively yet intelligent, aimed at Bloomingdales' shoppers rather than shoplifters. It would have the closing market prices, an authoritative business section and up-market consumer features, to attract *New York Times* readers on their way home. Some twenty million dollars was budgeted for the launch and the initial circulation target set at a modest 200,000. With a nice sense of retribution, the *News* people hired Clay Felker as editor.

The concept of *Tonight* had been devised by marketing strategists, but to those unversed in their mysteries there were some peculiar things about it. For one, it was going to be sold at newsstands only in Manhattan south of Harlem. The traditional *News* readership in the outer boroughs was to be ignored. Part of the reason for this decision lay in another dubious strategy. *Tonight* was not to be an entirely separate paper but an afternoon edition of the *News,* carrying many of the same feature articles as next day's morning paper. That is why there was no real attempt to sell it where the *News* already had a strong hold on the morning market.

Murdoch is energized by such blatant declarations of hostility. As soon as he had wind of the *News's* plan he summoned meeting after meeting of his executives to devise a counter-strategy.

"It was educational to watch him," one of them recalls. "He's not like most people expect in this kind of situation. He's fairly quiet, solicits opinions and listens. He asks a lot of questions. But he has incredible instincts and there's always a point at which he makes up his mind and that's it. He operates with almost a total absence of internal memoranda and stuff like that. He doesn't believe in channels. He'll pick up the phone and call directly. Most big companies are gorged with bureaucratic nonsense on paper but the *New York Post* is not."

When David Schneiderman went for one of his infrequent meetings about the *Village Voice,* he found Murdoch bubbling with enthusiasm for the impending battle with the *News,* asking advice on what moves he should make. "He was like a general in a war," Schneiderman remembers, and it was only with difficulty that he was able to steer the conversation round to the *Voice* at all.

The main decision was to meet the challenge by printing the *Post* earlier in the morning, to compete with the *News* on the newsstands and on railway stations while people were on their way to work. The time of the first edition was advanced to 7 a.m. There was a debate on whether to reduce the price from thirty cents to twenty-five. Most people advised him not to, but Murdoch, always a low-price enthusiast, did it anyway. As a result of these moves the *Post* won about 100,000 new readers, roughly the sales figure *Tonight* settled at after the curiosity impact had worn off. The *Post*'s price cut meant it would be out of the question for the *News* and *Tonight* to go up to thirty cents. With their large combined circulation, this cost them much more than the *Post* forfeited by its reduction.

Felker did not prove a judicious choice as editor. His recent experience and his greatest success had been with magazines. Many felt he might not be strong in news gathering and presentation—areas that are paramount in all newspapers but especially tabloids that appear in the afternoon. Most of his major hirings were of columnists and feature writers, such as Richard Reeves and Gary Wills, skilled at turning out exquisitely crafted and thoughtful articles of several thousand words—splendid stuff, but not the kind needed in an afternoon paper, which must first of all be a fast read. Of the handful of writers he lured from the *Post,* the most notable was Claudia Cohen, the successful young editor of the page six gossip column that had been one of Murdoch's earliest innovations. The circumstances of her departure illustrate the fervor with which Murdoch was conducting the war.

Roger Wood, the editor, was away on the day she announced she was leaving, so she handed her notice to John Van Doorn, deputizing for him. When Wood phoned to ask how things were going, Van Doorn told him about Cohen. "You'd better call Rupert," said Wood, although Van Doorn had not thought it necessary to inform the publisher of anything so trivial. Murdoch was in the South of France, but Van Doorn took the advice and phoned him. "Good," said Murdoch when he was told. "Have her out of the office by tomorrow." Van Doorn protested that she had given the required two weeks' notice and he saw no need to rush things. "Get her out, get her out," Murdoch insisted, apparently fearing she would use her final two weeks to damage the paper, to hit back at her enemies or steal secrets to take across to the *News.* Murdoch reinforced the instruction with a call to Wood, who phoned Van Doorn again. Cohen left within a couple of days.

Van Doorn sees that as evidence that Murdoch has an essential dislike of journalists. Soon after his arrival as managing editor he had a small problem with reporters who left for home after work without checking with him or another senior editor. He wrote a wry memorandum reminding the offenders of the news-room tradition of getting a "goodnight" from the news editor. Murdoch found this cordial approach to staff infuriating. "You treat them like that and they'll come after you," he said. "No sense in being funny, they'll get after you." This is consistent with his observation to Robert Ducas, when head of the *London Times* office in New York, that journalists are chronically idle.

It was soon clear that *Tonight* had been badly misconceived. It was not simply the long features; it just did not look newsy. The front page was too sedate, lacking the compelling urgency of the

Post's screaming headlines. And there was a confusion of identity with the morning paper. Readers could not remember whether the features and special sections duplicated those in that morning's *News* or the next morning's. Part of its circulation was taken from the old late-night edition of the *News,* on sale as people left theaters, cinemas and restaurants. They bought that because it was the next morning's paper. They were getting a jump on the news. That edition was stopped when *Tonight* was launched, but fewer night-owls were attracted to an afternoon paper, several hours stale.

By the spring of 1981 it was apparent that *Tonight* was a failure. Its circulation had struggled to barely over 100,000 copies a day and had then dropped below 80,000. They were having trouble giving it away: commuters from Westchester and Long Island were being handed coupons entitling them to take it free for a week, but even that did not convert many of them. When the sales figures for the six months ending on March 31st were available, the *Post* was able to trumpet that its circulation was up to 732,158 from 654,314 a year earlier.

Over the same period, despite the launch of *Tonight,* figures for the *News* were lower, at 1,491,556, as against 1,554,604 for the six months ending March 31st, 1980. Felker was replaced as editor of *Tonight* by Dick Oliver, a man with a background in hard news, and the paper became thinner as the controlling company in Chicago decided to cut losses. On August 15th, 1981, Michael O'Neill, the executive editor of the *News,* and Robert Hunt, the publisher, called the staff together in the news room and announced emotionally that *Tonight* would cease publication at the end of the month. Hunt had other rigorous measures to reveal—a wage freeze for all and a cut of 10 percent in the salaries of the company's eleven senior executives.

This substantial victory for Murdoch was sweetened by another success he was enjoying that summer. A few years earlier he had teamed up with the Australian film producer Robert Stigwood in a company called Associated R. & R. Films. (The initials are for Rupert and Robert. Had they used their surnames it would have come out as S. & M., indicative of films of a less proper kind than they planned.) Their first production was Peter Weir's *Gallipoli,* and Murdoch admitted that he had been drawn to it because of his father's role in that campaign. The film was released in New York in 1981 and was a deserved success. Lines formed outside the cinema on Third Avenue and 59th Street, where it had its first run, and Murdoch was not to know that at the end of some performances faint hissing could be heard from the audience when his name came up on the credits. That image problem again.

Although the *Post* had trounced *Tonight,* it was still losing more money than his other American enterprises were making. He was certain by now that the only way he could significantly increase his share of city advertising, short of driving the *News* off the market altogether, was to force his circulation up still further. There were already some phenomenal days when the *Post* was selling all it was physically capable of printing: on the day President Sadat was assassinated they sold 1,050,000 copies, but that was an isolated event. To try for a longer-lasting increase Murdoch turned to a device that had proved effective, though horribly expensive, in London and Australia: bingo.

This is a perfect gambling game for newspapers because it obliges players to buy the paper every day to see whether they have won. Long popular in Britain, where the non-newspaper variant is played in hundreds of converted cinemas all over the country, it involves each player checking numbers against a personal card. The first to check a complete line, or the whole card, wins the prize. Since in the newspaper version the numbers are available only in the paper, it is a cast-iron circulation builder.

The 1981 bingo craze began in Britain. It started on the *Daily Star,* a tabloid launched by Trafalgar House, the new owners of Express Newspapers. The *Star* was aimed at the bottom end of the market, competing directly with Murdoch's *Sun,* even to the extent of publishing daily pictures of nude women. But its circulation stuck at around a million—less than a third that of the *Sun* and the *Daily Mirror*—until the introduction of bingo. The *Daily Star* management mailed a million cards to householders, pointing out that the only way to find out whether they were winners was to buy the paper. Circulation rose by 75,000 within a week, and continued to climb.

Murdoch, characteristically, decided to fight back on a more ambitious scale. The *Sun* was to have a bingo game that every person in Britain would have the chance to play. Cards were mailed to every household in the country. Prizes would total a million pounds in the first few weeks. The impact on circulation was so sensational that the *Daily Mirror* had no alternative but to join in as well. The game, or versions of it, spread to London's two more sober tabloids, the *Mail* and the *Express*. Now everyone had to have bingo, just to keep up with the others. Once started, it was hard to see how the games could be abandoned without a mutual self-denying agreement among the proprietors—a device foreign to Murdoch's nature. He prefers to continue the games, and the drain of funds they involve, believing that his opponents will weaken before he does, and he will reap the reward. If bingo expenditures were to force the *Daily Star* to close, the *Sun* would be the beneficiary. It is part of the philosophy that makes Murdoch an advocate of uneconomic cover prices.

Delighted with the initial success of the London bingo promotion, Murdoch decided to do the same in Sydney, where it would, he saw, be an ideal way for his *Daily Mirror* to steal a march on its afternoon rival, the *Sun*. It worked there too and, like his London competitors, the *Sun* in Sydney had to improvise its own bingo game in the race.

From there, New York was a natural progression. With the *Daily News* demoralized by the closure of *Tonight*, it was time to press home the advantage. At the beginning of September 1981 the *Post* began mailing a sheet of weekly cards to every household in New York city and some of the inner suburbs—more than six million altogether. The name bingo was unavailable for copyright reasons, so it was called Wingo. At the *News,* something close to panic set in when they first caught wind of what Murdoch was planning. They threw together a rival game, calling it Zingo. If they were to compete they had no time to plan their own mailing, so the cards were printed in the paper itself and promoted by intensive television advertising. This is less effective than direct mailing, where the potential player has the card in hand, uncertain whether it is a winner of thousands of dollars but having to spend only twenty-five cents a day to find out. In the early stages the *Post*'s circulation vaulted by some 200,000 to nearly a million a day. The *News* put on readers, too—but fewer. As the circulation gap between the two papers narrowed, the *News* continued to be afflicted by a debilitating hemorrhage of confidence until in December 1981 the Chicago Tribune Company announced that it was for sale. It was still the largest-selling city newspaper in America but now it was limping and bruised, its spirit damaged, apparently mortally, by its brush with the formidable Australian. It had lost eleven million dollars in 1981 and the projections were for losses of thirty million in 1982 and fifty million in 1983. Not surprisingly, there was no immediate rush of buyers, but in the first weeks of 1982 a number of corporations were said to have made discreet inquiries.

On March 31st it was announced that Joseph Allbritton, a tough, fifty-seven-year-old Texas millionaire, would buy the *News* provided he could negotiate cost savings with the printing unions. Allbritton had bought the Washington *Star* in 1974, before selling it at a loss four years later to *Time* magazine, who have since closed it. In 1981 he bought the *Trenton Times* in New Jersey and made Draconian cuts in staffing. On April 5th he said he wanted to shed 1,600 of the 3,800 unionized full-time workers on the *News,* saving eighty-five million dollars from the 200-million-dollar annual payroll. Stanton Cook, President of the Chicago Tribune Company, commented: "If these negotiations fail we see no alternative but to cease publication of the *News."*

The Allied Printing Trades Council had since the 1978 strike engaged the inevitable Theodore Kheel as their permanent adviser. Kheel could see that Cook's naming of Allbritton as the buyer of last resort made the union's negotiating position dangerously weak. To offset that, he persuaded the Allied to investigate purchasing the *News* themselves under an Employee Stock Ownership Plan (ESOP)—a scheme offering tax advantages to companies selling stock to trusts for the benefit of employees. The union leaders, though, were nervous about such a departure from tradition and doubted whether they were capable of running the paper without a proper proprietor.

At about this time Kheel was at a dinner party in Manhattan and sat next to Donald Kummerfeld, president of News America, Murdoch's American operation. "It occurs to me that if the *News* survives, the *Post* will be in trouble," Kheel told Kummerfeld, to whom the thought had certainly occurred also. Kheel went on to say that the unions he represented were almost as concerned for the future of the *Post* as for the *News,* although it provided substantially fewer jobs for their members. "Why not call Rupert?" Kummerfeld suggested.

Relations between Kheel and Murdoch, having reached their nadir during the 1978 strike, had improved since the settlement of

Kheel's libel action against *New York* magazine—a settlement that some felt was made at the expense of the article's author, Richard Karp. The possibility of bringing Murdoch in as a second bidder, to outflank the *New*'s strategy of dealing only with Allbritton, had been dawning on Kheel for some time. The thought crystalized when Kheel and the unions were allowed to see the letter of intent Allbritton had signed to buy the paper.

As Kheel saw it, the terms offered meant that the Tribune Company were in effect paying the Texan to take the paper off their hands. In return for shouldering the potential burden of some thirty-seven million dollars in severance pay and around fifty million dollars of unfunded pension liability, Allbritton would receive assets worth about seventy-five million dollars. He was risking very little and, if he succeeded in negotiating the staff cuts he planned, he could make a profit of eighteen million dollars in his first year.

Kheel did not contact Murdoch directly but instead telephoned Martin Fischbein, his former employee, then a senior executive at the *Post*. (Fischbein died in a motor accident in 1983.) "Do you know the *News* is up for grabs for nothing?" Kheel inquired. A meeting was arranged between Kheel, Murdoch and George McDonald, the president of Allied, at Murdoch's apartment. Further meetings took place at the University Club, the restaurant "21" and other fashionable midtown locations. It was agreed that Murdoch should express his interest in buying the papers, possibly in partnership with the proposed ESOP.

The union leaders preferred Murdoch to Allbritton, largely because he was the devil they knew. For sure, he was a tough negotiator but at the end the deal was always struck. Allbritton was an unknown quantity. The outcome they sought most fervently was for the Tribune Company to change its mind and continue publishing the *News*, but Murdoch would be a good second best. They recognized the risk that he would close one of the two papers once he had acquired both; but there was in any case always the danger that after they agreed to Allbritton's manning cuts one of the papers would close anyway, leaving the other with a much reduced staff.

On April 7th Murdoch gave a press conference to stress that, to defend his trading position, he would have to insist on manning concessions at the *Post* equal to any negotiated for the *News*. The *Post*, he said, had lost twenty million dollars in 1981 despite its increased circulation. Asked why he had not sought such cuts

before, he replied that he had not then thought it possible to achieve
them. He said: "I feel passionately that the *News* ought to survive
and the *Post* ought to survive too." He left it to McDonald to make
public the suggestion that he might bid for the *News*. Murdoch,
although by now virtually committed to a bid, said for the record
only that he would think about it. Allbritton was furious at
McDonald's move. He suspended talks with the unions, although
the Tribune Company reiterated that the paper would close if he did
not buy it.

There was never any real doubt that Murdoch would go along
with McDonald's and Kheel's suggestion. Here was the chance to
end at a stroke the losses on the *Post,* which clearly could not
continue indefinitely at their present rate. What is more, a monopoly
of the New York tabloid press would put him in the pleasing position
of being able to turn his nose up at advertisers too proud to do
business with him: now it would be him or nobody. It was an
unmissable opportunity.

On April 12th he announced formally that he was in the hunt for
the *News*. The direct competition of the two tabloids, he declared,
was a "dance of death" that would end with the disappearance of
one or both of them. He would publish both papers, he promised, if
the unions would agree to cuts to cover their current losses. He
would spend $150 million on a new joint printing plant, with
modern equipment that would bring costs down to the level of those
on competing suburban newspapers. Employees would be allowed
to buy stock up to half the value of the new company.

The Tribune Company, fearing they might be forced to negotiate with Murdoch if Allbritton withdrew from the contest, persuaded the Texan to resume talks with the unions, whose bargaining
position had been strengthened by Murdoch's announcement. A
Tribune statement called the bid "a transparent attempt to destroy
and shut down the paper" and Stanton Cook made the point that
Murdoch, having shown no interest when the paper was put up for
sale in December, now declared himself through a press announcement. "This is really a curious approach, even for Mr. Murdoch, if
one is really seeking to acquire a property."

Though Cook declined to deal with him, Murdoch continued to
pour on the pressure, trying to dissuade the unions from agreeing to

Allbritton's terms. He hinted he might shut the *Post* if the unions gave so many concessions to the *News* that his paper could not compete effectively. The *New York Times,* too, said they would want to benefit from any new manning agreement. Five days later the talks between Allbritton and the unions broke down on his insistence on a wage freeze and a five-year contract, but Allbritton agreed to resume them after an appeal from Mayor Koch.

Then on April 28th the board of the Tribune Company met in Chicago, to discuss some disturbing advice they had received from their labor relations lawyers about possible liabilities if Allbritton's negotiations with the unions failed and they closed the paper. They were told that Murdoch's intervention might have changed matters radically. As well as severance pay and unfunded pensions, they might now be liable to pay off the job guarantees of a significant group of printers until their contracts expired in 1984, making a total liability of between $200 million and $300 million. The lawyers explained that the question would go to arbitration and that the ruling might go against the company if they closed the paper while another buyer—Murdoch—was willing to buy it. The chances were that the decision would be in favor of the company, they advised, but the snag was that if the arbitrator decided differently there was no appeal against his ruling. Payments on that scale would be quite insupportable, the board decided. The softer option—given their continued aversion to dealing with Murdoch—was to reverse their December position and continue publishing the *News,* after trying to secure concessions from the unions on something like the scale Allbritton had suggested. They announced this decision and fixed a meeting with union leaders for April 30th.

But Murdoch was still not finished. The day after the Tribune announcement he tried to contact Cook by telephone to formalize his offer and, on failing to do so, hurriedly dictated a letter to Cook's secretary. "Since there are apparently no other qualified buyers for the *News,*" he wrote, "I am advised there should be no legal barrier to purchase by News America Publishing, Inc. Under these circumstances I hereby offer to sign a letter of intent with Tribune Co. containing the same terms as those set forth in your letter of intent with Allbritton Communications Co.... Despite public speculation to the contrary, I do not wish to see the *News* closed. I believe it is in everyone's interest to seek a solution that assures continued publication of both the *News* and the *Post* under sound economic conditions."

This provoked a furious reply from Cook, which he published, along with Murdoch's letter, in the *News* under the headline: TRIB TO RUPERT: DROP DEAD. It began: "I acknowledge receipt of your message to me dictated by you to my secretary when you called my office yesterday after business hours. Although a public announcement of the availability of the New York *News* for purchase was made on December 18th, 1981, no representative of yours made any attempt to contact us until after a contract was signed by our company with the Allbritton interests on March 31st, 1982. Even then, your initial apparent communication to us was casual, vague and lacking in any substance or meaning. You now, on the eve of our meeting with the unions, present an 'offer' that is so contingent that it is patently illusory on its face.... You have no right to intrude upon or attempt to 'spoil' our negotiations with the unions and your only motive for doing so is anticompetitive. We view your claim that you are presently a qualified buyer of the *News* as an anticompetitive and predatory act and you should govern yourself accordingly."

It took six months for the *News* to complete its negotiations with the unions. They resulted in a potential saving of some 50 million dollars a year, while a five-cent price increase would generate additional revenue of 15 million. The contract with the unions was extended from 1984 to 1987, making it unlikely that the Tribune Company would think about closing the paper until then. In 1983 it made a useful profit, while Murdoch was still losing a million a month on the *Post*. The *News* began to hit trouble again when printing was transferred to a new out-of-town plant. The long transfer process and teething troubles with the new machinery resulted in distribution delays and the omission of late sports results from some editions. As the *Post* trumpeted in a full-page advertisement on 4th June 1984, since the previous June the *News* had lost 139,083 in weekday circulation and 191,164 on Sundays, taking its sales to an "all-time low."

In four years, said the advertisement, the *News* had lost 1,500,000 readers while the *Post* had gained 663,000. (Readership is not the same as circulation, because each copy is read by more than one person.) Yet over the past year things had not been too bright for the *Post,* either. Its growth had flattened and circulation had still not broken the magic million mark. While it was conceivable that its losses might be reduced at least to a seven-figure annual sum, there was no chance of its becoming profitable unless the *News* were to close.

Just after Allbritton began his ill-fated negotiations, he met Kheel and McDonald in his suite in New York's exclusive Carlyle Hotel, at Madison Avenue and 76th Street. Kheel raised the question of the impact any concessions to the *News* would have on the viability of the *Post.* Allbritton replied that there was no need for worry on that score. "Rupert's ego is so big that under no circumstances would he shut the *Post.*"

When Kheel reported that conversation to Murdoch, he responded: "Let me tell you something. We are now a public company and regardless of my ego I have to be concerned about continuing losses."

All the same, Allbritton was expressing a view widely held in New York. When McDonald was negotiating new contracts with *Post* executives in 1981 and they pleaded poverty, the union leader told them: "You make a profit in Australia and you've just bought the London *Times.* Here in New York you've elected a mayor and a governor and a president and you've got a loan of $380 million from the Export-Import Bank. The *Post* is worth a fortune to you. We have to look at the whole picture when you say you can't afford a pay increase."

It is hard, as McDonald implies, to separate Murdoch's political from his commercial interests. Although the *Post* had by now lost all traces of the liberalism that had characterized it under Dorothy Schiff, there remained one policy area where it stayed constant—support of Israel. No doubt this sprang partly from Murdoch's own conviction, but it was also true that the business people who had to take decisions on whether to advertise in the *Post* were overwhelmingly Jewish. In recognition of his stance, the American Jewish Congress in New York named Murdoch Communications Man of the Year in April 1982. "My whole life has been with newspapers and so has my father's," he said when he received the award at the New York Hilton. "You could say my destiny is to be in love with newspapers." The president of the Congress is Howard Squadron, his New York lawyer.

Soon afterwards Murdoch suffered an unexpected political setback that defined the limits of his influence. Mayor Koch had decided to seek the Democratic nomination for governor, largely at Murdoch's behest. (The pair had remained firm friends and mutual admirers over the years, to the extent that Koch had written to the Pulitzer Prize committee urging them to honor the *Post* for its editorial writing. He clearly detected in the editorials qualities that escaped the committee, for no prize was forthcoming.) The *Post* organized a ballot among its readers, who overwhelmingly urged the mayor to run for governor. After his landslide victory in the previous year's mayoral election, everyone assumed Koch would win the primary easily. But he hampered his own chance by giving an unguarded interview to *Playboy,* in which he rhapsodized about city life and characterized country-dwellers as "rubes."

In a statewide election you need votes in the rural areas as well as in the city, and the remark did not endear him to the out-of-towners, despite his subsequent assurances that he had not really meant it.

The *New York Post*'s attempts to minimize the damage were ineffectual, because the great majority of its circulation is in the metropolitan area. All the same, two days before the primary the *Post* loyally published an opinion poll that showed Koch with 51 percent of the vote and his old rival Mario Cuomo with only 27 percent. It lent a wry double meaning to the paper's bright red front-page headline when Cuomo won: MAGIC MARIO.

In the election itself, in November, the *Post* came out for the Republican Lew Lehrman, and did so in a way that illustrates the enthusiasm with which Murdoch's endorsements are followed through in all parts of the paper. On the day of the election the owner of a Brooklyn drugstore was murdered by a robber. Lehrman had been running strongly on a law-and-order campaign and Steve Dunleavy saw that this murder could give the candidate some last-minute help. He informed a member of Lehrman's campaign staff. Might it perhaps be exploited in the campaign, if Lehrman would issue a strong statement condemning it? He did. It was published with the front-page headline: LEHRMAN LASHES OUT, and the story inside headed: LEW ENRAGED BY ELECTION DAY MURDER. The candidate was quoted as asking "How many more mothers? How many more widows? How many more orphans?" A Lehrman aide subsequently told the *Los Angeles Times* that the statements attributed to him had been "greatly exaggerated."

Despite this last-minute help, Lehrman was narrowly defeated by Cuomo. Murdoch had temporarily lost the knack of supporting winners.

Undaunted by his continuing losses on the *Post,* Murdoch continued to bid for new properties. His next pass was at the *Buffalo Courier-Express,* the morning paper in the declining industrial city on the Canadian border. In August 1982 Cowles Media, the Minneapolis-based chain that had bought the paper in 1979, decided to close or sell it, because they saw no way of stemming losses running at $8,500,000 a year. They approached Donald Kummerfeld. After getting Murdoch's go-ahead, he began an investigation into the paper's viability. He and his team visited Buffalo and concluded that the paper could not make money without staff cuts so deep that the unions would not accept them, and they told Cowles they would not go ahead. On September 7th Cowles announced that the *Courier-Express* would close in twelve days' time.

The unions, keen to preserve at least some of their jobs, urged Murdoch to reconsider. Their leaders flew to New York to meet him and his senior executives, who laid down stern conditions for a takeover. Chief among these was a six-month grace period during which Murdoch's people would evaluate journalists on the staff and have the right to dismiss those they thought unsuitable. The object was to reduce the editorial staff of 157 to ninety, of which twenty would be brought in from Murdoch's existing publications. This meant that fewer than half the existing journalists would keep their jobs.

"We look at a newspaper somewhat differently than many other publishers," explained Bob Page, vice-president of News America. "We want control of the newsroom. We want to determine the quality of the staff. We want to put out the type of newspaper we want."

The staff had no illusions about what that meant. Richard Roth, a reporter and Guild official, put it this way: "They want people who can think like Rupert Murdoch and who can believe in his publishing objectives." Guild members concluded that they would sooner see the *Courier-Express* fold than be converted into an ersatz

New York Post and decided overwhelmingly to reject Murdoch's conditions. "We voted to die with dignity," a reporter told the trade magazine *Editor and Publisher;* and die they did.

Murdoch and his supporters find that attitude impossible to comprehend. To them, it is inconceivable that anyone should prefer to have no newspaper at all rather than one imbued with the Murdoch ethic. The Murdoch technique, as seen by those who practice it, is simply to make newspapers more accessible and therefore popular by eliminating high-minded pretension. They believe that college-trained editors and reporters, in their conviction that journalism-school values represent the ultimate in fine writing, have lost touch with the mass readership.

Murdoch prefers the techniques of Hearst, Pulitzer and Bennett, the great popularizers of the 19th and early 20th centuries. He does not appear to appreciate that what he dismisses impatiently as intellectual garbage is valued by those who write it and some who read it as journalism of a high and responsible standard, greatly to be preferred to the corner-cutting, dramatization and inevitable distortion inherent in the Murdoch technique. Serious-minded Americans do not object so much to his populism as to his undisguised scorn for the kind of journalism they admire and believe important.

His experience with the *New York Post* suggests that in the 1980s the market for that kind of paper and the cynical values it embodies is not attractive enough to advertisers to be served profitably. His paper does not lack readers, but the readers lack purchasing power.

In May 1984 the Public Broadcasting Service, in the course of a two-part series on Murdoch, interviewed readers of the *New York Post* on the street. Most said they bought it for the Wingo, but others admired its approach:

"I've heard it was sensational," said one. "A little bit too sensational. In other words, they lie a little."

"Do you mind that?" the interviewer asked.

"No, it makes it interesting."

On the same program Steve Dunleavy stated the Murdoch case, employing the breathless hyperbole characteristic of the *Post*.

"We don't cater to taste, we serve taste," he maintained. "Believe me, Rupert Murdoch has bosses. He has two million bosses out there in New York City. Are we to preach to them and tell them what they should be reading? Or should we be reacting to what they wish to know—*wish* to know. . . . They ask of us: 'We want this information, we want this kind of a story. . . . We want to know what is going on and you'd better tell us. Otherwise, pally, we ain't gonna buy your paper.' "

By now Murdoch had become one of the people newspaper owners automatically thought of when they wanted to unload their titles. And it was not only proprietors. His next acquisition came about partly at the instigation of an editor—who quickly qualified to join the long honor roll of Murdoch victims.

Bob Forst had been editor of the *Boston Herald American* since 1979. Some twenty years earlier, the *Boston Herald-Traveler* had been the city's leading serious paper, outselling its rival the *Globe,* which was then so folksy that its editorials were signed "Uncle Dudley." In the 1960s the *Herald-Traveler* declined, partly because of a debilitating law suit over a television station it owned. In 1972 it was bought by the Hearst Corporation, who merged it with their vigorous tabloid *Record American* to form a new broadsheet, the *Herald American.* The hybrid paper never did well. Editors came and went. Forst was hired from Hearst's *Los Angeles Herald-Examiner* to halt its declining circulation.

He had been there only a few months when he was surprised to get a call from Murdoch, asking whether he would like to be considered for editor of *New York* magazine. It was a tempting offer but Forst did not see how in conscience he could accept it. He was only just beginning to come to grips with the *Herald American.* He had hired some good new people and he felt it would be wrong to abandon them.

In 1981 the paper became a tabloid and achieved a small reputation for its snappy headlines: REDS' BREZH DEAD and GAUCHOS BLITZ BRITS were two of the more notable. But circulation remained stagnant. Forst detected dwindling interest from his proprietors in the unprofitable paper and in 1983 he thought it time to move on. So he telephoned Bob Page in New York and inquired whether Murdoch was still interested in him. The answer came back that there were no vacancies at present. Half in jest, Forst then asked Page: "Why don't you get Rupert to buy this thing?"

Not long afterwards Forst was summoned from an editorial conference to take a call from Page. "Rupert's coming to town," Page told him. "He wants to talk to you." Elated, Forst returned to his conference. "Do you hear that bugle?" he asked his executives. "It may be the cavalry."

At lunch in St. Botolph's, a discreet Boston restaurant, Murdoch quizzed Forst about the paper's commercial and editorial prospects, then invited him to spend a day at his recently-acquired country place at Old Chatham, in upstate New York. It was not a good day for Forst. He began by spilling coffee on the floor: the frugal Anna took the blame for having glued the handle inadequately on to a broken cup. Later, while walking in the nearby woods with his children, Murdoch sprung his surprise: yes, he was going to bid for the *Herald American* but no, he was not going to ask Forst to edit it.

To soften the blow, he invited Forst to stay on as assistant publisher during the first three months of the new ownership. Then he discussed other roles the deposed editor might play in his organization. Perhaps he would like to go to England for six months to work on one of his papers there? Or join the *Village Voice* as editor or publisher? Or maybe start a new financial weekly that Murdoch had been pondering for some time?

"It was like he was a waiter bringing the dessert menu over." Forst was to say later. "I didn't know whether I wanted the eclair, the chocolate mousse or the strawberry tart. I wanted it all." The offer, when it came, was a stale Danish pastry. He was asked to be third managing editor at the *New York Post,* which had never had more than two managing editors and probably needed only one. "It would be like going into a shark pool with neither a repellent nor a knife," he told his friends. He declined the offer and parted company with Murdoch.

"I found him very charming," Forst was able to say when the passions of the moment had passed. "He charmed me right out of my underwear."

Forst's *Herald American* was selling only 228,000 copies a day—less than half the circulation of the *Globe.* Murdoch offered the Hearst Corporation one million dollars for it, plus another seven million dollars out of any future profits. He hoped to save seven million dollars by cutting staff. The deal was concluded in his favorite combative style. It had been hard to get the unions to accept his proposed cuts and Murdoch accused the *Globe* of trying to sabotage the negotiations, much as he had himself been charged with spoiling by the *Daily News* in New York. The *Globe* had indicated they would want the same manning concessions the unions were giving to the rival paper. (They did not get them.) The last deal with the last union was struck only minutes before the deadline on December 3rd, 1982. The *Herald American* was his.

He quickly changed the name to the snappier *Boston Herald* and imported two of his best men from New York to change it into an authentic Murdoch tabloid—Joe Robinowitz from the *Post* and Leslie Hinton, an Englishman, from the *Star*. Bob Page was appointed publisher. The layout of four columns to a page, which Murdoch finds dreary and pretentious in a tabloid, was changed to seven narrow columns, designed for faster reading. The reporting and editing were made sharper, less leisurely. Murdoch and his disciples dislike the American habit of writing tricky introductions to news stories, which seem clever to the writer but often baffle the reader. (For example, a story in the pre-Murdoch *Herald American,* about a teenager breaking the windows of a taxi, began: "In the end, they shook hands and went their separate ways.")

As everyone expected, Murdoch introduced a Wingo game which produced the anticipated circulation boost. He also greatly expanded and improved sports coverage, forcing the *Globe* to do likewise. But what most people noticed was the change in tone, the introduction of a new stridency, the exploitation of readers' basic (some would say base) instincts and emotions. The ideal Murdoch story seeks out or creates its own heroes and villains. Heartless moms who abandon their children vie for attention with heroic pilots who steer their crashing helicopters away from crowded schools. (This latter incident rankled local Murdoch critics—Bob Forst among them—who pointed out that it did not take a great deal of heroism for the pilot to calculate that he would stand a better chance of survival by landing in an open field instead of on top of a classroom. But to present it as a self-sacrifice made it a much better story.)

Local crime was played up, as was gossip about the person-alities in Boston television stations. But not all the changes were in a down-market direction. Some months earlier Forst had removed the daily list of stock prices, to save money. Murdoch had them reinstated. And in an interview with *Boston Magazine* in May 1983, five months after his acquisition of the *Herald,* he surprised the staff by publicly criticizing them for printing over-prominent and sensational headlines.

"We need a more restrained front page," he said. "Boston isn't New York. We are not in competition with another tabloid here. While I'm on the subject, I think that the headlines are often too big at the *New York Post*. I personally don't like front pages that are *all* headline. I'd like to change some of that. Of course when you're pushing for more and more circulation, the bigger headline you write [in terms of size], the more papers you seem to sell. When you go up 20,000 papers in one day, there's an overwhelming temptation to come back the next day with the same size headline. You can't always give in to that."

On the broader issue of his aims for the *Herald,* Murdoch told the interviewer, Greg O'Brien: "I think the *Boston Globe* is vulnerable. It has an allegiance to the upper class, to the liberal attitude. Now there's nothing wrong with that. That's fine. But I think it causes resentment. We, on the other hand, can't and won't pander to a particular group. We will appeal to everyone—white-collar, blue collar and those in the middle. We will put out a thorough, competitive newspaper for *everyone* to read, and we will work hard to earn the respect of *all* segments of this city. Consequently, we intend some day to outsell the *Globe*. It's not a matter of whether we will, but when. . . . Now I don't think that's to say the *Globe* will become a worse paper. It may become a better paper because of us. All I'm saying is I think it's unnatural for a good tabloid *not* to outsell a good broadsheet. . . .

"Tabloid journalism has gone out of fashion in America, but I think it will come back. There's a market out there for papers that are not ashamed to include some human interest, that are not ashamed to entertain people. . . . There's a tendency today to judge tabloids by more traditional standards of journalism.

"There's an elitist attitude out there. One problem is that journalism students today are taught that papers like the *New York Times* and the *Washington Post* are the models, that what those papers do is responsible and what someone else does is irresponsible. By the time these kids are on the street [looking for work], they have a cynical approach to anything that is not traditional. Their goal seems to be to have Robert Redford play them in a movie."

Initially, the rival *Globe* showed distinct signs of panic at the prospect of the fierce new competition and began to act out of character. Surprisingly, they outbid the *Herald* for the serial rights in a revelatory book by the ex-wife of Mike Torrez, a former pitcher for the Boston Red Sox baseball team, full of the kind of steamy secrets with which the sober *Globe* would not normally be expected to concern itself. The *Herald* retaliated with a ruse straight from the streets of Sydney—they interviewed Mrs. Torrez, who revealed nearly all the secrets from her book, which the *Herald* proceeded to print before the *Globe* began its serialization.

It soon became apparent, however, that the *Globe* had little to worry about. For although the *Herald* put on readers quickly—100,000 in the first year of Murdoch's ownership—it was not taking them from the *Globe,* whose sales remained stable at just over half a million. More significantly, the *Herald* was suffering from the same disability as the *New York Post,* in that the greater circulation was scarcely being reflected in terms of advertising share. By the end of 1983 only 16.3 percent of the city's daily newspaper advertising was going to the *Herald*—a bare one percent increase over the previous year. The *Globe* held the rest.

The 100,000 new readers, attracted largely by Wingo, were presumably people who had not formerly read any newspaper, and they were not a group of much interest to advertisers. So the *Herald's* cheeky boast that "we've got the *Globe* on a string," made in advertisements and on T-shirts, proved empty, or at least premature.

Murdoch's next acquisition came in another historic American city with a formidable newspaper history. The 1930s play *The Front Page* had immortalized the highly competitive and sensational approach to journalism for which Chicago had been noted and which Murdoch has always thought of as the right way to produce popular newspapers. But in the last dozen years or so Chicago journalism—like that in other American cities—had changed. As Murdoch had remarked in his various interviews, reporters now came not from the blue-collar housing projects but from universities and schools of journalism, where paramount among the qualities instilled into them was an onerous sense of responsibility, the idea that newspapers were important as a tool of democracy. As a consequence the press now took itself more seriously. Both surviving Chicago papers—the *Sun-Times* and the *Tribune*—prided themselves on the sobriety and impartiality of their reporting, the wisdom of their editorials and the quality of their writing, even though the *Sun-Times* was a tabloid. (The idea that a tabloid could be a serious paper had emerged over the last dozen years or so. The best example of the form is *Newsday* on Long Island.)

The change in the *Tribune* had been remarkable. Under its notorious editor and publisher Colonel Robert McCormick it had been nationally renowned for its extreme right-wing brand of virulent populism. Indeed, the *Sun,* forerunner of the *Sun-Times,* had been launched primarily as a liberal antidote to it in 1941 by Marshall Field III, the department store magnate. In the 1960s the *Tribune* decided that if it was to prosper it needed to modify its political stance and redirect its appeal until it more closely resembled the *New York Times* and *Washington Post,* papers occupying the positions in their markets that the *Tribune* aspired to in Chicago.

The transformation was a success. By 1980, when only the *Tribune* and *Sun-Times* survived from the city's formerly flourishing raft of papers, the *Sun-Times* was indisputably the further down market. That was the year when Jim Hoge, on the staff since 1958, became publisher, succeeding Marshall Field V, grandson of the founder and joint owner of the paper with his half brother Frederick. Hoge turned the *Sun-Times* into a responsible liberal newspaper competing for approximately the same readership as the *Tribune,* attracting to its staff some of the best young products of the journalism schools, who won prizes for their work.

By 1983 both papers were making money, but the *Tribune* was by far the more profitable, outselling its rival by 756,877 to 654,597 on weekdays and by the hefty margin of 1,127,778 to 588,970 on Sundays. Frederick Field, who lived in California, had never felt at all committed to the *Sun-Times,* and believed that the money he could gain from liquidating his share in it would earn a better return elsewhere than the paltry three million dollars a year he was making from the paper.

At 31, eleven years younger than Marshall, the bearded Frederick (known widely as Teddy and less respectfully as "the weirdo") was an enthusiast for auto-racing and loved the fast Hollywood world of movies and television. It was in those areas, and in oil and gas, that he wanted to deploy his investments. Where was the glamor in owning a half share in a newspaper thousands of miles away?

Marshall is a more sedate character, and the two constituted an uneasy partnership. A slim, diffident man, nicknamed "the wimp" by caustic *Sun-Times* journalists, Marshall is a pillar of the Chicago establishment and a prominent patron of the city's symphony orchestra. When Frederick told him he wanted to sell his holding in the *Sun-Times,* Marshall had to decide whether to buy his brother's share or sell along with him. Since stepping down as publisher of the paper, Marshall had become increasingly absorbed in the real estate business and did not want to devote the necessary extra resources to the *Sun Times*. He decided to sell.

Rupert Murdoch had been keeping his eye on Chicago since soon after he arrived in America in the early 1970s, when he visited the city and went to lunch at the *Sun-Times* office with Marshall Field and a number of senior executives and journalists, including Hoge. Murdoch asked shrewd questions about the paper's commercial condition, made mental notes and went away for nearly ten years.

When, in the spring of 1983, the Fields announced that the paper was for sale, Hoge's thoughts sprang in some alarm to Murdoch. He decided that preemptive action was required. He went to see Marshall and, drawing a lurid portrait of Murdoch's publications, especially the *New York Post,* he sought to persuade his proprietor to rule out the Australian as a qualified bidder. Believing he had succeeded, Hoge assured his staff that any bid from Murdoch would not be entertained by the management. Murdoch, though, had other ideas. Apprehension and outright hostility to his approaches have always had the effect of stimulating rather than dampening his ardor. And there was the extra, irresistible challenge of opening a second front against the *Tribune* and Stanton Cook, who were giving him so much trouble with their revived *Daily News* in New York.

As he had shown in the *New York* magazine purchase, Murdoch is adept at exploiting divisions among owners of properties he wants to buy. He flew to California to see Frederick Field and put it to him that, in fairness, the *Sun-Times* should be sold to the highest bidder. Frederick needed little persuasion on the point and made it forcefully to his brother. Marshall now told Hoge that the rules had been altered a little. Murdoch would be allowed to make a bid, but essentially only for the purpose of pushing up the price to the eventual buyer. A final sale to Murdoch was still not anticipated.

That, however, was not at all how Murdoch saw it. So confident was he of success that, to familiarize himself with the paper, he spent long hours poring over microfilm copies of back issues. He had himself driven round the city to get a feeling for the suburbs as well as the downtown area. When an important acquisition is in prospect, he is nothing if not thorough. Learning from his New York experience that it is important to get ethnic matters right, he asked a casual acquaintance: "Which is the Catholic paper in town?" He was told that, to survive in Chicago, all papers must serve the substantial Catholic community.

Hoge was meanwhile forming a consortium of local business people, as Harold Evans (an old friend) had done for the *Sunday Times* in London. He raised 63 million dollars. This was scarcely enough to secure the paper and the Field syndication service that went with it, so the consortium bid for the paper only, leaving the syndication service, valued at 20 million, to be sold separately. This exceeded the *Washington Post*'s bid of 50 million but was seven million less than Murdoch's 90 million tender for the two properties—the most he had ever offered for a newspaper.

At 10:30 in the morning of November 1st, 1983, Field, Murdoch and Hoge walked into the expansive news room of the *Sun-Times,* with its view across the Chicago River into the downtown loop area. Word was already circulating that, despite what everyone believed to be his assurances of the spring, Marshall Field had decided to sell the paper to the highest bidder and not to the Hoge consortium. Most of the staff were horrified at the prospect. Some stood on desks to get a better view of the proceedings as Field announced the bald details of the sale. There was a tense silence after he had spoken, but emotional applause for Hoge as he declared, seemingly close to tears, that his consortium had been beaten "fair and square."

Murdoch then spoke briefly, assuring his listeners that there would be no change in the paper's essential character. Knowing what they did of his record, the newspeople had every reason to be skeptical; applause for the Australian was restricted to the bare minimum necessary to maintain a semblance of good manners.

The three men moved a few hundred yards to the Denver Room of the Marriott Hotel on Michigan Avenue for an 11:30 press conference. Marshall Field said that, left to himself, he would not have sold to Murdoch. "Hoge's offer was acceptable to me but not to my brother," he stated. "My sentiments were that we should try to have a local owner if possible; and I was willing to give up something to do that. To be perfectly frank, my brother felt that he wanted to maximize what he got for the paper. Our agreement is such that he has a perfect right to do that. So it took control out of my hands."

Reporters at the press conference were handed copies of a letter Murdoch had written to Marshall Field the previous day in an attempt to allay doubts about his intentions. The assurances he gave were of a similar nature to those that had been wrung from him at the London *Times,* and before the Australian Broadcasting Tribunal, although here in Chicago there was not even the pretense that they were legally enforceable. If he could so interpret his pledges to the national directors of *The Times* as enabling him to dismiss the paper's editor, and simply ignore his assurance to the tribunal that he planned to settle back in Australia with his family, there was little hope that he could be kept to the terms of the letter. Yet if it would increase his chance of acquiring the paper, he saw no reason at all why he should not write it.

"Basically," he wrote, "we neither plan or intend any substantial changes in the newspaper and we would strive to maintain the newspaper's high standards and its reputation in the community. . . . It will not look like any of our other papers so much as it will look like the *Sun-Times* in today's form. . . . I will be approaching the task of continuing the *Sun-Times* with great seriousness and no little humility. I plan to spend a great deal of time in Chicago in the early stages of our ownership." Asked at the press conference whether he considered the letter binding, he described it as "at the very least a moral obligation." But to whom? Certainly Marshall Field had no intention of holding him to its terms once the sale was finalized.

Murdoch parried questions about the sensationalism of his newspapers in his bland, practiced manner. "You ought to look at them before you spout those myths," he declared. "I'm very happy to stand on my record." His polished performance faltered only twice, when he spoke of the *Sunday Times* instead of the *Sun-Times*. An understandable slip by a man who owns so many newspapers in so many places.

Although Murdoch had asserted that he planned no substantial changes, he lost no time in telling senior staff about the changes he did plan. They seemed substantial enough to people who had been devoting their working lives to producing the best paper they could—a paper that, they were now being told by its prospective owner, was gravely deficient in many crucial areas. At a lunch following the press conference, he indicated the kind of changes that would be required. He spoke of switching from a four-column to a seven-column layout, as he had done in Boston. He said he wanted more competitions and more human interest stories. Taxed about the Son of Sam excesses in New York, he replied: "Journalists take the news too seriously. You guys ought to have more fun." He bore a similar message to a broader group of editorial staff at a dinner that evening at Crickets, a Chicago restaurant.

Hoge, for one, doubted whether there would be much fun for him in working for Murdoch and that hunch was confirmed a few weeks later when he read Evans's book, a cautionary tale for all those foolhardy enough to believe that, with their exceptional talents, they might be able to succeed in taming the beast where others had failed. On the day the sale was announced, Hoge declined to discuss his future in detail with Murdoch, promising only to do what he could to smooth the transition between owners.

In December they talked more fully. Murdoch said he wanted to feel free to intervene on the paper editorially. He had not spent ninety million dollars or more to let someone else have the fun. Hoge said he knew that was how Murdoch liked to operate, but he had his own ideas about the prerogatives of a publisher, which did not seem to square with Murdoch's. It was probably better if they parted company from the start, rather than implement Murdoch's suggestion of a three-month trial period to see whether they could work together.

Murdoch had a similar discussion with Ralph Otwell, the *Sun-Times*'s veteran editor. He grabbed a copy of that day's issue of the paper and, quickly flicking the pages, told Otwell just what, in his

view, was wrong with it. After that chastening experience, Otwell
was a little surprised to receive the same ninety-day offer, and
thought it prudent to decline.

Another of the paper's stalwarts was unhappy about the sale to
Murdoch. Mike Royko, who wrote a daily column, is without much
doubt Chicago's most celebrated and popular journalist. In the issue
of December 15th he devoted his column to a report of the annual
satirical revue staged by the Chicago Bar Association, and in
particular a skit about the sale of the *Sun-Times*. In it, a group of
reporters complained to the Field brothers about letting Murdoch
have the paper. A man supposed to be the Fields' lawyer sang a song
in their defence, to the tune of "The Gambler." It related how
Murdoch came in quest of the paper but the Fields would not at first
sell it to him because of his reputation.

Then:

> He said: "I can understand that.
> I appreciate your spirit,
> I admire your dedication
> And respect the way you feel.
> Would it help salve your conscience
> If I paid you ninety million?"
> They said: "Murdoch, you're a scoundrel,
> But you've got yourself a deal."

After writing that column—and complaining that the word
"sleazy" had been omitted from his description of some Murdoch
papers—Royko took himself off on leave pending the transfer of
ownership. Interviewed on television, he gave his opinion that no
self-respecting fish would want to be wrapped in a Murdoch-owned
paper, and advised the tycoon to "go kick a kangaroo some place."

The venom of Royko and others who opposed the deal was not
directed solely or even chiefly at Murdoch. Many believed Marshall
Field was principally to blame. In a television interview Royko said
Field would hold a position in Chicago's history comparable to Al
Capone's. And in his December 15 column Royko was scornful of
both Field brothers. "We all know about the ravages of inflation,"
he wrote cuttingly. "Many millions just don't buy as much as they

once did." And of Marshall Field's attempt to pin the blame on Frederick, Royko commented: "That's the way life is. If the devil isn't making us do something bad, then it's a kid brother."

The veteran broadcaster and author Studs Terkel commented: "Marshall Field selling to Murdoch is the best case I know of for a revision of the inheritance laws. . . . Here's a case of genetic accident enabling a man to alter the lives, the livelihoods, the reputations of hundreds of his betters, as well as the reading material of millions. . . . I feel Murdoch has utter contempt for the people he says he's catering to. They're not serving the people, they're demeaning them."

One veteran *Sun-Times* man was able to express his view more directly. Nick Shuman, about to retire early after 32 years with the company, was in an elevator when Marshall Field stuck his arm through the closing door and joined Shuman inside. Field smiled and joked that it was a relief that he no longer had to worry about breaking elevators. Shuman snapped back: "Marshall, you were an asshole when you owned the paper and you're an asshole now." So that Field should not mistake the outburst for merely momentary irritation, Shuman followed up the encounter with a letter accusing his former boss of allowing "an honorable American journalistic enterprise, a precious voice in the community, to be sodomized by Rupert Murdoch." He concluded: "Over the years, you have prattled about your 'legacy,' by which you meant your money. You never understood. The legacy left you by Marshall Field III and Marshall IV was honorable, creative service to their community. You have pissed on that legacy." Such are the passions Murdoch can arouse.

In December there was a break in negotiations for completion of the purchase. Murdoch found he would have to assume responsibility for the pension arrangements and that this would cost nearly ten million dollars. He wanted the price reduced to take that into account. A new local group—not including Hoge this time, but with cash from, among others, the *Boston Globe*—heard of the hiatus and entered a bid for 100 million.

Murdoch was obliged to match that and, despite renewed protests, the deal was confirmed. Field said he had received legal advice that his agreement with Murdoch could be made to stick in court, so the bidding could not be reopened. That this explanation was met with skepticism was in part a measure of the horror many of the paper's staff felt at the prospect of Murdoch and their hope that even at that late stage he could be thwarted; but he could not be.

Murdoch took control on Monday, January 9, 1984. The previous Friday Hoge, Otwell and two executive vice-presidents on the commercial side resigned from the paper. Bob Page came from Boston to replace Hoge as publisher. Roger Wood was summoned from New York to become editor temporarily, assisted for the first few weeks by Charles Wilson, a Scot bred in the British tabloid tradition who had recently been appointed executive editor of the London *Times* and was fresh from ruffling feathers there.

In Chicago, he was soon nicknamed McNasty. As much as Murdoch would have liked to appoint an American editor from the start, if only for the purpose of public relations, he knew of none he could trust to do things his way. His profoundly held belief that his kind of journalism is right and the rest of America's wrong limits severely the pool of talent from which he can draw.

Of Hoge's senior editors, only one survived the immediate change of control: executive editor Gregory Favre. After a few days he too was asked to resign after an argument with Wood over one of Murdoch's obsessions—the need to get people out of the office quickly once they have said they want to go. The man in question was Alan Mutter, the city editor, who had given two weeks' notice. When Favre said he should be allowed to stay until the end of that period, both he and Mutter found themselves on the street within hours.

Several dozen members of the *Sun-Times* editorial staff applied for jobs at the *Tribune* or in other cities, and by the end of January 67 people had left the staff, many taking advantage of the Guild agreement that allowed for severance payments after a change of ownership. Page had a derisive name for those who left or who complained about the new order: the boo-boys.

The loudest booing of all was still coming from Mike Royko, who quit the paper in a storm of publicity and litigation. When he was on vacation the *Sun-Times* customarily published old columns he had written a year or two back. That had been happening since he absented himself from the office in mid-December and Page continued the practice in the first issue for which he was responsible. It was widely assumed that the columnist would not want to work for the paper, given the uncomplimentary remarks he had already made about the new proprietor. On Tuesday, 10 January, the *Tribune* announced that Royko would in future be writing for them. Some thought he could take as many as 100,000 readers with him to his new paper, and Page, claiming he was in breach of his contract with the *Sun-Times,* said he would initiate legal action to prevent his leaving. "The *Tribune*'s malicious interference into our business is intolerable," Page stormed.

He sought an injunction to prevent Royko from writing for the *Tribune.* The following day, before there had been time for the case to be heard, the columnist had the rare distinction of being published in both Chicago papers. The *Sun-Times* printed one of his old columns and the *Tribune* the first of his new ones—inevitably about Rupert Murdoch.

Royko looked back on some of the jobs he had held before becoming a journalist more than 20 years earlier. He had worked in a bowling alley, a lamp factory, a department store and a bar. He had settled into journalism because he liked sitting down, but Murdoch was now contesting his right to sit in his new employer's premises. "Can you imagine a guy coming all the way from Australia just to tell me where to sit?" Nobody had ever threatened legal action to prevent him doing his earlier, non-sedentary jobs. "Ah, Rupert, where the hell were you when I needed you?"

Page did not get his injunction and Royko continued to write for the *Tribune,* but he took nowhere near 100,000 readers with him. Audit Bureau of Circulation figures showed that sales of the *Sun-Times* declined by 27,000 in the six-month period ended in March 1984, while the *Tribune*'s circulation was up by only 6,000. The discrepancy is because many people were in the habit of buying both papers and stopped taking the *Sun-Times* either because of the Royko switch or because they were out of sympathy with the new approach. In June the Medill School of Journalism at Northwestern University conducted a survey of the paper before and after Murdoch in which researchers asked James Engle, the circulation director, to explain the drop. He attributed only a third of it to the Royko factor and a quarter to the unfavorable publicity Murdoch initially received. The rest, he said, was accounted for by a headline in the early days of the Murdoch ownership: RABBI HIT IN SEX

SLAVERY SUIT, which he believed had cost substantial numbers of readers, especially in the predominantly Jewish suburb of Skokie. In their concern for the Catholic readership, Murdoch's people may have forgotten the susceptibilities of other ethnic groups.

The layout was quickly changed from four broad columns per page to six narrower columns and the tone in those early weeks was distinctly more sensational than readers were accustomed to. The front page headline on one of the first Sunday issues was: MEN BEAR CHILDREN?—which would have sat better in Murdoch's super-market weekly, the *Star.* There was increased use of eyegrabbing pictures that related to no news story, supported only by brief captions—a well-tried device seldom used in Hoge's time. The length of stories was cut and there was more coverage of crime.

Statements from the management reflected Murdoch's compet-itive approach. "While Jim Squires [the *Tribune*'s editor] is taking his siesta, we plan to eat his lunch," Bob Page told the *Wall Street Journal.* But by March—roughly coinciding with Charles Wilson's return to London, although not necessarily connected with it—there were signs of a restraining hand. Headlines were more decorous and coverage of hard news, especially local news, was strengthened. Murdoch, who fulfilled his undertaking to spend time in the city by flying in on lightning raids, was clearly aware of the danger of falling into the *New York Post* syndrome, where sensationalism frightens away up-market advertisers.

Politically, there was a distinct shift in the editorials to reflect Murdoch's conservative views, supportive of President Reagan. Some liberal columnists were replaced with commentators from the right. Ellen Goodman's column was first moved from the main editorial pages and then dropped. She went across to the *Tribune* and was replaced at the *Sun-Times* by Patrick Buchanan, a conservative. Garry Wills lost his spot in the paper after writing an unflattering account of the first weeks of Murdoch rule for *Vanity Fair,* a magazine edited in New York by Tina Brown, the wife of Harold Evans—one small act of revenge countered by another.

Almost immediately, and again true to form, the new manage-ment entered into disputes with the journalists' Guild. The first was about an item taken from the *Sun-Times* and used in the *Star.* It was from an award-winning series on homelessness that had appeared in the *Sun-Times* before Murdoch took control. The *Star* rewrote it in its own distinctive style and invented some quotes, offending the homeless family who were the subject of the piece. The Guild complained about that, and that the writer had not been paid for the extra use of his work. They were told that it was customary in the Murdoch organization for material appearing in one publication to be available for use in any other without cost. As for the invented quotes, they were told to take the matter up with the *Star,* which proved unrewarding.

The other dispute was over staffing. In the first six months of Murdoch's ownership, nearly 50 members of the Guild quit the paper and hardly any were replaced. Murdoch thinks most American newspapers are chronically overstaffed—a view not shared by the Guild. They objected to his increased use of freelancers and non-staff correspondents to fill the gaps—less expensive because the paper takes on no long-term commitment. Again, the Guild found the management unresponsive to persuasion.

Chicago had to wait until April for the launch of Wingo. For a warm-up, the *Sun-Times* started a game based on readers' social security numbers. The *Tribune,* which a few years earlier had borrowed Zingo from its sister *Daily News* in New York, countered now with a game called Trivial Pursuit. The advantage Wingo has over other games is that it involves the possession by readers or potential readers of a card that has to be checked daily. When it was introduced, circulation increased by some 80,000. The normal pattern is for a fifth or a quarter of new readers to stay with the paper after each game has run its 20-week course. At the *Sun-Times* that would take the readership to slightly below its level when Murdoch bought it. Future games, added to any editorial changes readers might find attractive, would gradually lift circulation until it approached that of the *Tribune*.

It would be surprising if Murdoch did not quickly increase the profits of the *Sun-Times*—one of the few profitable papers he has bought. Savings on staff and other overhead will improve the balance sheet even if revenue remains static. Yet the present signs are that any improvement will not be at the expense of the *Tribune,* for Murdoch is not competing primarily in markets where that paper is strongest. Hoge's aim was to try to make inroads into the *Tribune*'s long-time monopoly of upscale readers. A marketing strategy based on Wingo is, by contrast, likely to strengthen sales in the lower income groups. The Medill School survey found that the *Sun-Times* was strongest in poorer and less educated households, with the largest concentration having incomes between $10,000 and $25,000. On the other hand, nearly a third of the *Tribune*'s readers lived in households earning more than $40,000 a year. The *Sun-Times* did best in the inner city, while the *Tribune* had a firm grip on the wealthier suburbs. The researchers found that casual readership of the *Sun-Times* in essentially *Tribune*-reading households was likely to decline as a result of the change of ownership. Thus Jim Squires, despite Page's threat, seemed unlikely to lose his lunch— but a comforting factor for Murdoch was that the researchers saw no sign of heavy defections by *Sun-Times* advertisers.

As for content, the survey's detailed analysis confirmed initial impressions. The number of photographs had increased by a third over sample issues of the paper from 1976 and 1980. Coverage of crime was also up, especially rape. Whereas previously politics and government had been the largest category of news covered, it had now been overtaken by crime. Self-promotion items jumped from one percent to three percent of the news content. There was also a change in the placement of stories on the pages. Items concerning entertainment, celebrities, self-promotion, accidents and disasters were given greater prominence by the new editorial team.

It is hard to know how the researchers would have categorized a story that took up two-thirds of a page in the issue of 8th June, 1984. It reported the wedding of two people who were scarcely celebrities in Chicago, where they had only recently arrived. Since the groom was Bob Page, the *Sun-Times* publisher, it probably counted as self-promotion, particularly when you consider the venue. For the marriage was solemnized in the Lake Shore Drive apartment of Mrs. Maryland McCormick, a pillar of Chicago high society and, more significantly, widow of the legendary Colonel Robert McCormick, former editor and publisher of the *Tribune*. A large picture showed Page, Mrs. McCormick and the bride, Boston TV personality Nancy Merrill, standing beneath an oil painting of the colonel.

Mrs. McCormick had not for a long time been on the best of terms with her husband's successors at the *Tribune*. Page told his readers that she had been "wonderful" to him, adding: "When she heard that Nancy and I were planning to be married in Chicago she insisted, really insisted, that the wedding be here in her apartment.

She is a great and gracious lady." Another picture showed "Big Jim" Thompson, Republican Governor of Illinois, who attended the ceremony with his wife Jayne. A few weeks earlier Thomson had been pictured on the front page of the *Sun-Times* holding a Wingo card. And the newlyweds spent part of their honeymoon at the governor's official mansion.

This was all a typical piece of Murdochian grandstanding aimed at tweaking the nose of the opposition, and it worked better than Page could have hoped. The day the wedding report appeared, a furious Jim Squires sent a caustic note to Governor Thompson hoping that he and Murdoch would be happy together. Later, Squires explained why the event had so angered him:

"They're trying to occupy the political ground of the old *Tribune* and they tend to want to develop a cozy kind of relationship with politicians," he said. "That's a practice that Chicago newspapers used to do and one that got us all branded and resulted in reform. They're going back to pre-reform journalism where they use their newspapers to puff up politicians. . . . If you have the publisher staying at the mansion on his honeymoon you have some reason to question the independence and objectivity of that newspaper when it writes about the governor. That's a malady that hurt American newspapers badly in the 40s and 50s and 60s and one which the newspapers cured. Chicago newspapers don't cozy up to politicians."

Squires went on to articulate the objections that many serious American journalists have to Murdoch and his lieutenants:

"They are tacky people who seem to me to enjoy and pursue the kinds of things that are abhorrent to me and to people who have spent their lives trying to make American journalism better. . . . We've spent years here trying to live down and overcome a history of being a biased, subjective and partisan newspaper. Because of that we are extremely sensitive and perhaps hypercritical of people that do what he does. So many stories have to get thrown away, why should I spend more than half a page of newsprint on the wedding of my publisher? I think that our brand of journalism, the new kind that we're trying to practice in America, is more compatible with our system and a more positive force in our system than the kind he brings. . . . I would rather raise potatoes than do what he does or what he asks other journalists to do."

So Chicago was finding life with Murdoch very like what it had been led to expect from the experience of cities elsewhere. But if Governor Thompson thought he was gaining a permanent ally in the new owner of the *Sun-Times,* he had only to look at the fate of politicians who have received Murdoch's support, to have it suddenly and damagingly withdrawn: Gough Whitlam and Malcolm Fraser in Australia, Harold Wilson and Margaret Thatcher in Britain, Jimmy Carter in Washington. All have enjoyed the doubtful pleasure of being cozied up to by Murdoch, only to be discarded at his convenience—as indeed have business "friends" such as Clay Felker and, earlier, Sir William Carr. In the Murdoch world of deals and feuds, first-sight friendships and equally sudden enmities, nothing stays cozy for long.

TEN

Follow the Money

Rupert Murdoch more than commands the attention of this firm: he can write his own ticket here.
Herbert Allen, President of Allen and Co.

Murdoch would have loved to have been in Chicago in early January to supervise the assumption of control at the *Sun-Times* and mastermind the tussle over Royko. Instead he had to go to Switzerland, where he was negotiating a 45-million-dollar loan, shoring up his finances for the most daring enterprise of his American commercial career.

On January 4, 1984, at the meeting in Allen and Co.'s offices (described in the Prologue) he had rejected an offer from Steven Ross of Warner Communications and Herbert Siegel of Chris-Craft to buy back the Warner shareholding he had built up in the preceding months, even though the deal would have brought him a profit of 25 million dollars. If he was now to pursue his assault on the company, he would need some ready money. He had yet to decide finally whether—and, equally important, how—to go through with it. All the same, it was clearly prudent to have a cash reserve to fall back on should he decide to make further purchases of the stock. By the end of the week he was on his way to Switzerland.

Since making his pitches for Warner and the *Sun-Times*, Murdoch had increasingly attracted the attention of financial commentators and Wall Street analysts. Many felt, even before the Swiss loan, that he was overextended in terms of debt. In January 1984, News Corporation's long-term debt of nearly 400 million was almost equivalent to its shareholders' equity, whereas most American media companies kept debt to around a third of equity. He and his bankers justified a high debt/equity ratio by pointing to the healthy cash flow that newspapers generate, with income earned daily to cover interest payments. All the same, in an agreement with a consortium of banks in January 1982 for a loan of 75 million Australian dollars, News Corporation undertook not to let its total debt exceed 110 percent of the group's net worth without the consent of the participating banks. It was now running perilously close to that figure.

Murdoch has a powerful personal reason for preferring to borrow from bankers in circumstances where other companies would raise additional capital in the stock market. He is determined that News Corporation shall remain under his and his family's control. This has always been something close to an obsession, and its motive was succinctly explained to *Fortune* magazine by Richard Sarazen, the corporation's finance director: "His father was a manager who made fortunes for others. Rupert decided he'd never do it that way."

His network of businesses is constructed to ensure safety from predators. All stem from the Australian parent company, News Corporation, of which 46 percent is owned by Cruden Investments, Murdoch's family firm, and another 14 percent by nominees. Murdoch has said he would be prepared to dilute that family holding only if convinced it was urgently necessary to raise capital, but would not let it go below 40 percent—still effectively a controlling interest in all but the most improbable set of circumstances.

News Corporation has two wholly owned subsidiaries—its Australian holding company News Limited and the British holding company Newscorp Investments, which in turn owns all of News International save for the 12 percent of non-voting stock in public hands. His American holding company, News America, is half owned by News Limited and half by News International. The American newspapers and magazines are run by separate companies, all wholly owned by News America. The individual British companies are similarly owned by News International and the Australian subsidiaries by News Limited.

Shares in News Corporation are traded in Australia and over the counter in New York. Murdoch's reluctance to dilute his ownership of his companies more than is absolutely necessary was part of the motive for his characteristic attempt in June 1983 to buy back all the Special Dividend (non-voting) shares in News International. They were traded on the London market. These are the only vehicle for public investment in News International, created in 1980 when Murdoch, in an earlier move to strengthen his personal hold on the organization, bought out all the existing ordinary shares for cash plus an allocation of Special Dividend stock.

For some time the Special Dividend shares had been quoted at a little less than one pound until at the beginning of 1983 they began to increase in value quite sharply, like other newspaper stocks in London. The reason was a growing conviction that there were plans for a public flotation of Reuters, the international news agency owned jointly by major British and Commonwealth news organizations. It had in recent years become highly profitable due to the successful development of its financial information division. Murdoch owned 11 percent of the shares, a holding valued at 120 million dollars when they came to market. (Nearly half these, worth more than 50 million, had come with his purchase of Times Newspapers, making the 12 million pounds he paid Thomson's for the company look a bargain indeed.)

By June, responding to the Reuter rumors, News International non-voting shares stood at more than two pounds. It was then that shareholders received an offer from Morgan Grenfell, Murdoch's merchant bankers. The offer document disclosed that Newscorp Investments had been buying the shares in the market and owned 78.5 percent of them. Anxious now to acquire them all, they were offering £2.25 a share, the highest price at which they had recently traded.

The document said that because so many shares were now owned by News Corporation, it could become hard to market them in the future, and "it is possible that when the offer closes the price may fall significantly below the offer value." A similar warning was repeated in a follow-up letter in July, which noted that, after the initial response, News Corporation now owned 87.6 percent of the shares.

Some stockholders, though, held out, reasoning that if Murdoch offers £2.25 for something, it might well be worth substantially more. As if to punish these resistors, *The Times* stopped listing the price of the shares on its daily stock page. (They returned to the

list a year later.) But the holdouts were rewarded for their re-
calcitrance. By February 1984, with the intention to float Reuters in
the summer now confirmed, News International shares had more
than doubled in value to £4.60, and those who had accepted his offer
were left, like many Murdoch victims, wondering what had happened to their trousers. When the Reuters float was made, Murdoch
was the only major British newspaper proprietor to decide to sell
none of his holdings, keeping the shares as a further asset to borrow
against.

Murdoch clearly prefers to be answerable to banks rather than
to shareholders. In an interview with the *Economist* in February
1984, he said: "If you screw up, the shareholders may not throw you
out but the bankers will. Whatever happens, you're subject to the
disciplines of the market place. What it does mean is that you can
take long-term risks, like *The Times,* and back your judgment, take
a bad year or two and nobody's going to run at you."

Certainly shareholders would have been entitled to raise serious
questions about the financial debacle described in News Corporation's 1984 annual report. Although profits were marginally up by
about seven million dollars, the accounts showed an extraordinary
loss of some 70 million dollars attributable to misguided currency
speculation. Because it operates in three main currencies, the group
has considerable freedom of choice about which currencies to hold
and which to sell. In the past Murdoch managed to turn that to his
advantage, but in 1984 he appeared to have been gambling heavily
on a fall in the price of the U.S. dollar in a period when its value rose
consistently.

If shareholders had any voice in the company's affairs they
would have made trouble about that misjudgment, and also possibly
about the persistent heavy losses on the *New York Post.* Overall
Murdoch's American properties make money, mostly because of the
success of the *Star.* It earned 15 million dollars before tax in 1983—
but nearly all of that was wiped out by the 14 million loss on the
Post. It is by now apparent that the *Post* is unlikely to cut this loss
substantially unless it drives the *News* off the streets. Yet because it
represents his power base in the most important city in America,
Murdoch will cling to the *Post* long past the point where, in a more
conventional corporate structure, pressure from shareholders would
have forced him to consider closing it. That is the freedom his

family ownership affords him. But there is a reverse side to the coin of full personal control: it will never allow him to increase the capitalization of his company to the point where it can rank with the truly large multinational corporations, should that be his ambition. In the end, that was the crucial contradiction in his bid for Warner.

The *Economist* article showed that Murdoch's loss-making enterprises were funded to a large extent by his huge profits on the *Sun* and *News of the World* in London—$46,600,000 before tax in fiscal 1983,.up 88 percent over the previous year and amounting to 41 percent of the group's profits overall. Although it was demonstrably true that these two papers were acting as a "cash cow" to the group, as the *Economist* inelegantly phrased it, Murdoch was irritated to see it spelled out so clearly. As soon as he read the piece he was on the line to its author, Hugh Sandeman, protesting that when union leaders at *The Sun* saw it they would demand higher pay—a prophecy duly fulfilled the following July, when for some weeks the editor, Kelvin MacKenzie, brought out the paper virtually single-handed during a pay strike by journalists.

Murdoch has never given a convincing explanation of why he began his assault on Warner Communications in the summer of 1983. Some detect a pattern of personal revenge in many of his business decisions, but it does not seem plausible that he would base a high-stakes strategy simply on his desire to repay Steven Ross for having frozen him out of the cable TV deal he wanted to join. Part of the motive was that, like many tycoons, he found the movie business seductive. His success with *Gallipoli* had pleased and excited him and whetted his appetite for further screen triumphs. "We'd like to get closer to making films for television and theater," he told *Business Week,* and in another interview he said: "We have to prepare ourselves for possible challenges from the electronic media. We have to admit that in many areas there's a very thin line, or there's no line, between entertainment and news. Hence, we're looking forward to an expansion of our abilities and knowledge of the entertainment industry."

On a personal level, he was aware of Ross's reputation for socializing with a fast show-business set that included Frank Sinatra and Beverley Sills, the singer, who was on the Warner board. Murdoch thought he might enjoy all that. Another theory canvassed was that he sought the Warner film library as a source of programming for his satellite TV venture. But if that were the primary reason, why did he not abandon the bid when it was clear the satellite operation would be abortive—or seriously delayed at the very least?

His career as the first American tycoon of satellite TV was brief, dramatic and expensive. Television is a field he understands, and one that he believes makes a natural appendage to a newspaper empire. But he cannot buy control of conventional TV stations in America because of the law restricting holdings in them by foreign nationals to 20 percent.

No such restrictions apply to cable and satellite services. In April 1983 he bought a majority stake in the Inter-American Satellite Television Network and renamed it Skyband Inc. Almost simultaneously he acquired control of Satellite Television p.l.c., a British company providing programming by satellite to cable networks in Europe. Skyband was the more ambitious undertaking. It was to beam five channels of TV programs via satellite to individual homes, an alternative to cable in rural areas where the houses are too far apart to make cable installation economical. There are an estimated 26 million such homes in the United States. Each needs to be equipped with a dish for receiving satellite signals. Modern technology has reduced the diameter of the dishes and should in theory allow them to be sold at a price that makes individual ownership feasible.

Having bought the two companies, Murdoch made arrangements to lease the necessary five transponders on the SBS 3 satellite owned by Satellite Business Systems. In News Corporation's annual report in the summer of 1983 he wrote: "Within a few months we expect to be operating the first nationwide satellite-to-home broadcast network in the United States.... At first we will function essentially as a distribution system with programming purchased from outside sources. Eventually we will bring our own creative resources into play so that we can produce and broadcast our own entertainment and information services." In an interview, Murdoch told Michael Schrage of the *Washington Post* that he expected the American satellite network to gross some 325 million dollars by 1986, but he confessed it was a risky enterprise. Other companies had been making satellite plans, but he thought he would reap the advantage of being first in the field.

"What it's going to look like is either a bloody battlefield with a lot of red ink strewn around or a brilliant success," he declared. "The upside is enormous. It's well worth the risk but I would be the first to say that it will take three or four years to pay off." He told Schrage he hoped to use his tri-continental muscle to finance feature films and assure his satellite stations of a flow of programming.

Only weeks after that interview—and days after making the first million-dollar down payment to SBS—Murdoch announced that his plans to start satellite broadcasting would have to be postponed. There were two problems. The first was that the technology was less advanced than he had supposed and the small, cheap satellite dish not widely available. The second was a shortage of programs to transmit. He had to take a loss of twenty million dollars, most of it compensation to SBS for the cancellation of the satellite lease. It was a rare failure, but at least he had escaped before the cost reached a level at which it could cripple his other interests.

Murdoch began buying Warner stock on the open market in August, 1983. By the end of September he had accumulated around 1.6 percent of the company for some twenty million dollars. The news rated no more than a paragraph on most financial pages and provoked more bewilderment than alarm in Ross and his senior colleagues. It was scarcely conceivable that this relatively small outfit should be making a serious attempt to buy a company worth nearly two billion dollars—about five times the size of News Corporation. At the very least, they felt, he would need a partner, and they saw no evidence of another large buyer of the stock.

Not until the first days of December, when Murdoch notified the Securities and Exchange Commission that he now owned 6.7 percent of the stock, did the Warner management begin to concern themselves seriously about his intentions. He was now the largest single stockholder and they were scarcely mollified by Stanley Shuman's statement to the effect that he was "supportive of Warner management." They knew from Murdoch's record that his support can be ephemeral.

On December 9th Murdoch and Ross had the inconclusive meeting at which Ross explained why Murdoch's interest in the company could have adverse effects on his personnel and his television holdings, and Murdoch declined to back off. Four days later Murdoch disclosed that he had bought more shares to increase his holdings to 7 percent but stressed in his SEC filing that he did not seek control of the company or a seat on the board. Before the year ended Ross had finalized his defensive share-swap deal with Herbert Siegel of Chris-Craft—a man with an almost equally flamboyant reputation and with a record of lucrative investments in the movie industry. Siegel had made impressive profits on previous moves into Paramount and 20th Century-Fox, prompting the humorist Art Buchwald to nominate him for an award for having made the most money in the movie industry without having made a picture. By the following March, Murdoch might have been a contender for that honor.

The Chris-Craft deal was the signal for the legal battle to begin, and Murdoch was first out of the starting gate. On January 4th, just before going to meet Ross and Siegel in Allen and Co.'s office, he filed his complaint with the Federal Communications Commission about the effect of the share-swap on the parties' television franchises. The deal was technically between Warner and BHC Inc., a Chris-Craft subsidiary owning six TV stations, including one in San Antonio, where News America owns newspapers. Murdoch argued, first, that the agreement was in breach of the FCC's cross-ownership rules because Warner already owned cable TV services, and, second, that since he was a principal shareholder in Warner, the acquisition of a TV station in San Antonio would conflict with his ownership of newspapers there. He asked the Commission to halt the deal.

Two days later Murdoch went to the state court in Wilmington, Delaware—where Warner is incorporated—in an attempt to have the agreement halted. He argued that it was motivated simply by Ross's desire to keep control of the company and was against the interest of its shareholders—including Murdoch himself, who calculated that the deal was worth 100 million dollars more to Chris-Craft than to Warner. By issuing new shares to Chris-Craft amounting to 19 percent of the equity, the company had effectively prevented Murdoch and other shareholders from combining to get the 80 percent majority needed for certain actions, including the removal of directors. And a further protective clause allowed for Warner to buy back the stock allotted to Chris-Craft if a third party should ever acquire a third of Warner's equity—a provision described in Murdoch's suit as a "poison pill." The suit challenged the competence of Ross and the Warner management, especially in light of the Atari losses, and accused them of taking excessive personal remuneration for their services.

Three days after initiating the court action Murdoch, in Geneva negotiating his loan, had no inhibition about commenting on it. "We feel very hardly put upon by what has happened there," he told reporters. "We're extremely critical of that management. We're going to go on and our present plan is that if we're successful in the courts or before the regulatory authorities we will certainly have a proxy fight to remove that management." He spoke about "extravagance and mistakes" at Warner and concluded astutely: "How it will come out I cannot tell you. I can only promise you it will make some rich lawyers a lot richer."

On the same day Ross, attending a consumer electronics show in Las Vegas, characterized Murdoch's moves as "dangerous and disruptive." And a Warner executive commented to *Newsweek:* "If we had to pick somebody to lead a proxy fight against us we could have hardly picked somebody better than Rupert Murdoch, a thoroughly disliked foreign publisher of schlock newspapers."

By now the rich lawyers were working day and night to keep up with the mounting tangle of actions and reactions. On January 10th, the day after Murdoch's Geneva outburst, Warner filed a counter-suit against him in Wilmington federal court. Its purpose was to prevent Murdoch from going ahead with his share purchases, "apparently designed to inflate artificially the value of defendants' investment in plaintiff's stock and manipulate the market."

The suit said that Murdoch had been seeking proxies to topple Warner's management. It accused him of "deceptive and manipulative conduct" in not disclosing his true intentions when he began buying Warner stock. And it included wide-ranging imputations against the Australian publisher:

"Murdoch is now well known in the United States and England for purchasing reputable newspapers and converting them into a sensationalist format, emphasizing violence, scandal and sex. Murdoch has already destroyed the journalistic reputations of the *Post* and the *Herald* and there is widespread fear that he will do the same to the *Sun-Times.* ... Except in publications controlled by him, Murdoch has frequently been described as deceitful and untrustworthy by persons who have worked for him or who work in his industries. For example, Harold Evans, the former editor of *The Times* (of London) and the *Sunday Times,* stated that 'Murdoch issued promises as prudently as the Weimar republic issued marks.' On the other hand, in publications he controls, he is proclaimed as the savior of failing newspapers.... Recently, he has been using his newspapers to publicize his position concerning his relationship with Warner."

On the day that counter-suit was filed, more teams of Warner lawyers were at work in Washington, responding to Murdoch's complaint before the Federal Communications Commission. The response described the complaint as "but one move in a highstakes corporate strategy" orchestrated by Murdoch. It made the point that in raising the press cross-ownership issue he was in fact asking the FCC to protect the public against his own company's possible conflict of interest. And Warner undertook to divest itself of cable TV stations that conflicted with the newly acquired BHC stations.

The response concluded: "What is really involved here is the effort of News International and its controlling individual, Australian newspaper publisher Rupert Murdoch, to maneuver themselves into control of Warner. Petitioner is trying to use the Commission to stop a transaction which it believes would not further its designs for control. We submit that the Commission should not involve itself, particularly in the form of interim relief, in this kind of private, corporate battle." Whatever the merits of that argument, there was by now nothing private about the contest.

Two days later, on January 12th, the first of the judgments was handed down. Judge Grover Brown of the Delaware State Court declined to grant Murdoch his injunction against the Warner/Chris-Craft deal, saying he was not persuaded that it would result in irreparable harm to News International. Six days after that the Federal Trade Commission gave the go-ahead for the asset swap and Warner and Chris-Craft announced its completion. Murdoch, his 7 percent in Warner now diluted at a stroke to around 5 percent, spoke defiantly of his determination to fight on. "This is going to be won by whomever has the greatest willpower and the toughest hide," he told the *Wall Street Journal*. Ross, responding to his opponent's repeated slurs on his management capacity, said: "He has no chance of getting the company. I'm not interested in what Murdoch says about our ability to manage. Our record speaks for itself. Last year was bad but the 20 prior years were fantastic."

Up to this point, the legal skirmishes had been in the nature of spring training for the serious contests to come. Both sides, recognizing this, set about collecting as much damning evidence as they could find on their opponent's record and character. Warner hired a firm of Washington lawyers, specialists in investigative work, to delve into Murdoch's past in the hope of finding something murky.

Murdoch chose a less conventional method. He assigned Steve Dunleavy and two reporters from the *New York Post* to dig into Ross's business and personal history, using the pretext that they were working on an article for the paper. They telephoned the headmaster of his old school and several former Warner employees, asking questions about Ross's flamboyant life style and seeking examples of profligacy in management. When Dunleavy's assignment came to the attention of the press, some objected that it was improper for newspaper reporters to perform such tasks at the behest of lawyers, but Roger Wood, the *Post's* editor, breezily brushed such strictures aside, saying he saw nothing wrong in it as long as they weren't working for the paper at the same time.

News International's response to the Warner suit in Federal Court, filed on January 24th along with a counterclaim, owed something to Dunleavy's researches. It was a thorough piece of work. Even Harold Evans's wisecrack about Murdoch's reliability was answered with a quotation from an unfriendly review of Evans's book in the *New York Times*. But the meat of the response came in the counterclaim, in which News International sought an injunction and damages against Warner and Chris-Craft, alleging that their share swap violated the Racketeer Influenced and Corrupt Organizations Act. "Rather than serve any legitimate business interest," News International claimed, "the exchange was aimed at protecting Warner management's positions and extravagant compensation arrangements from any challenge by News International.... Their recent conduct is but the latest chapter in a long history of Warner management's entrenchment and fraud."

As examples of these allegations, the court document noted that Ross had received $22,500,000 in compensation in 1981, when he was said to be the highest paid executive officer in the country. (He dropped to third place in 1982.) "Other members of Warner's management enjoy similar extravagance," the document maintained, adding that the company owned a house in Acapulco, Mexico, for the use of management. It raised anew the 1982 fraud conviction of a Warner chief officer and made serious charges, documented at some length, that Warner management had misled the public over the Atari fiasco and had benefited from inside knowledge to the tune of more than six million dollars by selling some of their own Warner shares just before the heavy losses on Atari were announced. It sought to establish a pattern of illegal conduct by the management to manage Warner in their own self-interest, in violation of their fiduciary duties to shareholders, including News International. The latest example, according to the counterclaim, was the Chris-Craft deal, which "has no legitimate business purpose and is aimed at thwarting what members of Warner management perceive to be a threat to their positions and lucrative compensation arrangements by News International's shareholdings." For all these perceived injustices, News International sought a reversal of the deal, plus treble damages and costs.

While the case was meandering through the courts, both sides were also active in the stock market. On January 23rd, the day before the counterclaim was filed, Murdoch said he was talking with "other persons," apparently seeking allies. He said he had lined up 250 million dollars of extra financing and was still buying the stock. A week later his holding was back to the 7 percent he owned before the stock was diluted in the Chris-Craft deal. But Chris-Craft had been buying too, spending another $58,600,000 to bring its holding to 21.3 percent.

Still Murdoch talked defiantly . "We've made no decisions about where to go from here," he told the *New York Times*. "We're in the trenches for a long time." He claimed to be spending almost his whole time on planning moves in the battle and he continued his remorseless assault on the Warner board's competence.

"I think there is 50 million to 100 million dollars in excess overhead that could be cut right out in salaries and perks," Murdoch told an interviewer. "The more you look the more you see. The big problem there has been all the corporate adventuring—the move into Atari, all the wheeling and dealing." Coming from a man who only months earlier had lost 20 million dollars of his company's money in a reckless foray into satellite television, and was losing more in currency speculation, that showed some gall.

During February the price of Warner stock began to drop, indicating that neither side was now active in the market. It therefore did not come as too great a surprise when Warner announced in mid-March that they had bought back Murdoch's 7 percent stake for $31 a share, compared with the market price of $22⅞. Murdoch's profit of $41,500,000, plus eight million in reimbursed expenses, was much more than he had made on his last failed takeover bid, for the *Melbourne Herald* group. "I would have much preferred being a buyer than a seller," Murdoch said, and it might just have been true, for in a technical sense he had lost the battle.

"I knew we'd win," commented a relieved Ross, although his victory had been bought at great cost and the board had to face fresh legal action from aggrieved stockholders.

For Murdoch it was as though, some ten years after his first tentative steps in the United States, he had come of age. In Wall Street, the most effective route to gaining the respect of your peers is involvement in a high-profile corporate battle. From now on, whenever any action was detected in the shares of a media or related company, Murdoch's name figured prominently in the speculation. He was rumored, wrongly, to be making a play for the Disney film empire and a few weeks after that he put in a serious bid for the St. Regis paper and timber company—important suppliers of newsprint. On July 18th, 1984, having built up a holding of 5.2 percent of the company at an average price of $35.54 a share, he bid $52 a share for a controlling interest.

The St. Regis board reacted as Warner had done—they tried to fight the bid in the courts and took an ally to ward off the raider. On July 31st Champion International, another timber company, made a takeover bid, agreed with the St. Regis board, offering $55.50 a share for a 60 percent interest, giving Murdoch a profit of $36,600,000 when he sold his stake. Nobody knew where he would strike next.

A lesson he was beginning to learn from his Wall Street adventures was that images and impressions were more important than he had hitherto supposed. He had until now based his business strategy on the belief that money, determination and nerve were all anyone needed to succeed and be well regarded. It was not, he had felt, necessary to spend time impressing the press and public with his personal qualities. Indeed, he once thought abrasiveness and general lack of charm were positive virtues, as evidenced by his behavior at Thibault de St. Phalle's party soon after his arrival in New York in the mid-70s. The Warner bid had helped change all that. If his personality and record were to become issues in his corporate struggles, as they had in that case, then it was important that the image be burnished.

It had been his custom to turn down most requests for press and television interviews, on the grounds that they took up too much time and generally presented him in an unfavorable light. Now he began to make himself more available, especially to the business and advertising press. In January 1984, he was interviewed by *Business Week* and was the subject of a cover story in *Forbes* Magazine so flattering that he had it reprinted in his recently acquired Chicago *Sun-Times*. (It may not have been a coincidence that Murdoch's *New York* magazine published in their next issue an equally favorable profile of Malcolm Forbes, called "The High Life of Malcolm the Audacious." One good turn...)

January was also the month he accepted his first outside directorship of an American company when he joined the board of United Technologies. Harry Gray, chairman of the engineering conglomerate, explained: "Rupert Murdoch is a man of action, a builder. He possesses the kind of vision that our rapidly changing world requires of today's business leaders."

The following month *Fortune* took a more critical look at his business operations, pointing out that if he really wanted to become a mogul of the electronic media, he could not do it by making the kind of "bargain basement" buys he was accustomed to with his newspapers. In the spring Murdoch agreed to co-operate with the ABC television program *20/20* in a feature about him, including an interview with the redoubtable Barbara Walters. He let the cameras into his new triplex apartment on Fifth Avenue (he had just moved there from the duplex a few blocks south), was filmed romping in Central Park with his family and jogging outside his London apartment in Green Park. When Barbara Walters accused him of appealing to his readers' lowest instincts, he replied: "Well, there's nothing wrong with talking to the masses. You know, William Shakespeare wrote for the masses. I think if he was writing today, he'd probably be the chief scriptwriter on *All in the Family* or *Dallas*."

Anna Murdoch gave her opinion on her husband's future: "I don't think Rupert has finished yet. I don't think he has any plan that he follows, but I do believe that he still has things he wants to accomplish. I wish he would stop, I wish it would all slow down— we could have more time together, but I don't think that's going to happen." Miss Walters, noting that hostility towards him seemed to be abating as he accrued more power, asked him: "Do you think you could stand being liked and respected?" He replied: "Yes, yes, I think I could take it."

The ABC interview was in fact a step in his campaign for popular affection. That March he had taken another when he accepted a proposal by Thomas Kiernan, a New Jersey writer, for an "authorized biography," for which Murdoch would provide cooperation, access, contacts and a promise to review the manuscript before it was sent to the publisher. In the synopsis of his book circulated to potential publishers, Kiernan described in detail the dinner at an Upper East Side restaurant where he had discussed the project with Murdoch. He reported that when the Australian entered the room there was a ripple of excitement as everyone followed him with their eyes.

Kiernan stressed Murdoch's forceful and decisive style of speech when discussing business matters but noted too his contrasting uncertainty when the talk switched to his family: his daughter's problems that had led to her precipitate departure from an exclusive private school in Connecticut, and his sons' lurid tastes in video movies.

Kiernan is not the only observer to detect in Murdoch a latent lack of confidence. It manifests itself in a singular and unattractive habit of tinkering at the last minute with the seating plan at functions where he is the host. He did it at a Washington lunch he organized in the spring of 1984 to allow senior staff of his publications to meet members of the Reagan White House: he made sure he was sitting next to the most influential of them. And when he hosted a black-tie dinner to open an exhibition by Australian artists in New York that April, he strode to the seating plan and juggled it so that he sat next to Geraldine Ferraro, then a mere Congresswoman from Queens but already rumored to be a possible choice as Mr. Walter Mondale's vice-presidential running mate. Murdoch's speech to the unfamiliar audience of luminaries from the art world was notable for its brevity and his lack of poise in delivering it.

"What makes Rupert run?" is a question beloved of headline writers and amateur psychologists. There seems no real mystery in the answer. With Murdoch, what you see is what you get. He plainly wants to be the biggest and most powerful tycoon around, because he believes he does it better than anyone. And he sees nothing wrong in using his powerful position to promote the causes and political values he believes in. Owning newspapers in big cities is a path to political influence, and that is why it is likely he will acquire more of them.

The Hearst chain, from which he bought the *Boston Herald,* has papers in Los Angeles, Baltimore and Seattle that could be among his next targets. The political clout that the *New York Post* gives him means that he is likely to continue funding its losses for as long as he is able, as he will those of *The Times* in London and the *Australian* in Sydney.

Rumors that he is about to shut the *Australian* surface from time to time, as its editors come and go. One of them, Colin Chapman, set an unenviable record in 1982 when he sat in the editor's chair for less than forty-eight hours. Then Sir Larry Lamb, who left the group in 1981, returned briefly to take charge at the *Australian.* In September 1982, after a five-day strike, the management reduced the staff by thirty-nine and made fresh menacing sounds; but Murdoch has kept the paper going tenaciously for twenty years and it does not lose anywhere near the money the *New York Post* or *The Times* lose.

At *The Times,* despite intermittent strikes and the now almost routine threats of closure, things were looking up by the end of 1984. Circulation was growing steadily as a result of changes designed to make the paper accessible to a broader readership: more features on consumer affairs and more lightweight articles, plus the introduction of an easier crossword for those who could not master the traditional one (which was retained as well). The aim was to make inroads into the circulation of the *Daily Telegraph* and even the tabloid *Daily Mail.* The hiring strategy was significant: two men, a sports columnist and a new financial editor, came from the tabloid *Daily Express.*

Douglas-Home was a more reclusive editor than Evans and seemed more skillful at keeping Murdoch at arm's length. But he was not universally popular with the staff, many of whom disapproved of the down-market direction the paper was taking. And both he and his paper—as well as the *Sunday Times*—were made to look foolish in 1983 by trumpeting a "scoop" in the shape of Hitler's wartime diaries, which were quickly shown to be fakes.

Murdoch had taken a close personal interest in the negotiations to buy the diaries, which had also been featured in his American tabloid the *Star*. Those on the British papers who did have doubts about their authenticity knew that, in the peculiar corporate climate that Murdoch engenders, it would have been regarded as an act of disloyalty to raise too many questions. Characteristically, though, even this debacle was turned to profit. The Murdoch group received a full refund from the German source of the fakes, and the publication of the first installment, before the forgery was confirmed, gave the *Sunday Times* a useful circulation increase.

For some, the most remarkable evidence of a decline in traditional standards came in June 1984, when it was announced that *The Times* was to have its own upscale bingo game called "Portfolio," based on price changes on the London Stock Exchange. The idea had first been mooted during Harold Evans's editorship. Evans had been keen but it had taken Murdoch nearly three years to summon the courage to introduce it and weather the inevitable mockery and squeals of disapproval from traditionalists.

Like bingo and its variants, the game involved distributing individual numbered cards to readers. The numbers referred to specific stocks that varied daily. The reader with the day's highest overall gain in value—or lowest overall loss—would win or share £2,000, and there was a separate weekly prize of £20,000.

In terms of circulation the game was an instant success. It was a stroke of luck that the very first prizewinner was a student at Harrow, one of England's two most exclusive private schools. He fitted exactly the profile of the young, upscale reader that Murdoch was seeking to attract. Any readers who gave up the paper in disgust were greatly outnumbered by new customers. After the first two weeks of the 20-week promotion, circulation had gone up by 80,000, bringing *The Times* within range of the *Guardian* for the first time in six years. But executives expected anywhere up to three-quarters of the new readers to abandon the paper once the game period ended.

Circulation figures were looking good at the *Sunday Times* as well. These had been on a healthy upward trend since the summer of 1983, when Murdoch persuaded Frank Giles, his interim editor, to take early retirement. Most of the staff had assumed that Brian

MacArthur was being groomed to succeed him, but instead Murdoch went outside the paper's ranks and appointed Andrew Neil from the *Economist*. He had met Neil—at 34 younger than all the senior staff at the *Sunday Times*—at an occasion connected with satellite television, for which they shared an enthusiasm. Neil is fascinated by modern technology, and some of his initial changes reflected that: for instance, he introduced a page about technological innovation. The paper also took on a more strident conservative tone, closer to Murdoch's own views.

Hall's arrival naturally ruffled the feathers of staffers who felt passed over, and they had further cause for displeasure when two more senior jobs—deputy editor and foreign editor—went to outsiders. The new deputy editor, the brash 39-year-old Ivon Fallon from the *Sunday Telegraph,* announced on arrival that the trouble with the *Sunday Times* people was that they all had grown middle-aged together.

MacArthur, only two years earlier an apparently rising star in the organization, soon resigned and went to edit a paper in the west of England. Many other senior men left in Neil's first year, including the respected Washington correspondent Stephen Fay and the already demoted Hugo Young, who had just won an award as Columnist of the Year. Neil's was a characteristic Murdoch appointment.

On the seamier side of Fleet Street, *The Sun* and the *News of the World* continued to thrive and to help pay for other losses. In 1984 the *News of the World* made its long-expected switch to tabloid format and registered a useful circulation gain as a result. In the daily paper field there was the prospect of a poignant and costly new contest between Murdoch and his old rival Robert Maxwell, who in July 1984 finally acquired the daily paper he had sought for 15 years when he bought the *Daily Mirror,* the main mass-circulation rival to *The Sun*. Maxwell's first acts were to introduce a million-pound bingo game—which Murdoch matched—and cut the *Mirror*'s cover price by a penny. A notable feature of Murdoch's business career on all three of his operating continents is how the cast of characters, both friendly and hostile, remains remarkably constant.

As in New York, Murdoch had by the early 1980s gained a reputation in London as a dealmaker in business areas only marginally related to newspapers. He played a small but significant role in one of the most colorful stock market wrangles of the time, the attempt by Mr. Roland "Tiny" Rowland, chairman of the conglomerate Lonrho, to gain control of Harrod's prestigious department store from the House of Fraser.

The government's Department of Trade instituted an inquiry into the bid and found that Murdoch and Rowland gave conflicting accounts of a meeting between them in February 1983. Rowland, who had the previous year bought the *Observer* from Atlantic Richfield, said Murdoch had asked for the meeting to propose that Rowland try to acquire the Express Group of newspapers from Lord Matthews. Murdoch's plan, according to Rowland, was that Rowland would then close down the *Daily Star,* a paper that sells over a million copies a day competing directly in the *Sun*'s market. That would render the *Sun* substantially more profitable. It would also, if any such collusion became publicly known, cause both men trouble with the Monopolies Commission.

Murdoch denied that the subject of the Express Group had been raised at all at the February meeting. He said Rowland had asked him to buy 5 percent of the shares of the House of Fraser and then to ally himself with Rowland in a bid to get control of Harrod's. Murdoch said he declined. Rowland denied that version. The Department of Trade inspector said he was inclined to accept Murdoch's evidence in preference to Rowland's. Other observers found it hard to know which of these controversial tycoons to believe.

What next? The United States will be his major field for expansion from now on, because there is little scope for further advance in his native Australia—which he seldom visits nowadays—and because the Monopolies Commission in London will not allow him to buy any more British newspapers, no matter how many favors he performs for the government.

Now that he has acquired a taste for Wall Street maneuvers, more of those can be expected, as well as further newspaper purchases in large American cities. (In November 1984, he purchased 12 trade publications of the Ziff-Davis Publishing Company for $350 million, making it one of his more expensive American purchases, financed, as usual, with internally generated funds and bank borrowings. The publications, which include eight magazines, one newspaper, and three newsletters, deal primarily with the travel and aviation industries and are among the most dominant and profitable in those areas.) He thrives on risk and there will be failures as well as successes. That he has the realism and level head to absorb damage, as in his aborted satellite TV plans, limits the scope for the major disaster that critics have from time to time predicted although the 1984 currency fiasco was a serious and damaging misjudgment.

Despite his attempts to soften his image, Rupert Murdoch will remain unpopular with the gurus of the media, who believe he has undermined the standards of their profession, as well as with those unlucky enough to cross swords with him in business. He will continue to survive dangerously, bidding for almost anything that is going and buying some of it; hiring, firing, cajoling, telephoning, browbeating employees and politicians alike, living out of a suitcase, flying by the seat of his well-tailored pants.

Appendix

In the News Corporation Ltd. annual report for 1983, the company's interests were listed as follows:

Newspapers	Where published	Circulation
New York Post	New York	963,069
Boston Herald	Boston	325,086
Sunday Boston Herald	Boston	276,265
Sun-Times	Chicago	628,285
Sunday Sun-Times	Chicago	687,386
San Antonio Express	San Antonio	95,244
The News	San Antonio	79,314
Sunday Express-News	San Antonio	206,817
Houston Community Newspapers	Houston	265,410
News America Syndicate	Irvine	---
The Times	London	381,075
The Sunday Times	London	1,313,337
The Sun	London	4,186,907
News of the World	London	4,280,713
Times Literary Supplement	London	30,968
Times Educational Supplement	London	90,635
Times Higher Ed. Supplement	London	14,988
The Australian	Sydney	115,705
Daily Mirror	Sydney	329,472
Daily Telegraph	Sydney	299,797
Sunday Telegraph	Sydney	637,534
The News	Adelaide	175,772
Sunday Mail	Adelaide	248,665
Sunday Sun	Brisbane	375,459
Daily Sun	Brisbane	113,551
Sunday Times	Perth	252,352
Cumberland Newspapers	Parramatta	938,843
Northern Territory News	Darwin	16,425
Townsville Bulletin	Townsville	26,308
Northern Daily Leader	Tamworth	12,535
Wimmera Mail Times	Horsham	10,272
Other provincial newspapers	Australia	146,473

Magazines	*Where published*	*Circulation*
Star	USA	3,600,123
New Woman	USA	1,055,589
New York	New York	433,599
Village Voice	New York	151,109
New Idea	Australia	811,000
TV Week (50% owned)	Australia	836,000

Book Publishing

Bay Books	Sydney
Angus & Robertson	Sydney
Wm. Collins & Sons (41.7% owned)	Glasgow
Times Books	London

Television

Channel TEN-10	Sydney
Channel ATV-10	Melbourne
Skyband	New York
Satellite Television plc (73% owned)	London

Printing and paper

Progress Press	Melbourne
Eric Bemrose	Liverpool
World Printing	San Antonio
Townsend Hook & Co.	Kent, England
Convoys Group	London
Independent Newspapers (22% owned)	New Zealand

Other enterprises

Associated R & R Films (50% owned)	Sydney
Festival Records	Sydney
F.S. Falkiner and Sons (ranching)	Australia
Ansett Transport Industries (50% owned)	Melbourne
Computer Power (software—33% owned)	USA and Australia
News Air (aircraft leasing—40% owned)	Seattle
Shell Consortium (oil and gas—20% owned)	Bass Strait, Australia
News-Eagle Ptshp (oil and gas—95% owned)	Western Australia

Bibliography

Books

Brendon, Piers, *The Life and Death of the Press Barons*. Secker and Warburg, London, 1983.

Carydon, Les, *Paper Chase*. Herald and Weekly Times, Melbourne, 1982.

Cudlipp, Hugh, *Walking on the Water*. Bodley Head, London, 1976.

Edgar, Patricia, *The Politics of the Press*. Sun Books, Melbourne, 1978.

Evans, Harold, *Good Times, Bad Times*. Weidenfeld & Nicolson, London, 1983.

Freudenberg, Graham, *A Certain Grandeur*. Macmillan, Melbourne, 1977.

The History of The Times, 5 vols. The Times, London, 1935–84.

Inglis, K.S., *The Stuart Case*. Melbourne University Press, 1961.

Jacobs, Eric, *Stop Press*. Andre Deutsch, London, 1980.

Jenkins, Simon, *Newspapers—The Power and the Money*. Faber & Faber, London, 1979.

Koss, Stephen, *The Rise and Fall of the Political Press in Britain* (two volumes). University of North Carolina Press, Chapel Hill, 1981 and 1984.

Regan, Simon, *Rupert Murdoch, a Business Biography*. Angus & Robertson, London and Sydney, 1976.

Somerfield, Stafford, *Banner Headlines*. Scan Books, Shoreham, England, 1979.

Souter, Gavin, *Company of Heralds*. Melbourne University Press, 1981.

Thomson, Roy, *After I Was Sixty*. Hamish Hamilton, London, 1975.

Windschuttel, Keith and Elizabeth, eds., *Fixing the News*. Cassell, Melbourne, 1981.

Woods, Oliver and Bishop, James, *The Story of the Times*. Michael Joseph, London, 1983.

Zwar, Desmond, *In Search of Keith Murdoch*, Macmillan, Melbourne, 1980.

Articles

Brogan, Patrick, "Citizen Murdoch." *New Republic*, New York, October 11th, 1982.

Chubb, Philip, "The Murdoch Machine." A series of five articles in *The Age*, Melbourne, September–October, 1980.

Cockburn, Alexander, "Rupert Murdoch Tells All." Interview in *Village Voice*, New York, November 29th, 1976.

Deamer, Adrian, "Being Both Australian and National." *The Review*, Sydney, November 13th–19th, 1971.

The *Economist*, London, February 25th, 1984. "Rupert Murdoch: Is America a Leap Too Far?"

Hodgson, Godfrey, "Private Power and the Public Interest: The Case of Times Newspapers." *Political Quarterly*, London, October–December, 1981.

Kirkland, Richard I. Jr. and Kinkead, Gwen, "Rupert Murdoch's Motley Empire," *Fortune*, New York, February 20th, 1984.

Korporaal, Glenda, "Rupert Murdoch's Wall Street Connection," *Financial Review*, Sydney, December 9th, 1983.

O'Brien, Greg, "Rupert Buys Hub Rag," *Boston* Magazine, May, 1983.

O'Hanlon, Tom, "What Does This Man Want?" *Forbes* Magazine, New York, January 30th, 1984.

Raskin, A.H., "A Reporter at Large: The Negotiation." *New Yorker*, January 22nd and 29th, 1979.

Sheehy, Gail, "A Fistful of Dollars," *Rolling Stone*, Los Angeles, July 14th, 1977.

Welles, Chris, "The Americanization of Rupert Murdoch," *Esquire*, New York, May 22nd, 1979.

Zeitlinger, James, "O Tempora, O Mores," *Harpers & Queen* Magazine, London, September, 1981.

Index